Herbert Read
A British Vision of World Art

Herbert Read
A British Vision of World Art

Edited by Benedict Read and David Thistlewood

With a Foreword by Sir Alan Bowness

and contributions by Robert Burstow, Andrew Causey, Judith Collins, Hilary Diaper, Terry Friedman, Patrick Heron, Michael Paraskos, Benedict Read and David Thistlewood

Leeds City Art Galleries
in association with
The Henry Moore Foundation and
Lund Humphries, London

First published in 1993 by
Leeds City Art Galleries
The Headrow
Leeds LS1 3AA
in association with
The Henry Moore Foundation
and Lund Humphries Publishers Limited
Park House
1 Russell Gardens
London NW11 9NN

on the occasion of the exhibition
HERBERT READ: A BRITISH VISION OF WORLD ART
Leeds City Art Galleries
25 November 1993–5 February 1994

Illustrated works © the artists, their heirs and assigns 1993

Figs 48, 59 © Succession H. Matisse/DACS 1993
Figs 4, 29, 60, 62, 75, 80, 81 © ADAGP, Paris and DACS,
London 1993
Figs 15, 45, 56, 63, 64, 78, 79, 83, 84, 86, 95, 100, 128 © DACS 1993
Fig.27 © Estate of Edward Wadsworth 1993. All rights
reserved DACS
Fig.55 *Dead Mother* © Munch Museum/Munch Estate/BONO,
Oslo/DACS, London 1993
Figs 61, 82 © SPADEM/ADAGP, Paris and DACS, London 1993
Fig.74 © Fondation P. Delvaux – St Idesbald, Belgium/DACS 1993
Figs 51, 52, 53 © Nolde-Stiftung, Seebüll
Fig.162 © Sam Francis/ARS New York 1993
Cover image and Fig.102 © Karel Appel c/o De Tulp Pers,
Hilversum, Holland. Photograph by Brian Merrett, MMFA
Works by Ben Nicholson reproduced by kind permission of
Angela Verren-Taunt

British Library Cataloguing in Publication Data
A catalogue record for this book is available from
the British Library

Lund Humphries ISBN 0 85331 643 0
Leeds City Art Galleries ISBN 0 901981 58 3

FRONTISPIECE
Feliks Topolski *Portrait of Sir Herbert Read* 1962
Her Majesty The Queen and HRH The Duke of Edinburgh

Designed by Alan Bartram
Printed and bound in Great Britain by
BAS Printers Ltd
Over Wallop, Hampshire

Contents

TO MARGARET/LUDO

THIS VOLUME IS DEDICATED
BY THE PRINCIPAL PARTICIPANTS

2 Margaret Read (née
Ludwig) c.1930

Preface

In a passage in 'A Nest of Gentle Artists' (see p.59), referring to his equal allegiance to different groupings among the 1930s artistic avant-garde of London, Herbert Read compares himself to a circus rider with his feet planted astride two horses. As Chairman of the Herbert Read Exhibition Committee and at the same time co-editor of this publication, I could feel a certain appreciation of this role. And yet, just as my father unified the apparent contradictions of his sympathies in the integral oneness of his personal sensibility, so too I have found an overriding unity in the single focus of both operations on Herbert Read.

My involvement in both areas does place me though in a special position for expressing and defining indebtedness and thanks. Without the support of the City of Leeds who have provided funds through their Centennial Committee, the exhibition could not have taken place. On behalf of my exhibition and publication colleagues, and the Read family, I would like to thank the Committee, Councillor Bernard Atha OBE, Chairman of Cultural Services, and Christopher Gilbert, Director of Leeds City Art Galleries, for their support. Equally, without the support of the Henry Moore Foundation, both the exhibition and above all this publication could not have materialised in the form they did. To the Foundation's Trustees and its Director, Sir Alan Bowness, we are especially grateful.

The active interest and support of all members of the Exhibition Committee have been invaluable. But I am sure the others would not mind my singling out some in particular. Dr Terry Friedman, formerly Principal Keeper of the City Art Gallery and the Henry Moore Centre for the Study of Sculpture gave to the initial idea an impetus and momentum, as well as a professional attention, that have benefited us all and have mercifully persisted in spite of his recent retirement from his official positions. At the same time, quietly and seemingly unflappably, Alex Robertson, Keeper of Art at the City Art Gallery, has set the mechanics of organisation in motion and kept them going to an effective conclusion.

It has been a pleasure to work once again with John Taylor and his colleagues at Lund Humphries. I would single out once again, though, as far as the publication is concerned, the special contribution of my co-editor David Thistlewood, who successfully combines his extensive knowledge of and enthusiasm for Herbert Read with a practical and technical experience of editorial work without which I would have been considerably hampered.

A full list of other acknowledgements will be found elsewhere. For my own part I would particularly like to thank Michael Paraskos who, in addition to being the part-time Research Assistant for the exhibition, in which role he gave much needed help, also supported the project overall with his enthusiasm and interest. This in fact has been a widespread response to our preparations. Almost without exception the reaction of public collections and private individuals has been unhesitatingly supportive and enthusiastic. At every stage from all over the world new offers of help and information have been coming in, so that my hope is that far from providing all there is to say and show, we are offering for the moment a first, solid foundation for a new understanding and appreciation of Herbert Read and his work that can develop substantially from now on.

Finally, although by origin the Read family comes from the North Riding of Yorkshire, four generations have now found a home in Leeds (among which I am happy to be included). It seems fitting therefore that Herbert Read's centenary and that of the city's incorporation should be celebrated in partnership here in Leeds, also that this is done in conjunction with the city's partnership with the Henry Moore Foundation, whose originator was, as both families know, so close a personal friend of Read's. I am certain my father would have appreciated it.

BENEDICT READ
Henry Moore Lecturer in Sculpture Studies
University of Leeds

3 Interior of No.3 The
Mall, Parkhill Road 1933

Note
Illustrations marked *
are items formerly in
the Herbert Read
Collection

Herbert Read: A Foreword

Always at the still centre of Herbert Read's life was his creative work, as poet, novelist, autobiographer. Like his friend, T. S. Eliot, he quickly made a reputation as a literary critic, but, lacking private means, he needed a career. Eliot chose banking, Read the civil service though he soon gravitated to museum curatorship. It was at the Department of Ceramics and Glass at the Victoria and Albert Museum that Read was soon recognised as an outstanding young scholar and potential museum director: it was however the love of the objects in his care, and a wish to share that love with others, that changed his career.

Before he was forty Read had been Clark Lecturer at Cambridge (the basis of his Wordsworth book) and Professor of Fine Arts at Edinburgh, but it was the articles in the magazine *The Listener*, quickly to be collected in the book *The Meaning of Art* (1931, and many times revised and reprinted), that pointed the way forward.

Read was a great communicator, and an activist, who wanted to change people's ideas and make things happen. He espoused a large number of causes, promoted them by his writing and lecturing, and, by and large, saw them through to success. His view of modern art, as expressed first in *Art Now* (1933) and outrageously revolutionary in the England of the early thirties, was to become the orthodoxy. He campaigned for a reform in design, particularly design in industry. He was able to persuade the world at large of the importance of art in the education of children.

Had not war intervened, he would have set up a Museum of Modern Art in London. As it was he edited the *Burlington Magazine*, gave his publishing house, Routledge, an international profile, helped establish the Institute of Contemporary Arts and was its first President. The list could be continued.

Read was not a systematic or a particularly original thinker, but he was as passionately interested in ideas as he was in art and literature (despite his marriage to a musician he was curiously disinclined to write about music and the performing arts). Like most of us, his views were profoundly affected by personal friendships and the intellectual circles in which he moved. Meeting Moore and Hepworth and Nicholson changed his life. They stimulated his own creativity, and deepened his understanding of painting and especially sculpture.

There is a wonderful openness in Read's thinking. He was prepared to change his mind, and consider a different point of view. Perhaps this is what Andrew Causey calls his 'naturally dialectic way of thinking'. The rise of Hitler and the Spanish Civil War turned Read's attention to social and political issues. A mutually admiring relationship with Jung profoundly affected the later years, when Read's view of art and of the world perceptibly darkened.

Read's pacifist and anarchist convictions, pronounced so publicly during and after the Second World War, might be regarded as impossibly utopian, but taking this extreme position could also be seen as a beacon of sanity in a mad world. One had to respect the opinions of a pacifist who held the Military Cross, and an anarchist who could manifestly make organisations work. Read's position was attractive to many people of my generation, growing up in the war. Discovering the range and eloquence of his writing was a personal education that no one else provided.

Getting to know Herbert Read in the last decade of his life was a privilege and a delight. Not a great talker, there was a stillness about his presence that radiated insight and understanding. I cannot do better than conclude by adapting the words Read himself used about one of his heroes, Peter Kropotkin: gentle and gracious, infinitely kind and nobly wise – he was a seer, a prophet, but above all a scholar and a poet.

We salute Herbert Read for his achievements, in this the centenary year of his birth.

ALAN BOWNESS

Herbert Read: An Overview

Benedict Read

October 1933 saw the publication of *Art Now: An Introduction to the Theory of Modern Painting and Sculpture* by Herbert Read. The volume offered to a British audience a philosophical and critical defence of avant-garde European art of a range probably without parallel, for it included not just Abstraction and the School of Paris, but Surrealism and Expressionism also. The range of artists illustrated included Matisse, Picasso, Braque, Léger, Miró, Ernst, Klee etc, whom one might expect, but there were also particularly strong representations of Nolde and other Germans (Dix, Beckmann, Barlach, Baumeister) as well as Belgian Expressionists such as De Smet, Van Den Berghe and Jespers. It is true (and was acknowledged by Read) that considerable help in collecting photographs had been given by Douglas Cooper,[1] but there is also little doubt that many of the wider contacts were Read's own. Nolde for instance had sent Read a copy of his *Das Eigene Leben* in 1932 and lent Read the photographs for *Art Now*; we also know Read had at some time personal contact with the critics and artists of Belgian Expressionism.[2] Maintaining a definite presence also was the English avant-garde, particularly that centred at the time around Hampstead. Henry Moore had four works illustrated, Paul Nash and Ben Nicholson each two and others with single illustrations included Barbara Hepworth, Wyndham Lewis, William Roberts, Ivon Hitchens and Francis Bacon.

In 1934 Read wrote his only novel, *The Green Child*, in a wooden shed he had built for himself in the garden of 3 The Mall Studios, Parkhill Road, Hampstead. The work was thus written in a place and at a time when the author was both physically and intellectually immersed in the development of the Modernism in British art mainly associated with Moore, Nicholson, Hepworth and Nash, one which was soon to be further enriched and expanded by the passage through Hampstead of an army of European artists of all sorts and descriptions (see pp.63). Though the novel – which Read himself subtitled 'A Romance' – has a quite distinct character of its own, there are nonetheless elements in it that parallel the world of the visual arts the author was already so involved in.

There are elements of Surrealism in the work, in particulars like the stream now flowing in a completely contrary direction to what it had before, to the generally alien world to which the Green Child returns accompanied by the hero, Olivero, a world whose 'imaginative logic' results 'in a poem' that is the novel.[3] Within this world exist crystal objects whose form and function provide the key to the world – 'the study of the forms, properties and structure of crystals was the most esteemed of all sciences in this subterrestrial country; indeed it might be regarded as science itself, for on it were based, not only all notions of the structure of the universe, but equally all notions of beauty, truth and destiny'. The ensuing description of the aesthetics of these crystals, particularly in their (aesthetically) highest forms parallels some of the forms and thinking of exactly that time surrounding the work of Moore, Hepworth and Nicholson, and Herbert Read's writing on them: the

… whole aim was to make crystals which, while retaining the apparent structure of each class, departed from the strict natural order in some subtle way. Aesthetic pleasure was a perception of the degree of transgression between the artificial form and its natural prototype, and the greatest aesthetic emotion was aroused by those crystals which transgressed most within the limits of probability … no joy could equal the discovery of a form whose perfection was other than the perfection of nature.[4]

There are other ways (to which I will return) in which *The Green Child* illustrates many of the fundamental areas in which Read had a lifelong interest: under the guise of fiction it could be said to assemble a concentrated epitome of his multifarious concerns. For the moment one should perhaps appreciate what it constituted for Read's artist friends: a creative, poetic validation of Read as an original artist (for all its prose format), that along with his other poetry (published all through his life between 1915 and 1966) functioned as such for those artists with whom he was particularly associated and to whom he gave his most significant and crucial support. Moore, Hepworth and Nicholson were all to produce work directly tied to Read's poetry – Hepworth's drawing *The Poet Reading to his Children* of 1948, Moore a watercolour and an etching illustrating Read's poem '1945', Nicholson an etching in which his own design adjoins Read's holograph of his poem 'Tenement'.

Read's poetry, which represents in a way most truly the 'inner man', ties in directly with the visual arts in other instances: with Lucas Cranach, Giovanni di Paolo, a nineteenth-century statue of Cobden in Camden Town. One section of 'A World Within a War' refers to a painting sometimes attributed to Giovanni Bellini, *The Death of St Peter Martyr*, in the National Gallery, London;[5] an early part of the poem runs:

Sedate within this palisade
Which unforethinking I have made
Of brittle leaves and velvet flowers,
I re-indite a Book of Hours –
Would emulate the Lombard School
(Crisp as medals, bright but cool)
Talk mainly of the Human Passion

4 Marc Chagall *I and the Village* 1911. The Museum of Modern Art, New York, Mrs Simon Guggenheim Fund. Featured by Herbert Read as frontispiece to his childhood autobiography *The Innocent Eye* (1933)

5 Barbara Hepworth
The Poet Reading to his Children 1948. Leeds City Art Galleries (cat.no.107)

6 Henry Moore '1945' 1946. Private collection*

5

That made us in a conscious fashion
Strive to control our human fate:
But in the margins interpolate
Apes and angels playing tunes
On harpsichords or saxophones
Throughout the story thus maintain
Under a sacred melody the bass profane.

The historical range of the visual arts present in Read's poetry might surprise those who think of him solely as a champion of Henry Moore – 'A World Within A War' appeared in book form the same year as the first of the Lund Humphries monographs on Moore that Read introduced, 1944. But then anyone who actually inspected the Read introduction would see there also a range of historical art introduced to compare or contrast with Moore, just as anyone who thought more deeply about the matter would appreciate that the poet of 'Cranach' was working in the Victoria and Albert Museum at the time of its publication, the poet of 'Giovanni di Paolo', first published in book form in 1935, was at that time editor of *The Burlington Magazine* and about to publish there the first writings on such artists by John Pope-Hennessy. At one end of Read's poetic output, *Naked Warriors* was published in 1919 with a Wyndham Lewis abstracted design on the front cover belonging to the volume's publisher Art & Letters, with which Read was closely associated.

One should note this title with regard to the fusion of Read's interests. The idea of the magazine of this title went back to Read's days in Leeds where, in the creative atmosphere surrounding the Leeds Arts Club, he and Frank Rutter had first considered it. It was then through Rutter that during the First World War years Read made his first acquaintance with the London world – of art *and* letters, in that he met and came into close contact not only with visual artists like Ginner and Bevan, but also with Pound, Eliot and Wyndham Lewis – the latter, of course, active like Read in both visual and literary fields.[6]

At the further end of developments in the visual arts – and poetry – Read dedicated two of his *Vocal Avowals*, experimental word/sound poems of the later 1950s, to the French sculptor Etienne Martin and the Italian artist Alberto Burri. In an introduction to a catalogue of an exhibition of Burri's work Read wrote:

… in the first years after the war Burri created a new world of form; and it seemed that the more degraded the raw material of his experiments, the more his sensibility was challenged and the more surely it triumphed. No purer works of art have been created by an artist in the past fifteen years … Whatever he does – and this is the wider aesthetic significance of his work – his sensibility dominates the intractable material, to such an extent that a transmutation takes places, an alchemical process in which rubbish is redeemed in the alembic of the artist's sensibility, to become the 'perfect body' of a work of art.[7]

To this Read added in the catalogue his experimental poem 'basic black':

cry crew cry memory florida
masterly most crimson silt
shy masculine myrtle endeavour
sever christ cavalier host
ghost gonads sob linger
alleys lost singular wing
veins of love never ever cease
keep crestfallen thy cruise
dastard sap till sessions eventual
mortal leman entrance dry
wild hollow winter bruises
droop vocal illyrian avowals
kiss merciful o homily thy keel
england vesicles of delight
lost ever ever ever white pyx
residues of lust ah wax lack.[8]

In a note referring to 'A World Within A War'[9] Read commented: 'The poem is, like most of my long poems, divided into "movements" on the analogy of the musical sonata.' As a coda, so to speak, to his intermingling of poetry and the visual arts one should register a more limited but no less real correlation with music. An early poem 'Etude' was published in *Eclogues* of 1919. Later renamed 'Concert Party'[10] it begins briefly in simple description before moving on to a Nietzschean poetic rampage:

That white hand poised
Above the ivory keys
Will soon descend to
Shatter
The equable surface of my reverie.

To what abortion
Will the silence give birth?

Noon of moist heat and the moan
Of raping bees,
And light like a sluice of molten gold
On the satiate, petitioning leaves.

In yellow fields
Mute agony of reapers.

Does the metallic horizon
Give release?

Well, higher,
against the wider void the immaculate
angels of lust
Lean
on the swanbreasts of heaven.

A manuscript fair copy of this poem was inscribed by Read to his crucial early painter friend Jacob Kramer.[11] Later 'Legend' from *Poems 1934-34* of 1935 is subtitled 'for Viola and Pianoforte: Bax'[12] while 'The Visionary Hermit' is dedicated to the composer Michael Tippett.[13]

A new edition of *The Green Child* was published in 1945. Three years later Read sent a copy to Carl Gustav Jung with whom he had recently become directly involved as

6

1945

They came running over the perilous sands
  Children with their golden eyes
Crying: *Look! We have found samphire*
  Holding out their bone-ridden hands.

It might have been the spittle of wrens
  Or the silver nest of a squirrel
For I was invested with the darkness
  Of an ancient quarrel whose omens
Lay scatter'd on the silted beach.
  The children came running toward me

But I saw only the waves behind them
  Cold, salt and disastrous
Lift their black banners and break
  Endlessly, without resurrection.

Cranach

But once upon a time
the oakleaves and the wild boars
Antonio Antonio
the old wound is bleeding.

We are in Silvertown
we have come here with a modest ambition
to know a little bit about the river
eating cheese and pickled onions on a terrace by the Thames.

Sweet Thames! the ferry glides across your bosom
like Leda's swan.
The factories ah slender graces
sly naked damsels nodding their downy plumes.

---

publisher of the psychologist's complete works in English translation. Jung wrote back to thank Read, saying he was not naturally drawn to 'literature' but he was strangely attracted by genuine fiction, that is phantastical invention – 'it is a legitimate and authentic offspring of the unconscious mind and thus far it provides me with unadulterated information about the things that transcend the writer's conscious mind'. As for *The Green Child*:

I have read right through in one day and it gave me a rumbling in the depths that kept me awake for the better part of a night. It is, above all, wonderfully English: you go to bed without any particular forebodings and with no plans or intentions whatever and you wake up in the morning being the unaccountable proprietor of 30,000 square miles of virginal country, where you can't help being immensely useful and efficient.

On Read/Olivero's return and rediscovery of the green child and her 'other' world Jung comments:

What lovely unconventional things you have missed! From most enjoyable promiscuous battles upwards to the highest regions of wisdom! Here my Acheron began to shake. You touched upon the alchemical arcanum par excellence, the Philosopher's Stone, a really enormous problem, that is actually very much on my mind indeed …[14]

It is possible to interpret Jung's picking on, first, the element of political organisation in the work and, second, its psychological reverberations as identifying in *The Green Child* two more of Read's lifelong concerns. He had begun acquiring and reading the works of Freud and Jung in his twenties, and was to assemble by the end of his life a wealth of knowledge and experience in the works (in addition) of Adler, Klein, Burrow, Syz and others. The first major feedback from this interest came in his article on 'Psychoanalysis and the Critic' in volume three of T. S. Eliot's *The Criterion* in 1924-5. 'Myth, Dream and Poem' appeared in *Transition* in 1928; then Read's Clark lectures at Trinity College, Cambridge of 1929-30 investigated the work of Wordsworth in terms of psychology and personality, adding to the tracing of the poet's intellectual development a similar procedure with his emotional development, since Wordsworth, 'by

"BOY AT A STREAM."—BY J. H. FOLEY.

8

8 John Henry Foley
Youth at the Stream from
Illustrated London News
1851

9 The Wills Brothers
Richard Cobden 1863.
Camden Town, London

9

Cobden

COBDEN imperturbably stone
divides the flow of Camden traffic
frock-coated elevated stiff alone
– it is an academic trick
(petrification of the flesh
façade of an impassive mind)

Collisions happen in the milling mesh
to which we humans are consigned
but COBDEN neither sees nor feels
our common fate
nor hears the rumble of the wheels
early or late

Two larger tomes were an inexhaustible mine of delight ...
bound volumes of the *Illustrated London News* for the year of
the Great Exhibition ... full of the steel engravings of the
period.

The Contrary Experience, p.49

apostrophizing the mind ... hoped to conceal the significance of the body.'[15]

Read was using a psychological framework for inter-
preting the visual arts already by 1918 in his correspondence with Jacob Kramer, and it remained a
presence in such key works as *The Meaning of Art* of 1931
and *Art Now* of 1933. A more particular and substantial
application of the whole framework of psychology com-

prised the underpinning for *Education Through Art* that first
appeared in 1943, not just through analysing, describing
and identifying children's artworks in terms of psychological typology, but also through examination of the
nature of perception, aesthetics and imagery, culminating
in the essential argument of the book that psychological
integration, as discussed and explained, can only be
achieved by educating through art. While much of the
detailed casework and argument in the book was not
necessarily original to Read, the total coherent presentation of this complex manifesto contributed a great deal
to making it one of the author's most influential
publications.

10

11

In the 1950s Read was to use psychology as a basis of still more advanced, possibly even revolutionary theorising, as in *Icon and Idea*, the Charles Eliot Norton lectures in Poetry (note) at Harvard of 1953-4, in which Read set out to demonstrate that the icon, the image, precedes in the process of human creativity the intellectual, conceptual recognition of it. Finally in 1960 he published *The Forms of Things Unknown*, a series of lectures that had in the main been delivered at the Eranos conferences of philosophers and psychologists, under Jung's presiding genius. The book was concerned with the nature of the creative mind, with the ways in which such factors as image, symbol, myth and icon could and should be controlling influences in the development of human culture.

Read openly admitted in the Preface to *The Forms* that he wrote not as a scientist but as a poet, and this should remind us, in any attempted presentation of his life's work, of his lifelong involvement in literature – not just as well as everything else, but possibly more substantially than anything else. It was not just the poems that he began writing in his teens and first published in 1915, with *Songs of Chaos*. All through his life, as will by now be implicit, he wrote poetry on many themes, in many styles and and modes: metaphysical, philosophical, lyrical, classical, romantic. He also wrote *on* poetry, his own and others': sometimes more general theory – *Form in Modern Poetry*, 1932, *Poetry and Experience*, 1967; at other times on specific areas, such as the studies in English Romantic Poetry covering Wordsworth, Coleridge and Keats through to Hulme, Pound and Eliot, united in *The*

True Voice of Feeling of 1953. This was all against a background output of general literary criticism: his first ever recorded publication was in 1912, a letter to *The New Age* on pronunciation, with reference to a controversy over spelling.[16] Later came *English Prose Style* (1928), anthologies of prose and verse and a myriad of articles and reviews over what seem a thousand or more subjects.

The involvement with literature could be supportive as well as productive. There is little doubt that over possibly twenty years from 1939 when Read was involved as a publisher with Routledge & Kegan Paul he actively promoted poetry, to some extent in cahoots with his friend and colleague T. S. Eliot at Faber, in that the two would pass on to each other poets whose work they valued but did not feel fitted in with the necessarily distinct flavour of each house's imprint. In addition, literature was the occasion of as close personal friendships (as with Eliot or Bonamy and Valentine Dobrée) as were the visual arts.

The last major concern of Read's life that should not be ignored involves the political. Jung's identification of this in *The Green Child* is crisp but apt – Read/Olivero's waking up one morning to find himself the proprietor of a nation which he proceeds to run with ease and efficiency (see above). This was done through a devolution of most responsibilities to small local communities, with an enlightened philosopher/despot providing the initial impetus towards a self-regulating moral, economic and social well-being that no-one in their right (collective) minds would ever want to disrupt.

Read's initial political awareness had developed in Leeds

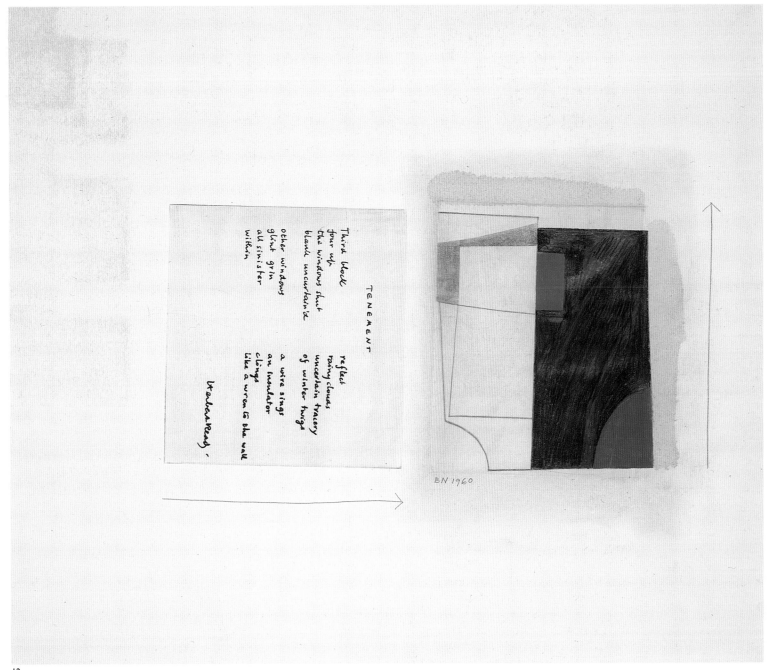

where ultimately (for him) a form of Guild Socialism, adeptly propagated in Leeds before the First World War, seemed the most satisfactory framework. In the years after the war, Read claimed, his position as a civil servant, which included his years at the Victoria and Albert Museum, precluded overt political commitment, though he did manage to review *The Letters of Sacco and Vanzetti*, the American anarchists for *The Criterion* in 1928-9.[17] But the changes in his employment in the 1930s, together with the rise of fascism in Europe, then the impact of the Spanish Civil War and the political elements of Surrealism made a clear political standpoint inevitable. Already in the introduction to the first edition of *Art Now* in 1933 Read inveighed against the systematic attack on modern

art immediately put into effect after the accession to power of the Nazi government in Germany. In 1937 Read declared his political affiliations in three articles entitled 'The Necessity of Anarchism'[18] to be followed by the book *Poetry and Anarchism* in 1938. As we have seen before, Read's concerns interweave and produce in this instance poems like 'The Brown Book of the Hitler Terror', 'Bombing Casualties in Spain', 'A Song for the Spanish Anarchists' and 'Herschel Grynszpan':[19]

> This beautiful assassin is your friend:
> …
> He lifts his hands in calm despair.
> The gesture loses its solitary grace
> and violence is answered by violence

13

listen to secrets in the night around you.
The light of the worlds beyond your world
beguiled you with hope of a harmony
wider than the anguish of our broken lives.
The wreckage of the day was hidden.

This beautiful assassin is my friend
because my heart is filled with the same fire.
…

It is feasible – and quite reasonable – to detect an underlying basis of libertarianism behind much of Read's writing on many topics.[20] *Education Through Art* champions the right of individuals to be true to themselves, and thereby and only thereby can social and political harmony be achieved. Read's defence of Abstract Expressionism blends the right of individual artists to express themselves this way on both psychological and (ultimately) political grounds. In effect one can see Read's persistent defence of artists of all sorts and grades of merit as a championing of the rights of the individual to freedom and expression.

A more active involvement with politics on Read's part included planning with George Orwell to set up a secret printing press as restrictions during the Second World War seemed increasingly to limit freedom of expression. Towards the end of the Second World War the police raided the premises of the Freedom Press, the principal anarchist publishers in London, and found what they alleged to be literature of a seditious character there and at the homes of Vernon Richards, his wife Marie Louise (née Berneri), Dr John Hewetson and Philip Sansom, all of whom were arrested and put on trial. This led to the setting up of the Freedom Press Defence Committee, with Read as chairman, and to the publication of two speeches by Read in their defence in a pamphlet entitled *Freedom Is It a Crime?*

To the very end of his life Read was prepared to argue and defend his views on art and its relation to society (inevitably a political stand) in language of which he was master. His last major public appearance was at an International Cultural Congress in Cuba in 1968, only months before his death. There he spoke on 'The Problems of Internationalism in Art' showing himself nonetheless able to recognise that there were still problems in this area to which he had devoted half a lifetime. He was still concerned in these last years with what he saw as threats to the rights of the artefact or the artist. In 1963 on a tour of Australia he was called on to testify in court that certain Aborigine works could not be considered obscene. Three years later, in 1966, he rose from his sickbed to appear in defence of an artist being prosecuted under the Vagrancy Acts of 1824 and 1838 for wilfully exposing to view in a public place – Leeds Institute Gallery, Cookridge Street – an obscene coloured picture 'Lost Love' and an obscene drawing.[21] The artist concerned, Stass Paraskos, with the trial looming, had written to a number of well-known personalities asking them to appear as defence witnesses.

until the sluggish tinder of the world's indifference
is consumed, consumed to the end.

Anger is now action. The white flame of justice
will dance wildly over Europe's dark marshes
until the morning air is everywhere
and clear
as on the hills of Hellas.

This beautiful assassin is your friend
walking and whispering in the night beside you.
His voice is the voice that made you

14

Herbert Read was included in this list because of his pre-eminence as an art historian, and the fact that he was thought of as a regional hero in Yorkshire, where the trial was to be held. The first reply to my appeal, by express post, came from Herbert Read who tried to reassure me, offered me the services of John Mortimer QC free of charge and promised to be an expert witness for my defence. There was a principle involved in the case and he was willing to defend it. He also made a joke about his usefulness as an expert in a court case under an Act designed to prevent vagrants from exhibiting deformed members of their bodies for profit.[22]

Read appeared as first witness for the defence, and was cited as a Trustee of the Tate Gallery. He did not think the works in any way 'depraving', they did not contain images of anything 'unnatural', no 'perverse' act, and were therefore a 'legitimate' representation of human sexuality.[23] In spite of this and further expert and eminent defence evidence, the case was lost, almost certainly through misapplication of legal technicalities.

Nevertheless it provided evidence (if any more were needed) that Herbert Read was prepared even at the end of his life to defend the causes of liberty and art. It is difficult to describe in limited terms an overview of a life so full of action and concerns. There are many smaller seeming anomalies unexplained: a pacifist who had acquired the DSO and the MC, an anarchist who accepted a knighthood, a poet and critic involved in all aspects of the Modern Movement who claimed the English poetry he most admired was that of the late sixteenth century (Peele, Daniel, Drayton and others) with modern affinities most with Hölderlin, Stefan George and Apollinaire. In the end I believe we must come back to the creative epicentre of all that he did, the poetry: we can do worse than take inspiration from the last two lines of 'The Heart Conscripted',[24] a poem which hints at some of the concerns I have mentioned and suggests finally the poetry should live on, the song which has no end:

The shock of silver tassels
the sledded breath ...
I who have fought my battles
keep these in a sheath.

The ulcer of exact remorse
from which the Lake poet perished,
the owl's indifferent hood –
these have vanished.

I hear only the sobbing fall
of various water-clocks
and the swift inveterate wail
of the destructive axe.

Lorca was killed, singing,
and Fox who was my friend.
The rhythm returns: the song
which has no end.

Notes

1 See Read, Herbert (1933) *Art Now* (London, Faber & Faber) p.9.
2 See correspondence between Read and Nolde, collection Stiftung Seebüll Ada und Emil Nolde, kindly brought to my attention by Dr Manfred Reuther. Evidence for the Belgian connections in Read's library.
3 See H. Read describing the drawing by René Magritte in his own collection in *London Gallery Bulletin*, no.1, April 1938, p.2.
4 Read, Herbert (1935) *The Green Child* (London, William Heinemann) pp. 228-9. In comparison see in particular the statement by Henry Moore in Read, Herbert (Ed) (1934) *Unit One* (London, Cassell) pp. 29-30, a statement Read himself may well have helped Moore to prepare: see Bowness, A. (1989) *The Conditions of Success* (London, Thames & Hudson) pp.21-3. Hepworth enters a much more classic, sometimes literally prismatic phase in 1934, at the same time as Nicholson's most strictly rectangular reliefs – with subtle counterpoints – are coming into production.
5 The passage in section 4 beginning 'Their feet upon the peat and sand …'
6 See Read, Herbert (1940) *Annals of Innocence and Experience* (London, Faber & Faber) p.176ff – the account given here was not entirely transferred to Read, Herbert (1966) *The Contrary Experience* (London, Faber & Faber), but the latter has additional information, pp.138ff.
7 London, Hanover Gallery, March–April 1960; reprinted in Read, Herbert (1962) *A Letter to a Young Painter* (London, Thames & Hudson) p.89.
8 Read, Herbert (1966) *Collected poems* (London, Faber & Faber) p.263.
9 Possibly published with the poem when it appeared in *The Sewanee Review*, LIII, 1945, pp.44-51.
10 Read (n.8) p.21.
11 Now in the Brotherton Collection, University of Leeds. The page is illustrated in Kramer, M. (Ed) (1969) *Jacob Kramer – A Memorial Volume* (Leeds, Arnold) p.5. The wording of the poem in manuscript differs very slightly from the published versions.
12 Read (n.8) pp.121-2.
13 *Ibid*. pp. 256-8.
14 Letter of 17 Oct 1948, published in full in C. G. Jung (1973) *Letters*, selected and edited by G. Adler and A. Jaffé (Princeton, Princeton University Press), vol.1, p.509-10.
15 Read, Herbert (1930) *Wordsworth* (London, Jonathan Cape) p.13.
16 (1912) *The New Age*, vol.12, p.95.
17 (1928-9) *The Criterion*, vol.VIII, pp.752-3.
18 (1937) *Adelphi*, vol.XIII, 458-63; XIV, pp.12-18; 44-8.
19 See Read (n.8) pp.137, 149-51. Herschel Grynszpan was a Polish Jew aged seventeen who assassinated Ernst von Rath, third secretary of the German Embassy in Paris on 7 Nov 1938.
20 This is understandably a strong element in the study of Read by the anarchist George Woodcock (1972) *Herbert Read: The Stream and the Source* (London, Faber & Faber).
21 See (1966) *Yorkshire Evening Post*, 19 Dec, p.1.
22 Paraskos, S. (1984) in *Homage to Herbert Read*, exhibition catalogue (Canterbury College of Art) p.42.
23 This account comes from the *Yorkshire Evening Post* (n.21) and the recollections of John Jones to whom I am most grateful.
24 Read (n.8) p.174.

15

15 Kurt Schwitters
*Collage with Herbert
Read* 1944-7. Private
collection

16 *New Yorker* cartoon,
inscribed on reverse
'Ludo from
Miriam Barbara
Gabo Ben'

"Oh, *that's* Herbert's muse."

16

17 Herbert Read *Figure Composition No.1* 1916. Private collection* (cat.no.185)

18 Herbert Read *Ethical Volition* 1916. Private collection* (cat.no.184)

Figure Composition - No 1   HRead. 1916.

17

Ethical Volition.   JHERead. 16.

19 Charles Ginner *Leeds University Buildings* c.1916. University of Leeds Art Collections (cat.no.96)

Herbert Read and Leeds

Michael Paraskos

Although not by birth an actual son of the city, Herbert Read's connections with Leeds were and remain strong. These connections are vital for understanding Read's development of thought and help to explain his unusually undogmatic approach to what often seem quite divers forms of art. Had Read not arrived in Leeds in 1908, it is unlikely his interest in the four key areas of his work – art, philosophy, literature and politics – would have developed in quite the way they did, or that he would have become the figure he did in the history of British and world art. In Leeds, Read found something unique and gained something unique; something which, perhaps, remains in the city to this day.

This uniqueness of the area Read acknowledged. Writing in the catalogue to the 1960 exhibition honouring Peter Gregory, founder of the University of Leeds Gregory Fellowships in the arts, he stated: '[Artistic] stimulus proceeds from intangible sources in the people; from a collective vitality that perhaps explains why so many of our best artists are born in Yorkshire'.

Leeds in the early years of the twentieth century possessed a remarkable cultural atmosphere which profoundly influenced Read. Two principal and two subsidiary factors contributed to this. The first concerns a new development in class politics, in which Read, because of his unfortunate family circumstances, was unavoidably a part. The second was the existence in the city of a climate for the strong promotion of, and debate on, art and culture, existing despite the apparent industrial degeneration of the city and the all too mockable philistinism of many of the city fathers. To these we might add the history of civic pride, which continued to find cultural expression in Leeds from the Victorian period until well into the twentieth century. And then there is the unquantifiable possibility that Leeds was accidentally lucky in having a number of talented people in its midst within a very short period of time, not least Read himself.

On the surface the Leeds Read arrived into was as far removed from Romantic ideals of culture as it was seemingly possible to get. Leeds was, Read wrote: 'a wilderness of stone and brick, with soot falling like black snow'. In the midst of this: 'Drab and stunted wage slaves drifted through the stink and clatter'. Even among all this 'dirt and drabness' however, Read cannot seem to avoid giving city life some of the poetic quality, the artistic potential, which many of the young Moderns, such as the Futurists and Vorticists, but also others, saw in it. The passage continues: '... tramcars moaned and screeched along their glistening rails, spluttering blue electric sparks'.[1] The scene is also one of beauty and excitement. As Read was later to assert: 'Inspiration ... is also to be found in the realities of our industrial civilisation'.[2] Yes, Leeds was a city of grotesque scenes, but the grotesqueries of industrial Capitalism were also made exciting by virtue of their very brutality and power.

Yet, although Leeds was one of the blackest slum-towns in the kingdom, still it was not without its cultural aspects, aspects which had allowed the Victorians to lavish praise on such cities that they were the rivals to the glory that was Greece and Rome. As early as 1846 Leeds had a formal school of art and design, which aimed to improve the artistic merit of local manufacture (something Read might well have approved of). Cuthbert Brodrick had given the city a magnificent town hall, in a grand Baroque Classicism, in 1858 and the Leeds City Art Gallery opened in 1888, although public art displays had been staged regularly before, at such unusual venues as the main hospital in Leeds, the General Infirmary. It was here the Prince of Wales opened the National Art Exhibition in 1868.

Leeds had also managed to cause something of a national stir with its statuary by Thomas Brock and Alfred Drury in City Square, newly laid out in 1903. These works represent one of the major civil commissions to be made in the progressive proto-Art Nouveau style of the New Sculpture; and while Brock's *Black Prince* remains a masterpiece in its own right, Drury's figures of *Morn* and *Evening*, holding their ice-cream cone lamps, soon became even more famous as the models for the poster advertisements for Ever Ready batteries.

But perhaps the most immediately important aspect of this type of civic pride for Read was the University of Leeds which in 1904 gained independence from the Victoria University, despised for its Manchester base by the proud burghers of Leeds, and by this time in terminal dissolution. Read's attendance at the University, from 1912 to his call-up for war in 1915, gave him a rare eclectic knowledge, involving, formally, the study of Latin, logic, law, history, French, English, geology, economics and politics. Such a breadth might put any modern student to flight, but Read studied extramurally too, particularly the works of ancient and modern masters of literature and philosophy, most notably Nietzsche, an interest which may be part of the key to Read's entrance to the Leeds Arts Club.

It was not that Read was following some standard course in university education. Partly due to his inability to decide which subject to study, he chopped and changed courses, eventually electing to take two degree

25

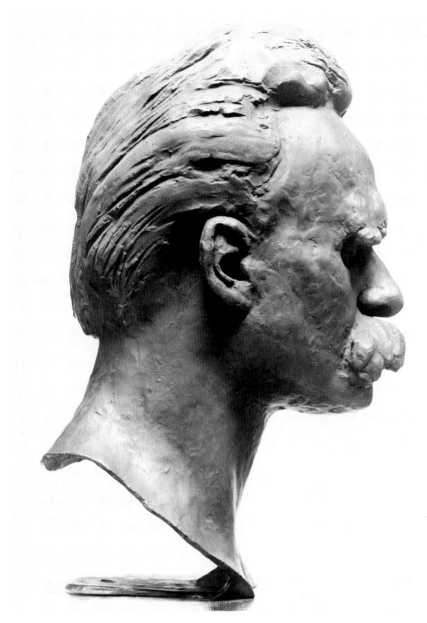

20 Max Klinger *Bust of Nietzsche* 1904. Museum der bildenden Künste, Leipzig (cat.no.119)

Nietzsche was a new world, and since my discovery of Blake, the most cataclysmic. For at least five years he, and none of my professors or friends, was my real teacher.

The Contrary Experience, pp.165-6

courses in tandem. He also had a profound dislike for the monological approach to education advocated, then as now, by the universities. He despaired of his fellow students who: 'were careful not to stray from the thin line which marked an easy path through the world of knowledge'.[3] This was not just morally wrong, but one might say he felt it was vulgar. The irony was that it was not just Read who felt this way about the University, but also its own Vice-Chancellor, Michael Sadler, and Read's professor of English, F. W. Moorman, who took Read under his wing, finding he had literary talent and ambition.

Leeds also had numerous local societies dedicated to more esoteric pursuits than the Art School, University or the city as a whole might have seemed likely to encourage. Bodies such as the Philosophical and Literary Society, the Mechanics' Institute (which had actually founded the Art School) and the Thoresby Society. Organisations such as these were responsible for the fact that during the late nineteenth and early twentieth centuries it was possible to attend lectures on art in the city at least two or three times a week. Yet, many of these institutions, even after the turn of the century, still reflected a Victorian bourgeois turn of mind – despite the demographic changes that were taking place, with the well-to-do Middle Classes, whose views these institutions tended to reflect, largely vacating the city for the countryside and small towns of Otley, Harrogate and York. So little impact had those who remained, the would-be young Turks of Modernism, made on the city's Establishment, however, that as late as 1917, when looking for an excuse to sack Frank Rutter from his post as Director of the City Art Gallery (for having helped Suffragette Lillian Lenton escape police bail) he was attacked for purchasing a somewhat tame, even by contemporary standards, modern painting by the late-Impressionist Camille Pissarro.

One organisation of great importance for Read which definitely did not reflect this Establishment attitude was the Leeds Arts Club. Founded in 1903, it may not on the surface seem so very different from the type of Victorian society that preceded it. Like them it organised lectures and debates, advocated social reform and self improvement and even promoted a form of the nineteenth-century guild movement. Its origins, however, were not the cosy bourgeois world of the nineteenth-century philanthropist, but rather the worlds of the Leeds Socialist and occultist networks, which, if truth-be-told, were not so very separate in 1903.

Its founder, Alfred Orage, was well integrated in both these worlds, as was his first discussion group, the 'Platonic Group' which the Arts Club succeeded. As well as advocating the Theosophic theories of Annie Besant the Arts Club promoted Nietzsche, an iconoclast of bourgeois society. It and its off-shoot, the Playgoers' Society, encouraged an interest in the New Realist playwrights, Ibsen and Shaw, and the New Symbolists, Strindberg[4] and Yeats. Despite its advocacy of Nietzsche, the Club also allied itself closely with the women's liberation movement. Consequently women were encouraged to join and, unusually for the time, made up a large minority of the membership. The radical fire of William Morris's Arts and Crafts Movement was also rekindled in the Club through the liberationist, even homoerotic, writings of Edward Carpenter, the Guild Socialism of Arthur Penty and the added coals of Orage's association with the Independent Labour Party and nascent British Communism. The Leeds Arts Club was indeed philanthropic, but this was not the philanthropy of the Victorian liberal con-

21

23

22

science; this was a revolutionary philanthropy of empowerment.

The large proportion of women members of the Arts Club was not the only significant aspect of its membership that should be noted. Most members were part of a new Middle Class, quite unlike the nineteenth-century bourgeoisie, yet which had grown up as a consequence of that bourgeoisie's attempts at education reform. Like Read, this new Middle Class had, by accident or birth, affinities with the Working Classes, but was clearly educated beyond being Working Class and by a Middle-Class education system. Many, like Read and Orage, were socially disenfranchised by the Establishment and its institutions which still dominated Leeds. A growing social group between the Working Class and the Bourgeoisie, it was almost inevitable that this class would create its own organisations, such as the Arts Club, and that these institutions would have a radical outlook.

Certainly Read seems to have been conscious of his socially ill-defined position and was, according to James King, 'haunted' by a sense of inferiority. In part this was based on his attendance at Leeds University where he 'felt cut off from the inherited traditions [Oxford and Cam-

21 Gerald Kelly *Portrait of Frank Rutter*. Municipal Gallery of Modern Art, Dublin

22 Francis Ernest Jackson *Portrait of Alfred Orage c.1920*. Leeds City Art Galleries (cat.no.116)

23 Mark Gertler *Portrait of Michael Sadler*. University of Leeds Art Collections (cat.no.92)

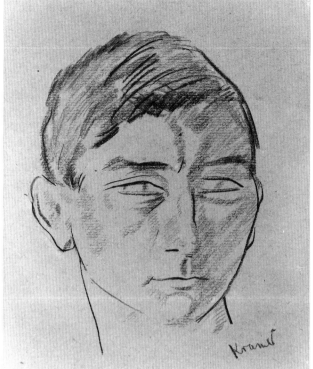

24

bridge] automatically bestow'. That this was more than just Read's personal feeling is perhaps testified by King's equal summary of Storm Jameson, who entered Leeds in 1909 and 'saw her institution as existing in another world from ... Oxford',[5] while Dickens as early as 1865 wrote of a man educated beyond his class, struggling to maintain his social position, in the novel *Our Mutual Friend* in the character of Bradley Headstone.

If King's assertion is correct, it is easy to see why a man such as Read would be drawn to the Arts Club. Increasingly his attention was being arrested by the condemnations of political agitators as he walked through City Square to work at the Skyrac and Morley Trustee Savings Bank. They, he wrote, 'gradually penetrated the armour of my inherited prejudices'.[6] The highly political lectures by Professor D. H. MacGregor and Arthur Greenwood at the Workers' Education Association classes Read attended before entering University may also have helped draw his attention to the Club, as both were members. By 1912 Read too was certainly enrolled and discussing matters with the first real artists he was to meet, Jacob Kramer and Bruce Turner. For all three the Arts Club was no doubt a vital haven from the deficiencies they found in the educational institutions, the University and Leeds School of Art, they attended.

Orage and his co-founder of the Arts Club, Holbrook Jackson, had already left Leeds by this time, in the case of Orage to edit a relaunched magazine, *The New Age*, on which Read himself would later work under Orage. Sadler and Rutter, however, had on their arrivals in Leeds been quick to involve themselves in the organisation, occupying a vacuum in it still apparent four years after Orage's and Jackson's exodus. They too no doubt found in the Arts Club something lacking in their occupational work.

Sadler and Rutter began to steer the Arts Club away from some of its more mystical extremes towards a more easily recognisable form of Modernist discourse. Yet, perhaps the holistic attitudes Read took, uniting art and life and seeing art as having a moral and social-reforming function, can be said to come from the earlier pre-Sadler/Rutter Arts Club, with its roots in the communalistic Arts and Crafts Movement of Morris. While at an Arts Club meeting, shortly after he had joined, Read had dismissed the ideas of one of Morris's chief protagonists in the twentieth century, and a stalwart to the Orage Arts Club, Arthur Penty, yet he later saw them as at least a possible means of achieving revolution, and certainly better than Fabian ideas. There is also evidence Read was in contact with Penty directly.[7] This suggests the discourse promoted by the earlier Arts Club survived and even developed under Sadler and Rutter, thus affecting Read. Certainly the type of art promoted by these two at the Club would support such a theory, with German Expressionism very much to the fore. Such art, after all, already had strong affinities with the existing Arts Club aesthetic, with its reverence for Nietzsche, revolutionary social theory and highly mystical content.

This mysticism is particularly evident in the works of Kramer and Turner. For them the use of the intuitive human faculties allowed the visualisation of a more expressive, and consequently 'truer', representation of reality. Others at the Club, however, such as Read, stripped the conclusions of such Club discussions of their mystical content, yet still retained a belief that by using one's intuitive faculties one could reach a 'truer' representation of reality. Whereas the spiritualists believed they were realising a vision of some barely perceived reality existing beyond human consciousness, somewhere in the ether (perhaps harking back to Orage's 'Platonic Group'), those such as Read believed they were visualising, in its purest form, reality as it is perceived by the human mind, what Read considered the *only* true reality. In effect we are witnessing a shift taking place, a stripping of art and artists of their quasi-religious function and instead a tying of them in to the world of early psychoanalysis; a shift which is paving the way for Read's later interest in Surrealism.

We have evidence of this difference of opinion in the Arts Club in an exchange of letters between Kramer and Read of 1918, when Read was still in the trenches of the First World War. Kramer had just given a lecture to the Leeds Arts Club's sister organisation, the Bradford Arts Club, in which he had effectively set out the spiritualists' case. He now wrote to Read to describe what he had said, suggesting: 'A spiritual discernment [in art] is more essential than the reproduction of the obvious'. Read accepted, in his extensive reply, that art did not need to be representational and also agreed with the general thrust of

25

Kramer's letter, which in effect amounts to an 'Expressionist Manifesto', but wrote specifically to correct Kramer on his use of the word 'spiritual'. This Read could not accept: 'I think you deceive yourself to this extent; the element of spirituality is not in the things, but in the image of the things in your mind'.

Tom Steele is undoubtedly correct when he says both men are here mining the same source for the terminology they use, that source being the Arts Club.[8] Both are re-engaging in a familiar Arts Club debate,[9] attested by Kramer's opening line in the letter: 'As you know Read that the degree of expression in a work of art is a measure of its greatness'. This was something Read certainly did know, as his response shows: 'I think we are agreed that

art is expression'. Both are reiterating a familiar concept which they must have been aware the other would concur with, at least if we are to take Kramer's confident assertion 'As you know Read' at face value.[10]

Yet the differences between Kramer and Read are nonetheless there, and remained throughout their lives. Read, for example, as late as 1968, in the revised edition of his book *The Meaning of Art*, ignored Kandinsky's blatant metaphysics, on which Kramer's ideas had been based, and stated the Expressionist imperative was the 'Expression of "the real process of thought" (Kandinsky called it the expression of inner necessity)' [Read's brackets]. There is nothing spiritual in this concept of Expressionism, it is rather, according to Read, an expression of

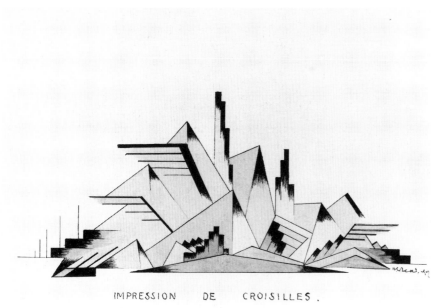

IMPRESSION DE CROISILLES.

26

26 Herbert Read
Impression de Croisilles
1917. Private collection
(cat.no.186)

27 Edward Wadsworth
Slag Heaps 1920. Leeds
City Art Galleries
(cat.no.207)

the reality of the mind, 'the real process of thought', almost exactly the same assertion he had made to Kramer fifty years previously.[11] The level of debate between Kramer and Read in this correspondence shows that the Arts Club was far from provincial in its outlook.

As well as avid involvement in the Arts Club, Rutter was not slack in trying to breathe new life into the City Art Gallery when he took over as Director in 1912, although this was usually in spite of rather than with his paymasters at the Corporation. So infuriating did Rutter find these officials, in 1913 he set up his own organisation, the Leeds Art Collections Fund, still in existence, to bypass them and raise funds specifically for purchasing contemporary works of art.[12] To the Arts Club itself Rutter brought encouragement for those advocating a 'non-pictorial expression', which seemed the logical extension of the Club's existing predilections. This would lead both Read and Kramer to experiment in this type of painting. Rutter also started the weekly habit of debating the lead articles in *The New Age* at the Club, thus tying its discussions into national and international discourses. The echoes of Croce which exist in the Kramer-Read correspondence may be a legacy of these debates. Yet there is also proof the Club was more than a mere receptacle of the outpourings of other people's debates, and that it in fact added to them with the 'Neo-Realist Manifesto', published by Ginner and Gore in 1914 in *The New Age*. As affinities between Neo-Realist ideas and the Expressionist Realism of Kramer and Turner might indicate anyway, Neo-Realism's ideas grew out of Arts Club debates in Leeds.

Rutter also brought Modernist exhibitions to Leeds, which Read would undoubtedly have seen, such as Gordon Craig's set designs and a 'Post-Impressionist Exhibition', including Cézannes, Gauguins, Van Goghs,

Kandinskys, Matisses, Serusiers and others of international repute, both in 1913. Very likely too, Rutter was instrumental in bringing Wyndham Lewis and a 'Cubist and Futurist Exhibition' to Leeds in 1914, although Kramer may have had a hand in this as well. This formed something of a dry-run for the soon to be named 'Vorticist Group' including as it did several of those subsequently given that title, such as Bomberg, Epstein, Wadsworth, Kramer and, of course, Lewis himself.

Despite its title, the *Cubist and Futurist Exhibition* also included work by artists such as Cézanne and Gauguin, perhaps those already owned by Sadler. Sadler's collection remains to this day a subject of great interest as it was probably the most progressive gathering of modern art in Britain at that time. Although initially ignorant of art, Sadler found buying paintings a palliative to depression. Even by today's standards Sadler's taste in anti-depressants seems impressive, including as it did the work of Kandinsky, Klee, Marc, Münter, Van Gogh, many of the leading English Modernists and, as mentioned, Cézanne and Gauguin. Gauguin's *Vision After the Sermon*, the 'Leeds Gauguin', was one of the principal works in the collection and must have seemed vindication to the Arts Club audience that saw it of their belief in the ascendancy of the spiritually charged, yet non-representational, use of colour and form in art.

This major proto-Expressionist work may have seemed

27

28

to point the way towards an abstract form of art, but Sadler's Kandinskys surely already demonstrated abstraction itself. Sadler began collecting Kandinsky's works before 1912 after seeing a number of woodcuts by the artist bought by his son, also called Michael, at an Allied Artists' Exhibition, organised by Rutter in London. Sadler's initial interest led him to journey to meet Kandinsky himself in Germany as well as to collect significant examples of his works, including the major masterpiece, *Composition VII* of 1913. There was even an attempt by Sadler to bring Kandinsky to teach in Leeds, but this was unfortunately prevented by the outbreak of war.[13]

Yet if Leeds narrowly missed contact with Kandinsky in person, it was still significant to the Arts Club, and consequently Read, that Kandinsky's principal treatise,

Über das Geistige in der Kunst, was translated by the younger Sadler. This placed the Arts Club members in a unique position at that time in Britain. Not only did they have high-quality works by Kandinsky and his associates in their midst, but direct and familial links with the translator of Kandinsky's ideas.

The works in Sadler's collection would have been very familiar to the Arts Club members as they were often used to illustrate Club talks, and even some meetings of the Arts Club were held at Sadler's home. Read also had a special, if unorthodox, access to the collection at other times. While Sadler's favourite, Kramer, was to be seen at the front door of Sadler's residence, Read had access through the back, with the help of his mother's friend, Miss Wallace, Sadler's housekeeper, with whom he took tea.

28 Paul Gauguin *The Vision after the Sermon* 1888. Scottish National Gallery of Modern Art

29

Read, like all the Arts Club members, would have been familiar with the debates going on at the time pitting Kandinsky's ideas against those of the remarkable philosopher T. E. Hulme, principally taking place in the pages of *The New Age*. Hulme attacked Kandinsky for Romanticism, lack of solidity in his forms and for using the falsehood of spirituality as a basis for his art. Instead he proclaimed a need for a new materialistic Classicism, hard and mechanistic. Both Read and Kramer took great interest in such debates and seemed to fall on either side of the divide. Yet in reality, as we have seen, the disagreements in Leeds were less clear cut than this. Read and

Kramer may have disagreed but they did so within a framework in which they both agreed. Perhaps it was only in a place such as Leeds, away from the physical presence of the protagonists and their parties themselves (which was probably just as well given the violent character of Hulme) that a third, compromise, position could have been reached. This compromise allowed for the incorporation of both Kandinsky's and Hulme's views into a single theory, as for the Arts Club there was not 'a barely negotiable divide' between them. Rather they were seen as twain points on a single spectrum; different but imperceptibly linked. It is an attitude which served

Read well throughout his career, as he 'could not see Romanticism and Classicism were mutually exclusive', according to Tom Steele; rather they were 'dialectically held in tension'. It was this holistic attitude that formed what amounts to a 'Leeds school of thought' in Modernism and which effectively unites Read and Kramer, despite their differences. Thus the Read who threw himself 'into the vortex', and was in fact to edit Hulme's papers after his death in the Second World War, still manages to have affinities with Kramer, an English Expressionist, both being members of that 'Leeds school of thought'.

The great importance for Read of the school of thought fostered by the Arts Club must be accepted, and accepted as of far greater importance than just for the immediate period in question. Here in Leeds Read first became engaged in the key debates of contemporary culture. His engagement was through a specific Leeds outlook, which was to be important for him throughout the rest of his life. Leeds also gave Read direct access to people who would be key figures in his life and development, such as Kramer, Rutter and Ginner, all of whom would later help introduce him to the major players in that other theatre of artistic debate, London. No doubt Leeds and the Arts Club association also helped Read gain his position on Orage's *New Age* in the 1920s.

Read left Leeds in 1915, following his call-up for the war, and was never to live in the city again. Yet he continued to revisit Leeds throughout his life, offering support for its artists and help for those, such as Peter Gregory and the Leeds Art Collections Fund, who sought to promote the arts in the city. His last visit, in 1967, shortly before he died, showed that even forty-four years after its collapse Read carried on the Arts Club's tradition of fighting philistinism in the city's Establishment, when he spoke in defence of a young artist being prosecuted for allegedly displaying obscene paintings (see p.18). One can only hope the city's memorial tribute to Read demonstrates it is a battle fought and won.

30

12 Rutter seems also to have been involved in another Victorian institution, the Philosophical and Literary Society, delivering to it a lecture series entitled 'The Evolution of Landscape Painting' from March 1913.

13 Although the dates seem to preclude a possible visit by Kandinsky to Leeds, Patrick Heron (see Heron interview) recalls that his father, Tom Heron, an Arts Club member, always insisted that Kandinsky did in fact visit Leeds as Sadler's guest. There is no other known confirmation of this assertion however.

30 Stass Paraskos *Lovers and Romances* 1966. Private collection (cat.no.174)

Notes

1 Read, H. (1963) *The Contrary Experience* (London, Faber & Faber) p.200.

2 (1960) Catalogue: *A Tribute to Peter Gregory* (Leeds).

3 Read (n.1) p.165.

4 An article on Strindberg by Read appeared in the University of Leeds magazine *The Gryphon*, no.XVIII, 1914.

5 King, J. (1990) *The Last Modern: a Life of Herbert Read* (London, Weidenfeld & Nicolson) p.24.

6 Read (n.1) p.200.

7 Penty is present in Read's address book from the period.

8 Steele, T. (1990) *Alfred Orage and the Leeds Arts Club 1893-1923* (Aldershot, Scolar Press) p.207.

9 Thistlewood, D. (1984) *Herbert Read: Formlessness and Form* (London, Routledge & Kegan Paul) p.33.

10 Read correspondence held by the library of the Victoria University, British Columbia, Canada. Kramer correspondence held by the Brotherton Collection, University of Leeds.

11 Read, H. (1931 [rev.1968]) *The Meaning of Art* (London, Faber & Faber) p.242.

31

I think it was in 1918, straight back from the front, that I first saw a collection of the drawings ... made as an official artist in France. I was immediately convinced, because here was someone who could convey, as no other artist, the phantasmagoric atmosphere of No Man's Land.

Introduction to *Paul Nash*, 1937

31 Paul Nash *We Are Making a New World* 1918. The Trustees of the Imperial War Museum, London (cat.no.153)

32 Wyndham Lewis *Mr Wyndham Lewis as a Tyro* 1920-1. Ferens Art Gallery, Hull (cat.no.128)

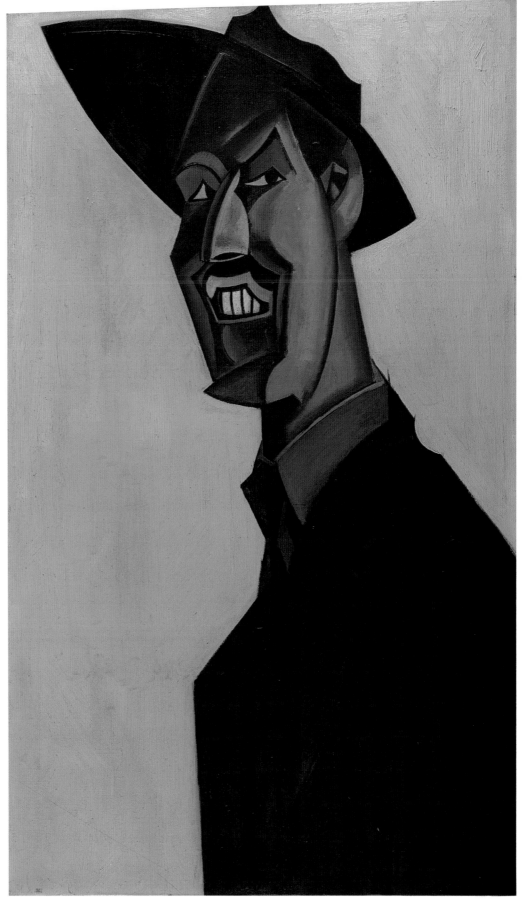

32

35

33

35

33-43
Original illustrations to
The Meaning of Art
(1931)

33 The La Grèze Bison.
Stone Age (Aurignacian
period); perhaps 20,000
BC. 1931 ed. fig.14

34 Stone figure. English;
late 13th century.
Collection Winchester
Cathedral. 1931 ed.
fig.29

35 *The Annunciation.*
Miniature mosaic.
Byzantine; 13th-14th
century. Collection
Victoria and Albert
Museum. 1931 ed. fig.27

36 *Orion crossing the sea.*
Bronze Mirror.
Etruscan; about 500 BC.
Collection British
Museum. 1931 ed. fig.3

34

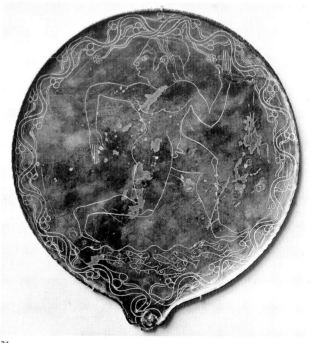

36

37

39

37 *The Twittering-machine.* Drawing by Paul Klee, dated 1922. Collection National Gallery (Kronprinzenpalais), Berlin. 1931 ed. fig.43

38 *Barbara.* Bronze by Jacques Lipchitz, 1942. Collection Buchholz Gallery, New York. 1968 ed. fig.60

39 *Abraham's Sacrifice.* From an illuminated psalter. English; about 1175. Collection Hunterian Museum, Glasgow. 1931 ed. fig.28

40 Stoneware jar. Chinese (Sung dynasty); 960-1279. 1931 ed. fig.9

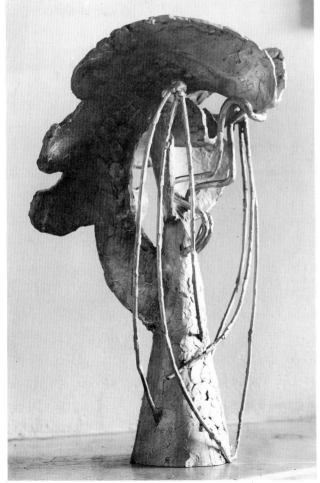

38

40

Herbert Read and the North European Tradition 1921-33

Andrew Causey

Herbert Read wrote less in the 1920s on the visual arts than on poetry and literature, and nothing at all on contemporary art. His energetic support for the Modern Movement later makes this seem strange, but the universal mistrust of radicalism and virtual absence of innovative visual culture in Britain after the war set different priorities. Between demobilisation in 1919 and his appointment to the Professorship of Fine Arts at Edinburgh University in 1931, Read was a civil servant, first at the Ministry of Labour, then at the Treasury, and from 1922 in the Department of Ceramics at the Victoria and Albert Museum. In so far as Read was identified with contemporary culture it was with the literary world of *The Criterion*, which T. S. Eliot edited and Read contributed to. It was a stern culture, anti-popular and concerned – outwardly, at least – more with standards than experiment. With watchwords like order, authority, tradition and the impersonal, it saw itself as reacting to the chaos in cultural and spiritual values that were perceived as resulting from the nineteenth century's twin legacies of mass materialism and Romantic individualism more than from the war.

Read shared the discontent with Romantic excess, art for art's sake, and the widely felt sense of the lack of spiritual authority outside dogmatic religion, which he rejected. He identified for a time with the cultural framework that grew up around Eliot, but it never entirely satisfied his feeling for the importance of the senses in aesthetic expression nor his preference for the synthesising power of intuition over the analytical tendency of the intellect. Read was attracted to Bergson in a decade when Bergson was seriously out of fashion. In the terms of debate that he acknowledged, Read in the 1920s was a classicist by affirmation, and, incompletely, by conviction; but underneath was a Romantic spirit deprived of its full expression.

The visual arts helped Read to find his way to a personal intellectual standpoint which fell into place rapidly from the time he started writing on art for *The Listener* in September 1929. Though he was by then ready to leave the Victoria and Albert Museum, it is wrong to think that the 1920s was a wasted decade in professional terms. The structure of the job suited Read in the early stages before his direction was clear, he made a useful range of contacts and his publications on art in the 1920s are more important than has been recognised. He was surrounded in the Museum by the art of all cultures and ages, and at a time when there was no stimulus from contemporary art, Read was able to discover from within the Museum's collections, and from contact with visiting scholars, new ideas and approaches that would eventually feed back into his views on contemporary art. He became interested in the way different cultures communicate their underlying 'will to form', their generic mode of expression, and his attention began to focus on nations and cultures as well as on chronological periods. He felt that the word art had become too identified with a single line of development, the classical, Mediterranean tradition, and, influenced by German thinking, Read turned to explore northern Europe. He was not concerned with works of art on their own: he was neither a critic in the limited sense of commenting only on art and events of the moment, nor was he an historian of changing artistic form. He was concerned with the wider issue of how art is represented within the broader cultural character of a society.

In 1921 A. R. Orage, familiar to Read from early days in Leeds, and editor of the influential *The New Age*, to which Read had occasionally contributed, presented him with two important openings: he offered him *The New Age*'s weekly 'Readers and Writers' column, which Read contributed during the second half of 1921, discussing a broad range of literary topics;[1] and through Orage Read was commissioned to edit for publication the papers of T. E. Hulme, the philosopher and earlier contributor to *The New Age* who had been killed in the war. Hulme was seminal for Read's thinking, and the book that resulted, *Speculations* (1924), was, as Read justly claimed in 1930, a key contribution to the thought of its period.[2]

In his column in *The New Age* Read kept track of French intellectual debates, as he continued to all through the 1920s. He liked the vigorous anti-Romanticism of Lasserre and Seillière, later became an admirer of Jacques Maritain's Neo-Thomism, and Read's belief in the need for active intellectual leadership to counter the threat from mass pressure for easy sensation led him later to support Julien Benda.[3] Read was élitist in the sense that he felt culture was the domain of the few and must be protected, but he was not an extremist, and never spoke with approval of French thinkers, such as Charles Maurras, leader of the far right movement *L'Action Française*, whom Eliot published in *The Criterion*, nor the xenophobic and anti-semitic Henri Massis who was translated into English and gained a following in Britain in the 1920s.

Read paid more serious attention in *The New Age* and all through the 1920s to Irving Babbitt,[4] leader of the American new humanists, and Eliot's former professor at Harvard, referred to by Eliot as 'the master'. Through Babbitt, as well as through Hulme, Read became conscious of the issue which he later regarded as the key to

41

42

43

41 Porcelain figure by Franz Anton Bustelli. Made at Nymphenburg, about 1760. Collection Museum für Kunst und Gewerbe, Hamburg. 1931 ed. fig.38

42 Tunny-fish in glass. Venetian; 17th century. Collection Victoria and Albert Museum. 1931 ed. fig.32

43 *Satan arousing the Rebel Angels*. Water-colour drawing by William Blake, dated 1808. Collection Victoria and Albert Museum. 1931 ed. fig.40

the intellectual debates of the decade, the polarity between Classicism and Romanticism. Babbitt had argued in his most recent book, *Rousseau and Romanticism* (1919), that Rousseau's naturalism had led to excessive dependence on the world of the senses, and thus on change, which is a feature specifically of the natural world, and that the whole Romantic period from Rousseau to the present day had become obsessed with novelty and the cult of the individual, leading to eccentricity and aberration. All of which culminated, Babbitt thought, in Bergson's belief that 'life is a perpetual gushing forth of novelties'.[5]

Babbitt wanted to restore the idea of a 'general nature' which is the core of normal experience, together with the Aristotelian doctrine of imitation as part of the creative act, and the classical belief in decorum and virtue as ethical values. Babbitt did not deny the importance of the imagination nor was he a dedicated opponent of Romanticism if it could be contained within an accepted cultural framework. Babbitt claimed to be an individualist, and to base his values on human experience; but, like Eliot in 'Tradition and the Individual Talent' (1919), he believed the individual only existed as the end product of a tradition, and that tradition was itself the historical representation of contemporary culture.

Read found support in the new humanists for his naturally dialectical way of thinking. Babbitt used the word 'monism' to describe the Rousseauesque permissiveness that enabled the individual to establish canons of value without outside check or authority. Babbitt, followed by Read, thought of Classicism and Romanticism not simply as good and bad but as tendencies that needed to be held in balance. Babbitt was almost as resistant to what he saw as the mindless Alexandrianism of Neoclassicism as he was to the anarchic individualism of Romanticism, and if his writing sometimes makes it seem that he thought otherwise, that is because excessive Romanticism and not Neoclassicism was the pressing problem of the day.

Read also found agreement in the new humanism with his belief that beauty should not be separated from ethics. He was concerned to find a way round the impasse of the Bloomsbury critics' formalism, as his comment that 'beauty is a quality of moral action as well as of significant form'[6] makes plain. Babbitt had pointed out that British eighteenth-century aesthetics had tended to see beauty as a product of feeling, and that, Babbitt thought, was where the rot set in. Read quoted Babbitt as saying that 'to rest beauty on feeling ... is to rest it on what is for ever shifting'.[7] For Read the divorce of beauty from ethics had opened up the possibility of aesthetics as a separate area of study, and this, he felt, ultimately led to the Bloomsbury cul-de-sac: the positing of a separate aesthetic emotion, which Read forcefully rejected, looking to both the new humanism and Hulme for support in doing so.

Read's criticism of Fry was muted at first, but more open by the beginning of the 1930s,[8] when his own growing interest in German and north-European art made him realise how much the dominance of the Mediterranean tradition in British criticism had led to stress being placed on beauty as opposed to other possible artistic values, such as expressiveness. Read continued to insist through the 1920s that the Mediterranean tradition should not be regarded as *the* tradition, challenging, for example, the American critic Waldo Frank in 1926 for asserting that 'there has been then for the entire term of history in the western world a common culture; a common whole'. In reply to Frank's assertion of the classical tradition as this common culture, Read countered with the tradition of 'the northern European or Gothic races ... the Gothic tradition', as transcendental, non-humanistic and different in nature from the classical.[9] This was to become a main thrust of Read's thought over the next few years.

Hulme had also stressed how the word 'art' had grown synonymous with 'the classical tradition in art', acknowledging as his source the German theorist of art Wilhelm Worringer.[10] The years 1500-1900, Hulme claimed, were a period of humanist values, and did indeed belong to the classical tradition, but the modern era was different. Hulme used the German theory of empathy, as adapted by Worringer from Theodor Lipps, to distinguish between art produced at times when people easily transferred their feelings onto external nature – periods of empathy, when the resulting art tended to be naturalistic – and times when people found the outside world hostile

and fled from the natural into a spiritual world – periods of abstraction. The modern period, Hulme asserted, was the latter.

Much of Hulme's thinking resembled that of the new humanists, but they diverged on the issue of modern art, which Babbitt rejected but which, in the form of Vorticism, Hulme supported. Read's views are not easy to establish. He had been committed to Vorticism to the extent of doing a small number of paintings in the Vorticist style, before giving up practising art. Read's comment in a review of the 1919 Bomberg exhibition that 'Bomberg's mind is that objective, scientific sort, which alone is capable of wonders',[11] said as much about the classical critical values Read then adhered to as it did about Bomberg, whose work at that moment was becoming increasingly individual. Vorticism was dead by the early 1920s, and because it remained virtually forgotten during Read's lifetime, he had no occasion to review it later. Lewis's virtual retirement from the visual arts for most of the 1920s is a sign of the almost total loss of confidence on the part of the avant-garde.

What ambitious art there was in England in the 1920s was largely concerned with landscape, a genre that neither Lewis and the Vorticists nor Hulme had been interested in, and which represented that very preoccupation with nature that much of the anti-Romantic onslaught in the 1920s was directed towards. Working on Hulme's papers between 1921 and 1923 would have brought home to Read the extent to which Hulme's preferences were for Egyptian and Byzantine art, whose non-classical, non-naturalistic types of expression were represented by means of relatively fixed styles maintained over centuries. Taken together these circumstances go a long way to explaining Read's silence on modern art.

Both through Babbitt, and independently in his 'Readers and Writers' column, Read came to comment on Lessing, the eighteenth-century German theoretician of art whom Read, referring to Lessing's *Laokoon* (1766), at one point described as 'the greatest writer on aesthetics since Aristotle'.[12] Read was interested in Lessing's theory that each artistic medium had separate properties which should never be confused, and he quoted Lessing's classic distinction 'that succession of time is the department of the poet, as space is that of the painter'.[13] Babbitt who, in an earlier book *The New Laokoon* (1910), had adapted Lessing's title and dealt with the same problem as Lessing, of the need to keep the separate spheres of the arts free from confusion, may well have introduced Lessing's ideas to Read.

The problem that both Babbitt and Read saw themselves facing was an indiscriminate naturalism and dependence on sensation resulting from the rise of a popular audience for art in the nineteenth century. The solution was to draw a protective line round each art, to define its role so that it could function unhindered by the potentially destructive force of popular taste. Thus far Read's commitment strongly resembles the classic

44 Ernst Barlach *Mors Imperator (Death the Emperor)* 1919. Private collection* (cat.no.17)

44

Modernism Clement Greenberg was to define two decades later partly through his 'Towards a Newer Laocoon' (1940), which implied in its title a link with Babbitt as well as Lessing. Greenberg was also to feel the need to assign the arts to protected territory at a time when their true expression was threatened by demand for accessibility.

But Read was by nature a synthesiser, and the rather rigid diagrams of what was virtuous in the arts that the classicists were drawing up did not really appeal to him. Rather than Lessing's 'separate spheres', Read naturally inclined to the doctrine of '*ut pictura poesis*', the likeness of poetry to painting, which Lessing had been engaged in discrediting. Read's affirmation of Lessing in 1921 came when the war was a recent memory and the ordering side of his temperament naturally held a certain sway. Others of a similar mind who had shared his experience at the front, notably Wyndham Lewis, maintained a severely anti-popular and anti-naturalistic stance right through the decade: Lewis's *Time and Western Man* (1927) is among other things a passionate defence of space as the province of the visual arts and time as that of poetry as Lessing had suggested. Lewis's book also included a

virulent attack on Bergson who was the focus, among contemporaries, of the anti-Romantics' attacks, as Rousseau was among earlier writers.

Read started to read Bergson immediately after the war[14] and came to him again when he was editing Hulme's papers. Hulme was devoted to Bergson in his early writings (1909-12), and though Hulme's subsequent criticism, of the Vorticist period, was more in key with the intellectual mood of the 1920s, Read was surely expressing his own values by re-ordering Hulme's writings in *Speculations* so that his comments on Bergson, composed into two chapters, appear as the climax of the book rather than the beginning. Bergson's concept of intuition presented an alternative to the constricting philosophies of the anti-Romantics and enabled Read to expand his intellectual position.

For Bergson the intellect was analytical: it divided, categorised and spaced things out. It was also artificial, in the sense that Bergson believed that reality was continuous and not divisible in this way. Reality was understood not through intellect but through intuition which he saw as instinct raised to a state of consciousness. Intuition was the root of the creative process: it synthesised rather than analysed, and was able, unlike intellect, to penetrate the world of reality. This was because reality was not a mass of objective detail external to the individual but a synthesis of past memories and present experiences, interpenetrating and inseparable, and conceived of as duration. Reality in this way became associated more with temporality, in the sense of endurance, than with space. What Read discovered from Bergson was an organic rather than atomistic concept of reality which, translated into the field of art, opened up the possibility of the genetic concept of art that Read was gradually to develop.

Read was also interested in Bergson's concept of intuition. He had been considering how psychoanalytic theory might provide a scientific basis for criticism, and without denying the role of the analyst in helping to elucidate the critical process, felt that art itself was intuitive and indivisible. 'Analysis', he wrote: 'involves the reduction of the symbol to its origins, and once the symbol is in this way dissolved, it is of no aesthetic significance: art is art as symbol not as sign'.[15]

This mistrust of the intellect as a reductive force grew, to the point where he wrote in 1930 that:

form, though it can be analysed into intellectual terms like measure, balance, rhythm and harmony, is really intuitive in origin; it is not ... an intellectual product. ... When we describe art as the 'will to form', we are not imagining an exclusively intellectual activity, but rather an exclusively instinctive one.[16]

The anti-Romantics worried particularly about the nineteenth century's easy satisfaction with naturalism and the world of sensation. Read did not dissent, but grew more concerned with a different and older legacy: the Cartesian division of mind and matter, which left the sphere of pure thought high and dry surrounded by a mechanistic world. Bergson helped to break down this division, and Read soon discovered in A. N. Whitehead – whose *Science and the Modern World* he described as the most significant publication in the combined field of science and philosophy since Descartes[17] – confirmation of many of Bergson's ideas.

Read came to see that the division between mind and matter, or man and the world, collapsed when the world was seen in Bergson's way. This was because of the key role Bergson gave to memory, which recorded the intersection of mind and matter in the past and brought the synthesis forward to the present, making the individual mind the carrier of the concept of reality as endurance. This dealt a blow to the idealism of the classicists with whom Read had identified because there was no longer an ideal structure or work of art out there waiting to be imitated. The individual was within a changing organic reality, the equivalent of which in spiritual terms is a kind of romantic pantheism. While Read was never a Bergsonian without reservation, Bergson certainly disposed once and for all of the fixed classical hierarchies he had been concerned with in the early 1920s.

45

Read's genetic theory of art, based on the study of art in relation to its origins and development within society, was only defined in *Art Now* (1933). *Art Now* opens with a contrast between the outdated – as Read saw it – idealism of the eighteenth century classical tradition and Giambattista Vico's theory in *La Scienza Nuova* (1725) of the function of poetry as the primary expression of a society's early consciousness of itself. Bergson is seen in *Art Now* as the appropriate philosopher with whom to end Read's account of the development of the genetic theory. There was a decade, however, between Read's learning about Bergson through Hulme and the publication of *Art Now*, and there is no question of Read's jumping directly from Bergson to Vico. Bergson was a liberating force, but it was German aesthetic theory that formed the immediate basis for Read's genetic theory of art.

Perhaps prompted by Hulme's knowledge of Germany, and aware of his having met Worringer in Berlin in 1912, Read at some point contacted Worringer with whom he remained in touch all his life. Having learned German between 1922 and 1925, he translated Worringer's second book *Formprobleme der Gotik* (1912) into English as *Form in Gothic* (1927); he was almost certainly instrumental in getting an article by Worringer on Expressionism, 'Art Questions of the Day', published in *The Criterion* in 1927, and he proof-read the English translation by Bernard Rackham, his head of department at the V&A, of Worringer's third book, *Egyptian Art* (1928). Read's *Philosophy of Modern Art* (1951) was dedicated to 'my esteemed master in the philosophy of art, Wilhelm Worringer'.

Worringer did more than anyone else to help Read develop the framework for a theory of art when he realised that the new humanism (to which he remained loyal in print till 1928)[18] was too negative. For Babbitt to counter Bergson's *élan vital* with his own doctrine of restraint, *frein vital*,[19] was not a happy solution for Read who, beneath the tidy classical carapace, did not altogether believe in restraint. It was not until 1933, in *Art Now*, that Read made the personal and entirely credible claim that 'art may flourish in a rank and barbaric manner from an excess of animal vitality; but it withers and dies in the arid excesses of reason'.[20] But already in 1925 he was happy to quote André Gide saying in a similar voice:

It is important to remember that the struggle between Classicism and Romanticism also exists inside each mind. And it is from this very struggle that the work is born; the classic work of art relates the triumph of order and measure over an inner Romanticism. And the wilder the riot to be tamed the more beautiful your work will be. If the thing is orderly in its inception, the work will be cold and without interest.[21]

Read's writing on art in the 1920s arose from his duties at the V&A. He co-authored *English Pottery* (1924) with Bernard Rackham, published *English Stained Glass* in 1926, and *Staffordshire Pottery Figures* in 1929. Apart from these, Read published specialist articles on ceramics and glass in the *Burlington Magazine*, *Apollo*, *The Connoisseur*, and *Country Life*. *English Pottery* is interesting for the way the authors stressed the peasant tradition in the medium, conscious that they were modifying the nineteenth century's high valuation of technical achievement. Read's 1929 book on Staffordshire figures picks up this point. 'These rather lonely remnants of English peasant art have suffered from unjust neglect' because nineteenth-century writers 'whose only aesthetic criterion was "elegance" scorned to notice their lowly existence'.[22]

Preoccupation with the peasant, the primitive and the pre-industrial was a part both of the 1920s' reaction against Victorian materialism and its search for innocence after the war. So far as the visual arts were concerned, a point of particular significance was reached with the discovery of the Cornish primitive Alfred Wallis by Ben Nicholson and Christopher Wood in St Ives in 1928. The consequences of that discovery, and the high valuation of the primitive and unspoiled, were to feed into the Hampstead artistic circle of the mid-1930s, of which Read was to be the intellectual leader. In the sense that Read's writing on Staffordshire focused on the primitive, it looked forward to his activities in the 1930s. In so far as it did this, however, it was a denial of the values of *The Criterion* circle, whose cultural orientation was sophisticated in the manner of an educated urban élite and who would have found in this valuation of the primitive an example of the Rousseauesque Romanticism they mistrusted.

46

English Stained Glass is primarily concerned with the Gothic, which Read divides into two: up to 1350 he calls the 'Age of Reason', and from then to 1500 the 'Age of Sentiment'. The first he calls a classical epoch because art is inseparable from the values of the whole of contemporary culture and cannot be studied in isolation. It is an integrated art with parts subsidiary to a total vision. The second period is romantic, and possesses variety and charm but lacks power and social worth. In late Gothic, Read thought, detail took priority over unity, each part was a display of artistic virtuosity, and the effect of the whole was lost. Read as the opponent of Romanticism and art for art's sake is saying that art cannot be treated as an isolated activity subject to its own laws without becoming enfeebled.

Read did not think of the development from the first to the second stage of Gothic simply as an aesthetic shift, but the mirror also of a spiritual and social change. In the 'Age of Reason', specifically in Thomism, Read saw the supreme intellectual achievement of the Middle Ages, the harmonious merging of the principles of faith and reason, matched in art by a corresponding resolution of the tendencies towards abstraction and naturalism. The 'Age of Sentiment', which saw the growth of anti-intellectualism in the Franciscan appreciation of the simple life, love of nature, and the introduction of religion to the masses on easily assimilated terms, was the equivalent of the period of Rousseauesque Romanticism. Read's cultural values are still anti-Romantic and anti-popular, he is still the true colleague of Eliot and Lewis in his mistrust of individualism and conviction that creativity is the privilege of the few. He plainly sees the universal and harmonic character of the earlier period of Gothic as diminished by the fragmenting individualism of Romanticism.

Read pays tribute to Worringer in the preface, and in one sense *English Stained Glass* is about the way Worringer's approach can supplant that of Ruskin and the kind of Romantic naturalism which had been discredited for Read. Ruskin is quoted as saying in *Aratra Pentelici*:

All this talk about abstraction belongs to periods of decadence. In living times, people see something living that pleases them; and they try to make it live for ever or to make something as like as possible that would live for ever … [they] would fain, if they could, draw every leaf upon the tree.[23]

Ruskin's limitation, in Read's view, was obviously his naturalism and inability to see the virtue of early 'classical' Gothic.

By contrast Read accepted the argument about Gothic ornament in Worringer's *Form in Gothic* (ornament alone being the subject of Worringer's study in the book). Worringer argued that the vitality of Gothic ornament was abstract not organic, and had nothing to do with the vitality of nature. The distinction held good that he had put forward in his first book *Abstraction and Empathy* (1908), between the will to abstraction characteristic of peoples fleeing the natural world in search of the spiritual, and the will to empathise with nature typical of peoples at ease in the world of organic form.

Read's position was different from Worringer's in one significant respect: the perfection of Read's 'Age of Reason' results not from the dominance of spiritual over naturalistic values, but in their reconciliation – the merging of reason and faith, the traditions of Classicism and the Christian Church, which he saw coming together in Thomism. Read's sense of this harmony formed by the merging of Aristotelian empiricism with the Christian tradition of faith through revelation showed that for him Classicism and Romanticism, the abstract and the organic, north and south European, were not irreconcilable, as for Worringer they were. Worringer had a mission to instate Gothic as *the* form of northern expression and one which was best when it was purest, uncontaminated by the naturalistic art of southern Europe.

Temperamentally Read, unlike Worringer, possessed a harmonising, synthesising disposition which was naturally drawn to Thomism which he understood chiefly through the writings of Jacques Maritain. Only when, in 1930, Read came to review the second English edition of *Art and Scholasticism* was Maritain's full importance acknowledged, with Read ranking the book second only to Hulme's *Speculations* in importance for the recent development of the philosophy of art. Worringer was still in his mind when he wrote that 'anyone born this side of the Alps must acknowledge, if he is honest with himself, the supremacy of Gothic. It is the only supreme expression of the northern will to form'. But at the core of Read's thinking on the Gothic was his acceptance of Maritain's argument that beauty is inherent in things and is not a product of the conformity of things to an absolute. The senses, Maritain is quoted as saying, may not alone suffice because the senses cannot realise the element of measure in beauty – 'but as the mind perceives, so the senses enjoy'.[24] Maritain showed Read a way out of the dilemma of how, as a 'classicist', to acknowledge the intuitive ordering, measuring facility of the mind without being deprived of the pleasure of the senses.

In *Form in Gothic* Worringer dismissed the 'autocratic claim of aesthetics to interpret the body of non-classical art'.[25] It was the same point that Babbitt had made in a slightly different way when he complained that the growth of an independent science of beauty in the eighteenth century had had the effect of detaching art from ethics. Read, too, was already conscious of the problem as being at the source of the fallacy of 'significant form'. What each in his own way was saying was that the growth of aesthetics as a separate discipline in the eighteenth century had pushed the wider role of art to one side in the pursuit of the inherently smaller project, the understanding of beauty. A convincing theory of art that was not merely a theory of beauty Read felt was urgently needed. In his brief introduction to his translation of *Form in Gothic*, which was published only months after *English Stained Glass*, Read stressed this point, emphasising Worringer's distinction between 'general aesthetics, or theory of beauty, and *Kunstwissenschaft*, or theory of art'. Beauty and art had become confused. As Read put it: 'Art is ordered expression, and the difference between art and beauty is not merely formal and historical, but a difference of values. Beauty is a sensational value; art is always an intellectual value'.[26]

Worringer believed that the spread of naturalism into northern art at the Renaissance had fatally compromised it, and later movements, like the Baroque and Rococo, in which he discerned the Gothic spirit, formed only a coda to the great periods of art before 1500. Twentieth-century German Expressionism was another late manifestation of the Gothic will to form, and Worringer's article on Expressionism in *The Criterion* in 1927 was a lament, first because of the 'elegiac classicism' that he saw already supplanting it (presumably the *Neue Sachlichkeit*), but more fundamentally because Expressionism, Worringer believed, had turned out to be a mere studio affair, 'the last revolt against the increasing social meaninglessness of art', a play of empty gestures on the periphery, not a movement stemming from the roots of society.[27]

Read did not share Worringer's pessimism. He preferred Hulme's belief that the modern period was essentially different from the post-Renaissance centuries, and did not engage with the problem of public versus private art, which was part of what made the Gothic unique for

Weekly Notes on Art

Distortion

DISTORTION is a word with unpleasant associations for listeners, but as some of the letters evoked by these weekly notes bear witness, it indicates one of the real difficulties in the appreciation of the visual arts. I should be prepared to say, in a very general and perhaps paradoxical way, that all art is distorted. Even classical Greek sculpture, which I dealt with last week, was distorted in the interests of the ideal. Was the line of brow and nose ever in reality so straight, the face so oval, the breasts so round, as they are represented in say, the Aphrodite of Melos? Of course not; and, indeed, it is difficult to find any work of art before the Italian Renaissance which does not depart in some way or other from actuality. In the sixteenth century, largely, I feel, from a misunderstanding of the purpose of classical art, a representational literalness did become dominant. But it did not last for long: the seventeenth and eighteenth centuries for one reason or another forsook the Renaissance conception of art, and it was only in the nineteenth century, that age of sham revivals, that the representational motive once more became normal.

There are, however, various degrees of distortion and no one, it will be said, objects to the idealisation of reality. It is only when nature is outraged that the spectator must protest. The line of brow and nose can be made straight, but the leg must not be twisted into an impossible shape. It is a question of degree, but it is arguable that the degree makes all the difference. But where can we draw a line? If we leave Greek art and consider early Celtic or Scandinavian art, we shall find that the distortion has proceeded so far that the representational motive has been entirely lost, and we are left with nothing but a geometrical pattern. In Byzantine art we find that the desire to give symbolic representation to an idea has deprived all human figures of their humanity. Christ on the Virgin's lap is not a child, but a miniature representation of the glory, majesty and dignity of Christ the man. In Gothic art all is made to contribute to the Cathedral's single effort to express the transcendent nature of religious feeling; the idealism of Greek art is united with the symbolism of Byzantine art; the result is not representational. In Chinese art, in Persian art, in oriental art generally, motives are used, not realistically, but sensually; that is to say, they merely contribute to the general rhythm and vitality of the artist's pattern.

All these departures from exact imitation are purposive. They are dictated either by the artist's will to form, his desire for a balanced or unified pattern or mass; or they are dictated by his desire to make a symbol for something super-real, something spiritual. I think it might be held that the second aim, the desire to make art symbolical, is not strictly æsthetic. I know of few works of art so impressive as the Byzantine churches at Ravenna; but the art is partly the work of time. The impression, that is to say, is not purely artistic, but partly historical, partly religious, partly atmospheric, and to that extent must not be credited to the power of the artist.

Isolate the art, and you are reduced to the elements of form and colour.

The psychological reasons which lead an artist (and the artist in all of us) to express himself in pattern are obscure, though no doubt they can be explained physiologically. But the instinct that leads us to put unnecessary buttons on our clothes, to match our socks and ties or hats and coats, that makes us put the clock in the middle of the mantelpiece and the parsley round the cold mutton, is the primitive and uneducated stirrings of the instinct that makes the artist arrange his motives in a pattern. The carver of the Chinese horse illustrated opposite might without much trouble have made his horse more realistic; but he was not interested in the anatomy of the horse, for the horse had suggested to him a certain pattern of curved masses, and the twist of the neck, the curls of the mane, the curves of the haunches and legs, had to be distorted in the interests of this pattern. The result was not very much like a horse —in fact, this horse is often mistaken for a lion—but it is a very impressive work of art.

The Chinese horse happens to belong to the greatest period of Chinese art; it must be all right, the sceptic is willing to admit. But when it comes to a modern work of art, to a painting like the one by Schmidt - Rottluff reproduced here, then for some reason a deep sense of hostility is aroused. The principle involved, however, is exactly the same. Schmidt-Rottluff is not interested in the living model, but the model has suggested a pattern, and the pattern achieved is a legitimate work of art.

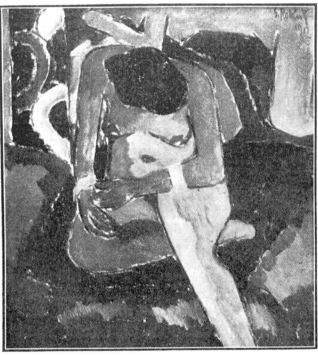

Nude, by Karl Schmidt-Rottluff

Kunsthalle, Hamburg

But does pattern constitute a work of art? That was the very pertinent question raised by a correspondent a few weeks ago. My provisional answer was that although a work of art always involves a pattern of some kind, all patterns are not necessarily works of art. Such a statement needs some definition of its terms. A 'work of art' generally implies a certain degree of complexity; we refuse the term to a simple geometrical design of circles and triangles, and even to the intricate but accomplished design of a machine-made carpet, although such patterns may be well-balanced or symmetrical.

What we really expect in a work of art is a certain personal element—we expect the artist to have, if not a distinguished mind, at least a distinguished sensibility. We expect him to reveal something to us that is original—a unique and private vision of the world. It is this expectation which, blinding the plain man to all other considerations, leads to a confirmed misunderstanding of the nature of art. Such a man becomes so intent on the meaning or message of a picture that he forgets that sensibility is a passive function of the human frame, and that the objects received in sensibility have their objective existence. The artist is only concerned with this objective existence. When he passes from sensibility to moral indignation or extra-sensuous states of any kind, then the work of art to that extent becomes impure. This means that a work of art is fairly adequately defined as pattern informed by sensibility.

Andrew Causey   45

48

48 Henri Matisse *Repos du Modèle* from *The Meaning of Art*, 1931 ed. fig.42

Worringer. Vorticism had been an expressionist movement, and its line is vital but non-organic, fitting Worringer's definition of Gothic ornament. Rejecting Worringer's notion of a steady decline, Read came increasingly to believe in the importance of German Expressionism as part of the tradition of northern art, and his articles in *The Listener* suggest that it was German art, as much as French and much more than English, that kindled his interest in the twentieth century.

In September 1929 Read was asked to contribute an article on 'The Meaning of Art' to the BBC's new journal *The Listener*. It was subtitled 'An Introduction for the Plain Man', and led to Read's being commissioned from 1 January 1930 to write a 'Weekly Notes on Art' column, in which he reviewed current exhibitions and new books. He continued the series, missing only one week, to 15 April 1931, when his appointment as Professor of Fine Arts at Edinburgh University compelled him to scale down his commitments, and he alternated first with Paul Nash, and then with other critics and writers.

Towards the end of 1931 the articles appeared in book form as *The Meaning of Art*. There were omissions and a loss of emphasis as articles were re-ordered to tell a more or less chronological story, and the book was differently illustrated as if – in respect of modern art, at least – the intention was to make it as accessible as possible. Thus an article on 'Distortion',[28] accompanied in *The Listener* by a 1910 painting by Schmidt-Rottluff, a German artist then unknown in England, was illustrated in the book by a 1916 Matisse. In ways like this the adventurousness of Read's ideas was sometimes lost.

Though the articles were very broad in their cast, contemporary art was well represented from the beginning. In January 1930 Read was writing about modern Italian art, in March he discussed Picasso, and in April Surrealism. In November Read wrote two articles on modern German art, introducing names from *Die Brücke*, post-war Expressionism and the *Neue Sachlichkeit* that were scarcely known in England.[29] Though Read was writing weekly for *The Listener* in the style of a freelance art critic, 1930 was in fact his last full year as a museum officer and civil servant. He had little direct experience of some of his subjects, and he was working in what was for him largely uncharted territory. An element of self-education existed in his writing, and while he engaged easily with some kinds of contemporary art, he had difficulty with others.

The area where Read seemed least at ease was Surrealism. Neither his article 'Beyond Realism', which focused on Surrealism, nor his 'Psychoanalysis and Art',[30] which referred to it, were reproduced in *The Meaning of Art*. 'Beyond Realism' reflects Read's existing pattern of thought in the way he contrasts Surrealism as romantic, because it dealt with emotion and sentiment, with Cubism as classical, on account of its concern with measure and proportion. (Cubism here, and still in *Art Now*, meant post-war Cubism, including what we would now call Purism). 'My own preferences are classical: that is to say I derive most pleasure from a work of art ... in which expression is achieved with some degree of formal precision. But I could never see why, though a classicist, I should be forbidden the enjoyment of romantic art'.[31]

Read admitted to having seen little Surrealist art, and there had been very little discussion of it in the English press. As Read based his analysis of Surrealism closely on Freud, his 1925 article 'Psychoanalysis and the Critic' might have been a way into Surrealism for him, including, as it did, a measured summary of the psychoanalytic ideas of Freud, Jung and Adler. But it was a cautious article, warning against the use of analytic methods to explain works of art ('art is art as symbol and not as sign'), and it was not until 1932, in *Form in Modern Poetry*,[32] that Read adopted a more confident approach to psychoanalysis and literature. Read was interested in 1925, as always, in new ideas, but at a time when he was beginning, through German theory, to explore the psychology of style as a collective or cultural manifestation, art as mirror of the psychological make-up of the individual would have been less relevant to him.

Though the year 1930 was to be a turning point, Read still had a residual loyalty to the new humanism and the *Criterion* circle. He published that year a pamphlet in support of Julien Benda, whose best known work *La Trahison des Clercs* explored his theory of the need for the intellectual to uphold reason against sentiment. Benda's seminal work *Belphégor* (1914) also appeared in English, in 1929, with an introduction by Babbitt,[33] in which Babbitt added Surrealism to the things he disliked about the Modern Movement. As the expression of a literary historian, Babbitt's Surrealism focused on Joyce, and he associated Joyce's stream of consciousness with the sense of impermanence and lack of structure he felt Joyce inherited from Bergson. Read's first comments on Surrealism in 1930 were also connected with Joyce, written in a tone that was cautiously explanatory rather than enthusiastic. Read associated Surrealism with Romanticism and liked, especially later in the decade, to view it as part of the English cultural heritage. In doing so, Read avoided consideration of the political dynamic of Surrealism in France which cut right across the traditionalist leanings of humanism.

Read's article on Picasso was a review of the German Wilhelm Uhde's unusual book *Picasso et la Tradition Française* (1928), in which Uhde associated the Spanish and German art traditions as sharing a common search for the transcendental. Read followed Uhde in drawing a distinction between the two great leaders of Modernism, describing Matisse as having a defined place in the history of modern art because of his ancestry in Cézanne and the French tradition, while Picasso's contribution was less well understood because, Read inferred, he belonged to the northern, spiritual tradition which had not yet been properly acknowledged. Though irritated by Bloomsbury's idolisation of minor French masters, Read was not attempting to diminish France's contribution to Modernism, and was saying here that Matisse is somebody we understand while Picasso should be our particular concern at this point because his 'northern' affiliations are an issue of the moment.

Writing about Derain in 1932,[34] Read saw that Derain's early departure from Cubism fitted into the classical recall to order which, in its literary form, he himself had approved of ten years earlier. To describe Derain's paintings he used words like 'virtue' in what he called 'the old sense' – meaning the way the word had been used in pre-Romantic times to value rationality and moderation. The prestige of Derain's being, like Matisse, a master in the French tradition enabled Read to stretch a point and name him 'probably the most important living artist'. But at the same time he asked 'how can a reactionary artist like Derain continue to interest us?' The answer was that Read could value a reactionary artist because he had not yet fully disclaimed the classical values he had espoused at the beginning of the 1920s, and

49

would not do so until the consolidation of fascism in Germany in 1933. Until then, but not after, Read was happy to be called a classicist.

Read hung on to his earlier values while evolving new ones through stress on transcendentalism and spirituality, and the northern will to form. When he spoke of Spain,[35] he placed it in a contemporary light, by pointing to the meaning that the mystic tradition of El Greco had for the present day in a way that the courtly style of Velasquez no longer did. He referred to the way Spain had escaped the familiarising process of the Grand Tour, and described Catalan Romanesque frescoes as the most beauti-

49 Henry Moore *Half-figure* 1932. Tate Gallery. Bequeathed by E.C. Gregory 1959 (cat.no.140)

50

accepted canons of British taste when in 1930 he described George Grosz as 'undoubtedly a very great artist', and he knew the way Grosz and Otto Dix would be received in Britain when he described how they 'scandalise art for art's sake critics'. In championing art which 'shared the common life of the people ... [which has been] reduced by the war to disillusion expressed in a negative vision through irony, satire and invective',[37] Read had finally left behind the standards of the new humanism and its belief in universal sentiment as opposed to the particulars of everyday life – seen in the work of Grosz and Dix at its most dislocated. Read was now saying that art was about the whole of human experience and could not necessarily be reduced to the typical. In the terms that Read had used ten years earlier the art he now defended was romantic.

There is no disputing that Read's priorities were changing, though the lines of the debate in his mind were still those established by Worringer. In discussing the development of animal ornament in the Middle Ages, Worringer had argued that the real world, though it was unfriendly and did not permit empathy – and did not, therefore, lead to organic or naturalistic form in the manner of Mediterranean art – was nonetheless an actual part of people's lives, on which they could not turn their backs. The combination of the tendency to abstraction, which Worringer believed to be the natural expression of northern art, and this pressure of actuality, which reflected the everyday but did not give rise to naturalism, led, according to Worringer, to caricature.[38] A very similar account of abstraction coming together with the actuality of an unfavourable post-war environment and emerging in forms that are often close to caricature can be used to explain the art of Grosz and Dix. Read's connection with Worringer ('actuality' was Read's word, the translation of Worringer's *Wirklichkeit*) helps to explain how he arrived, apparently so suddenly, at what was at the time a very un-British taste.

Read's passion for German art peaked with his friendship with Max Sauerlandt, to whom he dedicated *Art Now* (1933) 'in admiration of his knowledge of the art of all ages and in recognition of his devotion to the cause of modern art'. An Italian Renaissance specialist who had branched into other areas of the fine and applied arts, Sauerlandt had been since 1919 director of the Museum für Kunst und Gewerbe in Hamburg.[39] He had been a regular visitor to the V&A in the 1920s and first met Read there in April 1923. They had fairly regular meetings in London and at least one in Hamburg over matters of curatorship, but their friendship blossomed only about the time Read left the Museum. In February 1931 the sculptor R. P. Bedford, whom Sauerlandt had just met with Read, and who was also on the staff of the V&A, showed him his own studio where Sauerlandt was surprised and impressed by Bedford's collection of negro artefacts. Read and Sauerlandt also visited Henry Moore, from whose exhibition in April at the Leicester Galleries

ful in the world (which was careless: what he meant was not beautiful but expressive). All this time he was pointing, in Worringer's terms, to the abstract side of Spanish art, the side that would link it, according to Uhde's method, to northern transcendentalism.

Read saw German art as 'a queer mixture of vision and sensuality',[36] always conscious of the spiritual world as something not only endowed with grace but also full of mystery and menace – in contrast to the rational and humanised world of France. He stepped right outside

50 Barbara Hepworth
Kneeling Figure 1932.
Wakefield Art Gallery
(cat.no.104)

51 Emil Nolde *The
Family* 1931. Ada und
Emil Nolde Stiftung,
Seebüll. Repr. *Art Now*,
1933, pl.5 (cat.no.168)

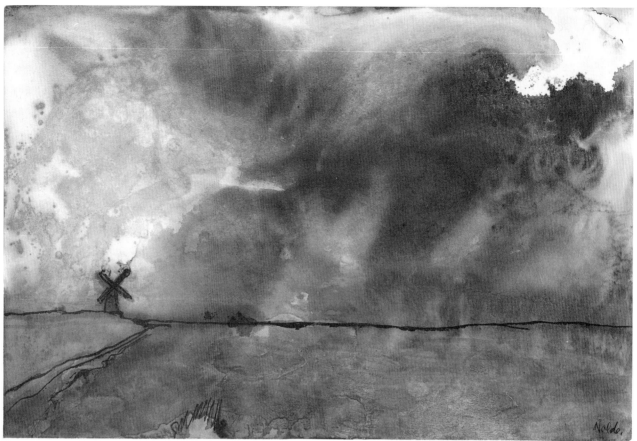

52

Sauerlandt purchased a sculpture for his museum. Read reviewed the exhibition for *The Listener*,[40] and the article became the only piece on modern British art in the first edition of *The Meaning of Art*.

Apart from being a distinguished scholar of older art, Sauerlandt was interested in the contemporary: in 1921 he published a book on Emil Nolde, a German artist whom Read was to single out in *Art Now*, and was honorary director of the Landes Kunstschule in Hamburg. Wherever he travelled he looked at contemporary art museums, and in June 1927 lamented the poor representation of contemporary art in the Tate, imagining how it would look with a collection of modern German pictures. He may have shared such ideas with Read at the time, but it was only when Read left the V&A to go to Edinburgh, and had time to explore the twentieth century, that Sauerlandt broached with Read the possibility of organising a big modern German exhibition for London. They discussed it when Sauerlandt stayed with Read in Edinburgh in January 1932, and their discussions would have been given reality by the Edvard Munch exhibition – the first in Britain – organised by the Society of Scottish Artists, that was being shown in Edinburgh at the time. Read had reviewed it for *The Listener*[41] and was so impressed that Munch became for him the founder of modern north-European Expressionism and the artist who saved German art from being overrun by France.

Sauerlandt followed up their discussions by pointing to the success of a big German show in Oslo. That, however, had been limited to Post-Impressionism, and Sauerlandt's ambition was an exhibition of post-war painting, and not only, by then, for London but for the whole of Europe. He knew that such a project would have powerful opponents among conservatives in Germany, and he pressed Read to set up a committee straight away so that the initiative could come from outside Germany, and Sauerlandt would assist with representations to the authorities in Berlin. The project not only came to nothing, but his championing what was to become forbidden art certainly contributed to Sauerlandt's downfall, as he was one of the first museum directors to be dismissed, on 5 April 1933, when the National Socialist Government came to power.

Sauerlandt remained in contact with Read who by the end of 1933 had left Edinburgh to become editor of the *Burlington Magazine*. Sauerlandt was also interested in English art and had written a long review for the *Hamburger Fremdenblatt*[42] of the *Mediaeval English Art* exhibition at the V&A which Read particularly commended his *Listener* readers not to miss.[43] Read's first editorial contribution to the *Burlington Magazine* was a survey of English art published in the first issue he edited in December. The article[44] was to be a turning-point for Read whose interests were to become directed increasingly towards England, and it also stimulated Sauerlandt to suggest contributions to the *Burlington Magazine* from himself. Their relationship had begun to turn from German priorities to English when, two weeks later, at the beginning of January 1934, Sauerlandt died at the age of fifty-four.

As Read finished *Art Now* in July 1933, three months after Sauerlandt's dismissal, the dedication was made in the knowledge that his friend's career had been destroyed, and Read's preface, which refers to the ignorant pretensions of the new German government in artistic matters, must have been written with Sauerlandt especially in mind. *Art Now*, with its long introduction on German aesthetic theory and its favourable view of German art (within a text which is, however, carefully balanced) marked the climax of Read's interest.

Read, however, kept an emotional commitment to German art, writing a preface to a Penguin special *Modern German Art*,[45] on the occasion of *Twentieth Century German Art*, the English response, held at the New Burlington Galleries in July 1938, to the *Entartete Kunst* exhibition shown in Munich the year before. Read again referred to the artists' use of irony and satire:

Some say these are literary characteristics and have nothing to do with the true, or formal, qualities of art. But that is precisely one of the distinctions that derive from our Latin prejudices. German art is not to be dismissed on such a quibble. It has its own safeguards against sentimentality, which is the only literary vice we need fear.[46]

Sauerlandt's importance for Read was exactly as Read described it in the dedication: it was the influence of a scholar 'of the art of all ages' who could combine this with 'devotion to the cause of modern art'. Read was drawn to German writers on art because of the ambitious terms they set themselves and, at least in Sauerlandt's case, because modern art was not seen as a different subject to, or needing different treatment from, any other.

Part of Read's plan for *The Listener* articles had been to expand on the idea of a northern art. Modern art was but one aspect of this and Read was certainly not trying to become an authority on the twentieth century to the exclusion of other interests. His two articles on modern German painting in November had been immediately preceded by three on Flemish old master painting following a visit to Antwerp.[47] Read believed that the Flemish exhibition at the Royal Academy in 1926-7 had been undervalued, partly because of Fry's influence with the public and his lack of understanding of Flemish art. He attacked Fry severely in *The Listener* in 1932, partly on this issue.[48] Having discovered that the kind of argument he had used to defend Grosz and Dix could be used in favour of Flemish art – with its comparable concern for 'actuality' – Read had another strand of his plan to define a northern art in place. In addition, Read found Fry's critical authority irksome, and there is sense now in which, having found his feet as a reviewer, Read was beginning to challenge Fry's authority.

'English art', Read was to say a year later,

53

suffering from the lack of any native lead, has grown feeble in a quite unnatural attempt to follow the French lead, which is Latin and antipathetic. I know that too much can be made of racial differences in art and literature; but they can also be too easily ignored, and the whole history of European art since the age of the great migrations shows the two opposed principles, which are rooted in the broad racial distinction of Germanic and Latin. Any complete fusion of these principles seems impossible, and even today when political and economic factors have done so much to obliterate real racial distinctions, it is still worth considering whether a certain fidelity to native traditions in art and literature would not be more fruitful in enduring works than the barren cosmopolitanism of contemporary fashions.[49]

54

Read's polemics on behalf of contemporary British art
over the next few years were more persuasive because he
had clarified in his mind the tradition into which he saw
them fitting.

Notes

1 For Read's relationship with Orage, see Martin, Wallace (1967)
The New Age under Orage (Manchester University Press).
2 Read, Herbert (Ed) (1924) *Speculations. Essays on Humanism and
the Philosophy of Art by T.E.Hulme*, International Library of Psychology, Philosophy and Scientific Method (London, Kegan
Paul, Trench Trubner). The claim is made in Read's article 'Art
and Scholasticism', *The Listener*, 19 March 1930.
3 Read's comments on Lasserre and Seillière are in *The New Age*,
4 Aug 1921. There is a reference to Maritain in Read, Herbert
(1926) *English Stained Glass* (London, G.P. Putnam's Sons) and
more substantial discussion in Read's essay on Descartes in
Read, Herbert (1929) *The Sense of Glory. Essays in Criticism* (Cambridge University Press), and in his 'Art and Scholasticism'
(n.2). For Read's views on Benda see Read, Herbert (1928)
'Humanism and the Absolute', *The Criterion*, Dec; Read, Herbert
(1930) *Julien Benda and the New Humanism*, University of
Washington Chapbooks No.37 (Seattle, University of Washington Bookstore) – later reprinted in the Beacon paperback edition
of Benda, Julien (1955) *The Betrayal of the Intellectuals* (Boston),
and Read's introduction to (1933) *The English Vision* (London,
Eyre and Spottiswoode) p.xi ff.
4 For Read's review of Babbitt's *Democracy and Leadership*, see *The
New Age*, 1 Oct 1921, and *The Criterion*, Oct 1924. See also Read:
'Humanism and the Absolute' (n.3).
5 Babbitt, Iriving (1919) *Rousseau and Romanticism* (New York,
Houghton Mifflin) p.xii.
6 *The New Age*, 1 Oct 1921.
7 *Ibid*. Read is quoting from *Rousseau and Romanticism* (n.5) p. 207.
8 See especially Read, Herbert (1932) 'The Painter Critic', *The
Listener*, 7 Dec.
9 Read, Herbert (1926) 'The Attributes of Criticism', in: *Reason
and Romanticism* (London, Faber and Gwyer) pp.5 ff.
10 See *Speculations* (n.2) p.82 ff.
11 Read, Herbert (1919) 'David Bomberg', *Arts Gazette*, 13 Sep.
12 *The New Age*, 1 Oct 1921
13 *The New Age*, 29 Nov 1921.
14 See Read, Herbert (1963) *The Contrary Experience: Autobiographies*
(London, Faber & Faber) p.277.
15 Read, Herbert (1925) 'Psycho-Analysis and the Critic', *The
Criterion*, Jan.
16 Read, Herbert (1930) 'Form and Expression', *The Listener*, 17
Dec, reprinted in Read, Herbert (1931) *The Meaning of Art*
(London, Faber & Faber) pp.7-8.
17 Read reviewed *Science and the Modern World* in *The Criterion*, June
1926, and Whitehead's *Religion in the Making* in *The New Criterion*,
May 1927. He discussed Whitehead again in his essay on
Descartes in *The Sense of Glory* (n.3).
18 See 'Humanism and the Absolute' (n.3).
19 See *Rousseau and Romanticism* (n.5) pp.150, 200.
20 Read, Herbert (1933) *Art Now* (Faber & Faber) p.30.
21 'Réponse à une enquête de la Renaissance sur le classicisme',
8 Jan 1921, from *Morceaux Choisis*, p.453, quoted in 'Psycho-
Analysis and the Critic' (n.15).
22 Read, Herbert (1929) *Staffordshire Pottery Figures* (London, Duckworth) p.21.
23 *English Stained Glass* (n.3) p.5.
24 'Art and Scholasticism' (n.2).
25 Quoted from Worringer, Wilhelm (1927) *Form in Gothic* (trans.
H. Read) (London, Putnam) p.8.
26 *Ibid*. p.ix.
27 Worringer, Wilhelm (1927) 'Art Questions of the Day', *The
Criterion*, Aug.
28 *The Listener*, 26 Nov 1930, illustrated by Schmidt-Rottluff, *Nude*,
1910, then coll. Kunsthalle, Hamburg. The article was reprinted
in *The Meaning of Art* (n.16) pp.11-14 without this illustration.
29 'Modern Italian Painting', *The Listener*, 22 Jan 1930; 'Picasso',
5 March; 'Beyond Realism', 16 April; 'Modern German Painting', 29 Oct; 'Post-War Art in Germany', 5 Nov.
30 'Beyond Realism' (n.29); 'Psycho-Analysis and Art', *The Listener*,
April 1930
31 'Beyond Realism' (n.29).
32 Read, Herbert (1932) *Form in Modern Poetry*, Essays in Order, no.
11 (London, Sheed and Ward).
33 (New York, Payson and Clarke).
34 'André Derain', *The Listener*, 5 Oct 1932.
35 In 'El Greco', *The Listener*, 12 Nov 1930.
36 'Modern German Painting' (n.29).
37 'Post-War Art in Germany' (n.29).
38 *Form in Gothic* (n.25) pp.61-2.
39 Information on Sauerlandt is mainly from Dingelstadt, Kurt
(Ed) (1957) *Max Sauerlandt. Im Kampf um die Moderne Kunst. Briefe
1902-1933* (Munich, Albert Langen/Georg Müller).
40 'Henry Moore', 22 April 1931.
41 'Edvard Munch', 2 Dec 1931.
42 'Englische Kunst des Mittelalters', 15 Oct 1930.
43 'English Gothic', *The Listener*, 14 May 1930.
44 'English Art', reprinted in Read, Herbert (1952) *The Philosophy
of Modern Art* (London, Faber & Faber). It was inspired by the
Royal Academy's winter exhibition 1933-4 of British Art.
45 Introduction to Thoene, Peter (1938) *Modern German Art*
(Harmondsworth, Penguin) pp.7-8.
46 *Ibid*.
47 1, 8 and 15 Oct 1930.
48 'The Painter Critic' (n.8).
49 'Edvard Munch' (n.41).

Weekly Notes on Art

Edvard Munch

EDVARD MUNCH is an artist whose work is little known in this country, but there is no doubt that he is one of the most important influences of the last fifty years. He occupies, in relation to the modern German movement, very much the same position that Cézanne occupies in the French movement. We might say that he saved German art from being swamped by the consequences of Cézanne's inventions—from being overwhelmed, that is to say, by a mode of expression that would have been quite foreign to the Nordic genius. Munch's work is therefore of peculiar relevance to us, for English art, suffering from the lack of any native lead, has grown feeble in a quite unnatural attempt to follow the French lead, which is Latin and antipathetic. I know that too much can be made of racial differences in art and literature; but they can also be too easily ignored, and the whole history of European art since the period of the great migrations shows the persistence of two opposed principles, which are rooted in the broad racial distinction of Germanic and Latin. Any complete fusion of these two principles seems impossible, and even to-day, when political and economic factors have done so much to obliterate real racial distinctions, it is still worth considering whether a certain fidelity to native traditions in art and literature would not be more fruitful in enduring works than the barren cosmopolitanism of contemporary fashions. That at least is the lesson which Munch has to offer, and I find a happy augury in the fact that the Society of Scottish Artists, in their annual exhibition at Edinburgh this year, have included a representative loan collection of Munch's works.

Munch was born in Löiten in Norway in 1863. After studying in the local technical school, he went to Oslo and there became a pupil of Christian Krogh, who represented the new impressionist movement in Norway. From 1889 to 1892, and again from 1895 to 1897, he was in Paris, but Paris had little to teach him, or little that he cared to absorb. His characteristic individuality is already shown in a picture like 'Das kranke Mädchen' ('The Sick Girl') painted in 1885, and his later developments are all implicit in a work like this. Between his visits to Paris, and from 1897 to 1909, Munch lived in Germany, and there he felt free to develop in a sympathetic atmosphere. That sympathetic atmosphere soon crystallised into a following, the most significant group in the history of modern German painting, a group known as 'Die Brücke' ('The Bridge') and including artists like Heckel, Kirchner, Schmidt-Rottluff, and Emil Nolde—names sadly unfamiliar to English ears. This group acknowledges Munch as their master, and from it originated that much wider movement in modern

The Dead Mother, by Edvard Munch

German art known as Expressionism—a movement entirely distinct from the contemporary French movement, and one which, in my opinion, ought to be much more sympathetic to our own northern consciousness.

What are these characteristics in Munch, and in the modern German school generally, which distinguish it from modern French art? I can perhaps best convey an impression of them by describing one of Munch's early pictures. There is one, to be seen in the art gallery at Bremen, called 'The Dead Mother'. Across the background is a simple couch, rather vaguely defined; at one end of this couch, only too terribly defined, is the emaciated dead face of the mother. In front, to the left of the picture, is the figure of a little girl, staring towards you with wild, unseeing eyes, her arms uplifted and her hands pressed to her ears as if to shut out the unholy silence that now reigns in the death chamber. Nothing more. The picture, you see, is a kind of dramatic symbol; it is the abstract idea of death symbolised by a human figure represented at a moment of spiritual crisis, and that generally was the character of Munch's early work. He must have felt the extraordinary superficiality of the French Impressionists, occupied to the exclusion of all other interests with problems of light and colour, texture and composition. Such problems had their interest for Munch, too; but beyond them was the great problem of human life, and everything else must be subservient to that.

This emphasis on subjectivity in art, on the element of human feeling, was one influence which Munch passed on to German Expressionism; but there was also the technical side. The early pictures of Munch are already painted in a bold, vigorous manner; as Munch's art develops this quality grows more emphatic. Roughly speaking, there are two alternative methods in painting—tone or line. If you desire depth and plastic cohesion, you must develop your tonal relations at the expense of linear outline; but if you desire movement and rhythm, you must develop linear qualities at the expense of tone. On the whole, we may say that Munch has sacrificed tone to line, and in this the modern German movement has to a great extent followed him; but there has been an attempt, which you can trace in the works of Munch, to obviate the limitations of the linear or graphic method, and to make it, in spite of everything, expressive of what we may call spiritual or psychological values; and this has been done by developing a quality which might be called monumentality. Lines enclose planes, and these planes, in terms of paint, are so solid in form and intense in colour, and so firmly organised in a structural sense, that they gain, as it were, the depth and atmosphere of real things. Art is no longer imitation, nor representation, but creation.   HERBERT READ

Preface to *Art Now*, 1933

This book, dealing with the most recent developments in painting and sculpture, is not an attempt to defend extremes of expression in a partisan spirit. Like many other people, I enjoy modern art with an enthusiasm which I try to keep free from intellectual prejudices. I am willing to admit that enthusiasm, being an emotional attitude, is a prejudice of another kind; but it is, in honest men, an inevitable one. Positive criticism begins as an impulse to defend one's instinctive preferences; but it only deserves the name of criticism if it reaches beyond the personal standpoint to one which is universal – that is to say, philosophical or scientific. This has become a commonplace of modern literary criticism, but it needs to be affirmed in the sphere of art criticism, which in this country has not been in any sense systematic.

The pragmatical Englishman is habitually content with such a state of affairs, especially since it justifies him in a hearty scorn of a phenomenon so disturbing to his complacency as modern art. The modern artist – by which term I mean the artist modern in sentiment as well as in circumstance – is in this manner gradually isolated. The public in general will not accept him at his face value, and is far too cautious to be convinced by a partisan enthusiasm. That such a situation has its dangers is proved by recent events in Germany. Before the coming into power of the present dictatorship, modern art enjoyed in Germany an esteem unequalled in any other part of Europe. Most towns of any importance had representative collections of modern painting and sculpture; in some cases these collections were as contemporary as a modern exhibition of motor-cars or Paris fashions (to take two spheres in which an obscure will to art does find adequate expression). Most of the leading German artists held positions as teachers in official art schools or were in more in direct ways supported by the State; museums and galleries were directed by the kind of informed criticism which I have indicated as desirable. Indeed, a happy state of affairs. But with the access to absolute power of a group of men, who, whatever may be said of their political abilities, can hardly be described as distinguished by any particular sensibility for the plastic arts, this state of affairs was suddenly destroyed. Artists and museum directors were dismissed from their posts, modern paintings and sculpture were relegated to the cellars or suffered worse indignities. This was entirely the result of a monstrous illogicality which identified modernism in art with communism in politics. The word 'Kulturbolschewismus' was invented, and under that cry a far-reaching vendetta was declared on those movements in contemporary art which are the subject of this book. My 'apologia' for modern art was not written with this situation

in view; but the object of this Preface is to claim that the theories I put forward involve a complete denial of the cultural identity of the modern movement in art and the communist or bolshevist movement in politics. A few modern artists may be Communists, and some are undoubtedly Jews – a fact which may have more to do with the matter than the German politicians would admit. But the majority of modern artists are neither Jews nor Communists, nor racialists or politicians of any kind. They are just artists, and, if anything, the more 'modern' they are in spirit as artists, the more disinterested and detached they become. In short, the good artist is very rarely interested in anything but his art.

So much is a matter of present fact; but in this book I hope I have shown further that even in its origins and development the modern movement in art has nothing whatsoever to do with sentiments external to its nature. You may, if you like, connect it inevitably with the general course of culture and civilisation since the Renaissance; but not only modern art, but modern ideas of every sort, including certainly the ideas underlying fascism and nationalism, are the outcome of the same tendency. Modern art is inevitably modern; but its modernity is expressed in terms which are strictly artistic, and these are the result of developments within the technique and science of art. The great artists who have most determined the course of modern art – Constable, Turner, Cézanne, Matisse, Picasso – have been and are singularly devoid of ideologies of any kind. They live in their vision and their paint, and follow the inevitable course dictated by their sensibility.

That their reliance on their sensibility may have had revolutionary consequences is perhaps to be admitted; but that too is an inevitable tendency of the modern spirit. The more mechanical the world becomes (not only the visible world, but the actual process of living) the less spiritual satisfaction there is to be found in the appearances of this world. The inner world of the imagination becomes more and more significant, as if to compensate for the brutality and the flatness of everyday life. That process of compensation has taken place in other historical periods, and art as strange and incomprehensible as any to be seen to-day may be found in the past. But not in the immediate past. The prejudice against modern art is, I am convinced, the result of a confined vision or a narrow range of sensibility. People forget that the artist (if he deserves that name) has the acutest sense of us all; and he can only be true to himself and to his function if he expresses that acuteness to the final edge. We are without courage, without freedom, without passion and joy, if we refuse to follow where he leads.

56

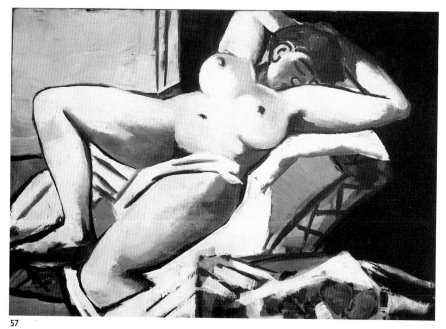

57

59

58

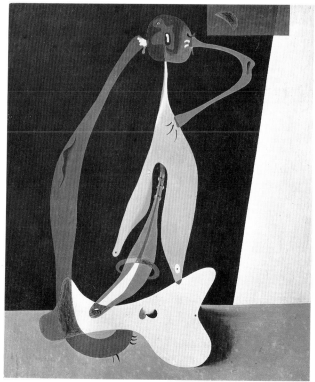

60

57 Max Beckmann *Nude*
1929 (pl.14)

58 Karl Hofer *Still Life*
1930 (pl.25)

59 Henri Matisse
*Portrait of a Girl in a
Yellow Dress* 1929-31
(pl.1)

60 Joan Miró *Femme
Assise* 1932 (pl.102)

61

63

62

64

61 Max Ernst *Couple Zoomorphe en Gestation* 1933 (pl.98)

62 Jean Hélion *Painting* 1935-6 (1948 ed. pl.161)

63 Paul Klee *Lady with necklace* 1932 (pl.119)

64 Paul Klee *Pavilion with Flags* 1927 (pl.120)

65

65 Ben Nicholson
Composition 1933 (pl.73)

66 Alfred Wallis
Harbour 1933 (pl.27)

66

A Nest of Gentle Artists

Herbert Read

(1962) *Apollo* Vol.LXXVI, No.7 (new series), September, pp.536-40. Reprinted by kind permission of the Editor

I am often asked to write my 'reminiscences', by which people mean my memories of the famous men and women I have known and of the movements and events in which I have been personally involved. Unfortunately, I do not possess what American writers sometimes refer to as 'total recall'. Recollection in my case is a completely arbitrary process, visual rather than auditory, and entirely unreliable. I can retrace the growth of my mind, the ever widening range of my interests, but I have a distressing lack of curiosity about people – or rather about their origins and associations. This is true even of some of my lifelong friends. I do not know who their parents were, where they went to school, how many times they have been married, or the maiden names of their wives. I offer these excuses for the vagueness of the present puny essay in the genre, which I have written because I think I may be the only participant who is likely to record an event of some importance in the history of English art: the existence for a few years of a close community of artists out of which emerged all that was to be most significant for the modern movement in England.

In April 1933 I left Edinburgh, where I had been a professor for two years, somewhat precipitately, and was under the immediate necessity of finding accommodation in London. I had already formed a friendship with Henry Moore – he has reminded me recently that it began one day in 1928 when we were introduced to each other by Sir Eric Maclagan at the Victoria and Albert Museum. Maclagan was the Director of that institution, and I was acting as his personal assistant. Moore had then asked me to come to his studio to see his work, and he relates that I came, saw all, and in true Yorkshire fashion (which he could appreciate) said nothing. He had spent the evening speculating with his wife (he had recently married Irina Radetsky) on my opinion, and then the next morning I had telephoned to ask if he could possibly let me have some photographs of his work because I wanted to write an article about it for *The Listener*. This was, I believe, the first time that a general article had been devoted to his sculpture and my appreciation of it was the beginning of a firm friendship and a mutual understanding that persist to this day.

This must have been the reason why I turned to Henry in my need and why he at once responded with an offer to lend me his studio since he was going abroad for a few weeks. So there I was, installed in the sculptor's studio, and it is an illustration of the kind of memory I do possess that I can still distinctly remember several pieces of sculpture that were in the studio at this time, and even their exact positions in the studio. They included the *Reclining Figure* in brown Hornton stone, now in the Leeds City Art Gallery, and the 'butter girl', as we used to call her, a boxwood figure of 1932 now in a private collection in London.

The studio was situated at No.11a Parkhill Road, on the frontier that divides the two worlds of Hampstead and Camden Town. A few yards along the road, behind the wall of the Priory Church, there was (and still is) a row of studios called the Mall, approached by a private path, and in one of these Ben Nicholson and his wife Barbara Hepworth had recently settled. Henry, Barbara and myself all came from Yorkshire – we had all received some degree of education in the same city of Leeds. This may have given us some initial basis of sympathy – at any rate, we were at the core of the group that was to grow to intimacy in the following years. Within a short time I found that I could acquire one of the studios in the Mall (No.3) and there I set up house with my second wife. We stayed there until our first child was imminent, and then, just before the outbreak of war, moved out into Buckinghamshire.

Another artist from the North (he too had studied at the Leeds College of Art) lived at No.6 – Cecil Stephenson, and he too became one of the group and shared our aspirations. Then to a house in Eldon Grove, on the other side of Haverstock Hill, came Paul Nash, already a friend of some years' standing. Paul was always the *grand seigneur* to us all – if one wanted to be unkind one would say he was a little pompous, but as I got to know him better this proved to be a superficial mannerism which I fancy he derived from a commander in Greenwich who had unsuccessfully prepared him for a career in the Navy. He, too, became one of our group, easy of access and radiating a more polemical spirit than most of us.

For five years I lived in friendly and intimate association with this group of artists, visiting their studios almost daily and watching the progress of their work. At the back of the studios were small gardens, and in mine I built a wooden hut, about six by four feet, and there, during the first summer, I wrote *The Green Child*. It was the happiest period of my life. I remember how when we had just moved into the studio and freshly decorated it, woodwork pale blue, walls white, Ben Nicholson came in to see the result. 'Wait a minute', he said, and retired, coming back a few minutes later with a round cork table-mat which he had painted scarlet. He seized a ladder and nailed the scarlet disc high up on the white wall. The whole place

67

Nicholson, we invited John Armstrong, John Bigge, Edward Burra, Tristram Hillier, Edward Wadsworth and the architects, Wells Coates and Colin Lucas, to be associated in this manifesto, and each of them contributed an article on his own aims and ideals. An exhibition of their work was held at the Mayor Gallery under the direction of Mr Douglas Cooper and Paul Nash wrote a challenging letter to *The Times*, which surprisingly was published (but this was on the formation of the 'Unit', in June 1933). Later in this same year, 1934, Anton Zwemmer published my first book on Henry Moore. Meanwhile in Germany events were moving to a crisis and the first refugee artists began to arrive. Walter Gropius came in 1934 and lived in one of the flats in Lawn Road which Wells Coates had built for Jack Pritchard. Moholy-Nagy came in 1935 and Naum Gabo the same year; and finally, in 1938, came Piet Mondrian, who set up a studio in Parkhill Road alongside the Mall. The presence of Gabo and Moholy-Nagy greatly strengthened the Constructivist element in the group, and in 1937 they felt strong enough to issue their own manifesto, the volume called *Circle* which was published in 1937 with Leslie Martin (a new accession on the architectural side), Ben Nicholson and Gabo as joint editors. Between *Unit One* in 1934 and *Circle* in 1937 the foundations were laid for the art that was to develop in England during the next twenty-five years.

Except for the Surrealist intrusion! An intrusion it was, an invasion from Paris which took place in 1936. Again I edited a manifesto, the volume published by Faber and Faber in 1936. Henry Moore and Paul Nash willingly participated, and indeed a surrealist element had been present in their work from the beginning. John Bigge and Edward Burra, who had been members of Unit One, also took part in the new manifestation, together with Eileen Agar, John Banting, Cecil Collins, Merlyn Evans, S. W. Hayter, Humphrey Jennings, Len Lye, Roland Penrose and Julian Trevelyan. There is no denying that a tension was created between the two extremes represented by the Circle group and the Surrealist group, and that I was in the position of a circus rider with his feet planted astride two horses. I tried to argue, and I still believe, that such dialectical oppositions are good for the progress of art, and that the greatest artists (I always had Henry Moore in mind) are great precisely because they can resolve such oppositions. As a poet I had to give my allegiance to the only vital movement in poetry – that represented by Rimbaud, Lautréamont and Apollinaire. The Surrealist movement, always essentially literary in its inspiration, was nourished at these sources. If I contradicted myself, then I embraced my contradictions. As I write two pictures face me on the wall, one a pure abstraction by Ben Nicholson, the other a surrealist fantasy by Paul Delvaux. By chance their colours harmonise; if there is any contradiction in their forms, it must correspond to a contradiction in my own mind, for both appeal to me with equal force.

was transformed by this accent of colour, perfectly placed.

The group worked intensely, in loose association with other artists. In 1934 I edited a volume called – for no good reason that I can remember – *Unit One*, the sub-title boldly asserting that it was 'the modern movement in English architecture, painting and sculpture'. In addition to Barbara Hepworth, Henry Moore, Paul Nash and Ben

68

69

All the actual contradictions that had grown up by 1939 were to be violently resolved by the outbreak of the war. As a group we were dispersed and were never to reassemble. But what was to be done for the future of art in England had been done. For a period of six or seven years a coherent group of artists had worked together in close proximity, generating some vital intimacy and enthusiasm. Within this inner group that worked within five minutes' walking distance of each other in Hampstead I do not remember any quarrels, any jealousy or spitefulness. It was a 'nest' of gentle artists (I am thinking of Turgenev's *Nest of Gentlefolk*), a spontaneous association of men and women drawn together by common sympathies, shared seriousness and some kind of group criticism. There were no polemics and no programme. In his letter to *The Times* Paul Nash said that 'the peculiar distinction of Unit 1 is that it is not composed of, let us say, three individuals and eight imitators, but of eleven individuals. And yet there is still a quality of mind, of spirit perhaps, which unites the work of these artists, a relevance apparent enough to any intelligent perception.' There was a prevailing good temper, an atmosphere in which art could grow. The war came and destroyed it all.

67 Herbert Read in No.3 The Mall, Parkhill Road. Howard Costa photograph, National Portrait Gallery, London

68 Ben Nicholson *Collage with Spanish Postcard* 1933. Aichi Prefectural Museum of Art, Japan*

69 Ben Nicholson *Profile* 1933. Private collection* (cat.no.160)

70

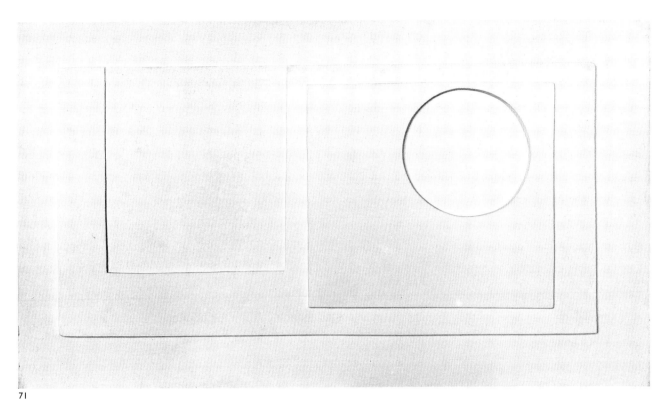

71

Such a feeling of unanimity was never to exist again after the war, but English art had come of age. Within the next decade it was to become, what it had not been for a century, an art of international significance.

'An Event of Some Importance in the History of English Art'
Postlude by Judith Collins

When Herbert Read returned rather precipitately to London in the summer of 1933 with his future wife, Margaret Ludwig,[1] he briefly occupied Henry Moore's studio flat in Hampstead (while Henry and Irina were away in Kent),[2] before moving with her into No.3 The Mall Studios, Parkhill Road. Over the next five years he was to meet artist friends on an almost daily basis, and watch the progress of their work. As the 1930s unfolded, Read was to be the eloquent advocate for this work. If he had remained in Edinburgh during the 1930s his contact with the Hampstead-based artists trying to forge a new language for British art during those years would have been severely diminished. By the happy accident of living and working in their midst he was the first to share their progress and to be readily on hand as their mediator. Read described this situation in a letter written in 1945 to the painter Cecil Collins: 'When one has grown up with the people of one's own generation, shared their hopes and fears, their moments of success and disappointment, one feels a special obligation to them'.[3]

The arrival in Hampstead of Continental artists threatened by the impending war – Marcel Breuer, Naum

72

73

73 Ben Nicholson
Gouache 1936. Private
collection* (cat.no.162)

73 Ben Nicholson
Gouache 1936. Private
collection* (cat.no.162)

Gabo, Walter Gropius, Piet Mondrian, and László Moholy-Nagy – fed into the work of the indigenous nest and made this community the centre of most that was modern in British art of the 1930s. Though Read was not the only critic and writer who lived in Hampstead at this time – there were also H. S. Ede (Henri Gaudier-Brzeska's biographer), Geoffrey Grigson, Roland Penrose, Adrian Stokes and John Summerson (who was married to Barbara Hepworth's sister, Elizabeth) – he was in the fortunate position of being at the pivot of the cross-currents of contemporary British and European art.

Read shared the concern of his artist friends about motivation and exhibition venues. He felt that a strategic communal front should be encouraged, with artists 'united against the common enemy, an indifferent public'.[4] Sympathetic exhibiting venues were a priority and the newly-opened Mayor Gallery was the most prominent of these. It had operated from an address in Sackville Street in the mid-1920s and reopened at

18 Cork Street in April 1933 with a major exhibition of recent paintings by English, French and German artists. Two of its directors, Fred Mayor and Douglas Cooper, were very well informed of recent developments in European art, and when Read's first major assessment of modern European painting and sculpture, *Art Now*, appeared in October 1933, the Mayor mounted a complementary show at the same time. The book received strong critical invective, and in Read's foreword to the exhibition catalogue he described the gallery as 'an unexpected harbour ... during the worst storm I am likely to encounter'.

The gallery held a similar complementary exhibition the following year, 1934, to mark the publication of the manifesto Unit One. In his introduction to the volume, which he edited, Read announced that the grouping of the eleven painters, sculptors and architects into the loose conglomerate of *Unit One* was a strategic move in order to promote themselves as a cultural power base in

74

London, postulating that such a group could fulfil the cultural functions undertaken by the Royal Academy, a national artistic institution that Read considered now moribund. Read was obviously in favour of artistic brotherhoods. Early in his introduction to the book *Surrealism* (1936) he wrote that this artistic movement was: 'the spontaneous generation of an international and fraternal *organism* in total contrast to the artificial manufacture of a collective *organisation* such as the League of Nations'.[5] The design of the book *Unit One* was aggressively modern, showing influence in page layout and typography from recent Bauhaus publications. Walter Gropius, the Bauhaus architect and director, had arrived

in Hampstead in 1934, and Read's already strong knowledge of European modern movements would have been immeasurably increased by this first-hand contact. The 'nest of gentle artists' was beginning to become less insular in outlook.

Henry Moore's greatness, which Read recognised as early as 1931[6] on the occasion of his second one-man exhibition at the Leicester Galleries, lay in his intuitive and empathetic relationship with his material and his capacity to translate meaning from one material into another – in the case of a mother and child from flesh and blood into stone. His creativity was described as:

a four-dimensional process growing out of a conception which

74 Paul Delvaux *L'Appel de la Nuit* 1938. Scottish National Gallery of Modern Art (on loan from a private collection, England) (cat.no.63)

inheres in the mass itself. Form is then an intuition of surface made by the sculptor imaginatively situated at the centre of gravity of the block before him. Under the guidance of this intuition, the stone is slowly educated from an arbitrary into an ideal state of existence.[7]

By the time Read wrote the pioneering monograph *Henry Moore Sculptor: an Appreciation*, published in 1934, he had decided that the ideal state to which great sculpture like Moore's should aspire was that which related to the vital rhythms and structures of natural forms. The key word that Read used for Moore's essential quality was 'vitality', a quality represented by:

> ... archaic types of Egyptian, Greek and Etruscan sculpture, very definitely by ancient Mexican sculpture, but perhaps with the greatest sureness by the long tradition which spread from the East and permeated from North and West known to art historians as the Animal Style ... [From] an intense awareness of the nature of the animal, its movements and habits, the artist is able to select just those features which best denote its vitality, and by exaggerating these and distorting them until they cohere in some significant rhythm and shape, he produces a representation which conveys to us the very essence of the animal. The same significant vitality is developed, perhaps from the same origins, by the Romanesque and gothic sculpture of Northern Europe. It is from such a point of view that we must approach the sculpture of Henry Moore.[8]

It is most interesting that at this same time, 1934, Roger Fry was giving the Slade Lectures in Cambridge, and one of these was devoted to the concept of Vitality. Fry found that this powerful quality first emerged in art in Scythian animal brooches, in works categorised by the term Animal Style, exactly the same conclusion reached by Read. Fry did not give an example of a contemporary artist who displayed such a quality, but instead found it in Italian art at the time of Giotto, then again at the time of Masaccio and Fra Angelico. From them, it jumped centuries to Rembrandt and Rouault, and that was as far as it came.[9] Fry died unexpectedly on 9 September 1934 with his Slade Lectures incomplete. His death removed an eloquent and charismatic art critic and lecturer from British cultural life. It came at the very time when Read was beginning to fill the role of proselytiser for modern English and European art just as Fry had done for the French and English Post-Impressionists twenty years earlier.

Read's composite essay on Fry, included in his anthology *A Coat of Many Colours* (1945),[10] was a mixed tribute containing affectionate praise tempered with sharp criticism, and it clearly revealed Read's own critical priorities. Commended for his introduction into English art criticism of the formal analysis of a work of art, and his wide-ranging and deep knowledge of art history, Fry did not, however, concern himself with the new ordering of society or the polemics of art, and tended instead 'to retreat into the private world of his own sensibility'. He also had serious blind spots, or as Read christened them 'black outs': abstractionism, Surrealism, Turner and the

75

whole of German art. Read could have been more generous and conceded that the foundations of his role as a critic had been painstakingly laid by Fry.

Read's main point in an essay (in fact, the text of a lecture he had given for the Artists International Association in 1935 with the title 'What is Revolutionary Art?')[11] was that revolutionary art should be abstract. It should not concern itself with literal representations of hammers and sickles, factories and machines but instead follow 'the vitality and intellectual strength of the new architecture', by which he meant that practised by Gropius and the Bauhaus in Germany. Read believed that the term 'abstract' could cover artists as diverse as Mondrian and Ben Nicholson at one end of the scale and Miró and Henry Moore at the other. However, Read had to acknowledge that such abstract artists were not alone in their avant-garde position, for there were actually two revolutionary movements currently being explored by English and European artists. The other was Surrealism, which Read described as 'literary, subjective and actively Communist', while abstraction, 'sometimes called non-figurative, constructivist, geometric' was 'plastic, objective and ostensibly non-political'. Read concluded his revolutionary art essay by acknowledging Surrealism's agitation: he saw it as negative, and destructive, 'the art of a transitional period'.

Although Read had considered Surrealism of *temporary* significance in 1935, he was prepared to champion its cause the following year. He was well aware that some of the artists he admired – Moore, Nash and Burra – were working in a manner that could be described as Surrealist, and he decided to examine this manifestation. The suggestion to hold an international exhibition in London in 1936 came from Roland Penrose, a Hampstead neighbour, but it was Read and Penrose who subsequently visited artists to look for work for the show. This took place at the New Burlington Galleries in June and July and Read wrote an introduction to the catalogue, where he claimed an English rather than a French source for Surrealism and began his campaign that 'Superrealism' was a better term than Surrealism: 'A nation which has produced two such superrealists as William Blake and Lewis Carroll is to the manner born. Because our art and literature is the most romantic in the world, it is likely to become the most superrealistic.'[12] Superrealist for Read meant work freed from the 'prejudice of naturalism', an artistic path which he constantly promoted.

In *Surrealism*, published in November 1936 and edited by Read, he looked back for Superrealists in English art history, and was perhaps a little hard on Turner: 'A little dogged in spirit, he lacked the final courage to take leave of his senses – the vacation which every hard-working artist owes to himself'.[13] Much praise was however given to Blake: 'In the whole of his writings I feel the presence of an instinctive dialecticism which is of the greatest interest'.[14]

It gradually becomes obvious from a study of Read's writings that 'instinctive dialecticism' was a state highly to be sought, and one that Read believed that he shared with Blake. Read felt that a person would sink into mental passivity and become stale and inert if he or she did not indulge in dialectical activity. By this he meant that a sentient human should actively develop *personal* ideas, and if contradictions occurred, then this was healthy. He defended himself in the introduction:

I am often accused of contradictions, and do not doubt that these exist in my critical writings. But I must confess that I am not particularly uneasy about them. They are related to the contradictions of my personality … and I do not choose to present a falsely regular facade. I have a strong dislike for people with symmetrical faces; if not criminals (an attested fact), they are at any rate stupid or depraved.[15]

Section 54 of *The Meaning of Art*, published in 1931, had been devoted to an examination of Realism: 'The kind of art which we might strictly call realistic would be one that tried by every means to represent the exact appearance of object, and such an art, like a realistic philosophy, would be based on a simple faith in the objective existence of things'.[16]

Read quotes the Impressionists as aiming for this, and more significantly the Netherlandish school of painters, for example Breughel. Read's anthology of collected essays, *A Coat of Many Colours*, contains one entitled 'Realism and Superrealism', in which he gives precedence to Superrealism over Realism and writes of Realistic or naturalistic art in a pejorative manner.[17] Not surprisingly,

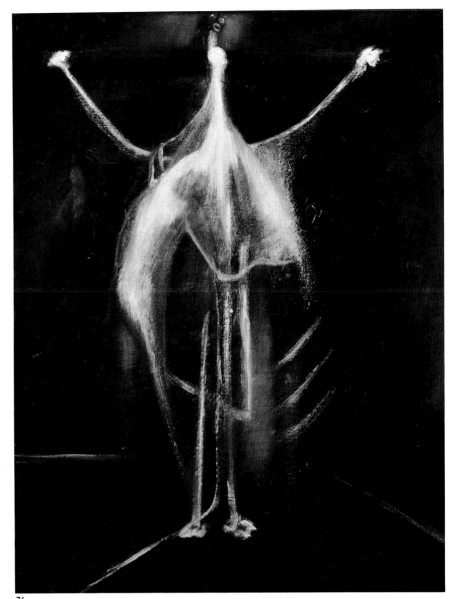

76

77

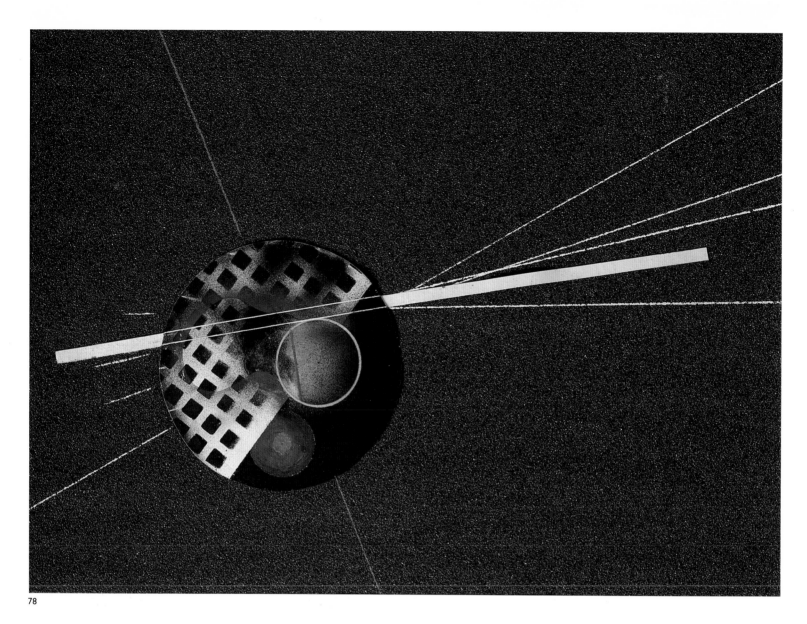

78

Read dismissed as minor and unnecessary the kind of art propagated by the Euston Road School of Drawing and Painting, a private art school opened on 4 October 1937 at 12 Fitzroy Street, London, with a teaching staff which included William Coldstream, Victor Pasmore and Claude Rogers. It had strong backing from Kenneth Clark, then Director of the National Gallery. It aimed to train the observation of its students, to train them to copy accurately the colour and shape of the object before them, and inevitably animosity grew between some members of the School and Read. The AIA organised a public debate between the Realists – represented by Graham Bell (an artist and critic), Coldstream and Peter Peri – and the Surrealists – represented by Humphrey Jennings, Penrose and Julian Trevelyan – held on 16 March 1938 at the Group Theatre Rooms, London and chaired by the painter Robert Medley. Read did not speak but reviewed the debate in *The London Bulletin* for April 1938. He was damning in his treatment of two of the protagonists:

We have tried to remember anything contributed to the debate by Graham Bell and William Coldstream ... but there is only the stammer and the sweat ... they are reduced to talking about the camera and Courbet. Actually our English Realists are not the tough guys they ought to be but the effete and bastard off-spring of the Bloomsbury school of needlework.[18]

The work of the Euston Road painters had been relegated to the level of decorative art.

However, Bell was not prepared to accept Read's criticism allied to his growing position of authority and had already begun to return fire as early as January 1937 in a series of articles and reviews for *The New Statesman & Nation*. In the 2 January issue he reviewed Read's book *Surrealism* under the title 'The Unthinking Read'. Another article, 'Escape from Escapism', printed in *Left Review* for December 1937 and primarily a review of an exhibition of work by the London Group, pronounced that 'abstract art' meant 'escapism'. The way to avoid escapism was to concentrate on 'things depicted [rather]

79

than in the manner of depiction' – in other words to follow the precepts of the Euston Road School.

Anthony Blunt, beginning his art historical career in the mid-1930s, also took up the Realist cause. He greatly admired the figurative sculpture in concrete made by Peter Peri, a Hungarian who arrived in London in 1933 after making a reputation as a Constructivist. For Peri's

exhibition in Cambridge in April 1937 Blunt wrote two reviews, both praising Realism above Superrealism and Abstraction:

If art today is not to stand still it must escape from the dead end of abstraction and obscurity which it has reached. You cannot go on making squares for an indefinite period, and though it is possible to continue on the lines of the Superrealists and spin

80 André Masson *Mass at Pamplona* 1937. Private collection (cat.no.132)

80

out your dreams for many years, only an artist who is entirely out of touch with the real world around him can fail to realise in the end that this is an unprofitable pursuit. The only hope for the arts at the present time is to come back to a simple contact with the problems which seriously concern the ordinary man, and to give up the ivory-tower existence to which it has grown used in the last generation.[19]

The ivory-tower élitism to which Blunt alludes could well have been a covert attack on Read. The two critics had shown themselves in direct opposition during 1936-7 when they took sides over the reputation of Picasso. Blunt described Picasso's *Guernica*, on show at the 1937 Paris World Fair, as 'not an act of public mourning, but the expression of a private brainstorm'.[20] A little later in the year he followed with 'Picasso's life has been spent in the holy of holies of art'.[21] Read had long considered Picasso to be a major artist who was not in any way remote and he provided an article for *The Listener* called 'The Triumph of Picasso', published on 27 May 1936. Picasso, Read wrote, 'worked emotionally, instinctively and not in accordance with a rational programme'.[22] He was bold enough to suggest that Picasso and Moore worked in the same manner: 'their most powerful creations are perhaps

just those in which the extremes meet in some kind of tension or equilibrium'. This was another way of saying that instinctive dialecticism was the key to their success.

Read's opposition to the more 'conservative' strains of English art is also evident in his relationship with the sculptor and graphic artist Eric Gill. In October 1928 Eric Gill moved from Wales to a large house and workshop, Pigotts, at Speen, near Beaconsfield, Buckinghamshire, a few miles away from Read's house at Seer Green. Their paths crossed many times in the 1930s, particularly in the correspondence columns of magazines, where in lively fashion they aired their views on each other's new publications. They would sometimes meet and talk in a pub in High Wycombe on a Sunday morning. In October 1929 Read was responsible for securing for Gill a major commission. On his recommendation the sculptor was offered by the Governors of the British Broadcasting Corporation the possibility of providing sculptures for a new headquarters about to be built in Portland Place. He accepted the commission and spent most of 1931-2 carving five large works *in situ* – the group of *Prospero and Ariel* above the main door, three *Ariel* reliefs above other doors, and a figure of *The Sower* for the front hall.[23]

Read respected Gill as a sculptor and as someone who would be likely to carry out this commission successfully, even though he was not in agreement with Gill's Christian standpoint. Read described himself in his *Annals of Innocence and Experience* (1940) as an agnostic, nor did he agree with Gill's belief that the Christian Church was the most appropriate agent for revolutionary reform. He thought revolutionary change could be achieved through art. Equally the two friends disagreed on the power of the content of a work of art. Gill's thesis was simple: the artist, whether he likes it or not, makes work which strongly expresses meaning or values. In contrast Read did not place meaning as the primary communicative function of a work of art. Gill put forward his view on Read in a letter written in October 1933, and it summed up their differences:

As for Herbert Read: he is a nice man & has a v. wide knowledge of ancient & modern art and an appreciation of the latter possessed by few. But I do think he's greatly in error in important matters of philosophy & religion so that while he is to be trusted in his appreciations of ancient works he is only to be trusted in his appreciation of those modern works which he can regard as 'pure' art – i.e. art without thesis, pure form.[24]

Read's power and influence was not confined to the 1930s but it can be argued that that was the decade in which his achievements reached their apogee. He himself recalled that although decades '... are arbitrary divisions of the flow of time ... we can look back on the years 1930-40 [and] we can have no doubt that they were decisive in the history of art in England'.[25] English art emerged from its 'slumbering provincialism' and aimed at an 'international status'. Although the Second World War brought a chaotic end to this productive decade, Read felt that what was needed to be done had been done.

After the common experience of that decade, the scattered artists were able to go their own ways, but with a sense of confidence and a courage that they might not have possessed but for their common experience. There may be a profound lesson to be learned from this chapter of art history: for not the least significant forces in the history of art are social and even intimate; schools and academies, publications and exhibitions are no substitute for the spontaneous enthusiasm that is generated when an arbitrary chance brings together in one place spirits with the same ideals and aspirations.[26]

Notes

1 Read resigned his post of Watson Gordon Professor at Edinburgh University on 28 June and he and Margaret eloped to London in July.

2 See Garrould, Ann; Friedman, Terry and Mitchinson, David (1982) *Henry Moore: Early Carvings 1920-1940* (Leeds City Art Galleries) p.11, for a photograph of the studio in 1932.

3 Letter from HR to Cecil Collins, 4 April 1945, Cecil Collins Papers, Tate Gallery Archive.

4 H. Read, 'British Art 1930-1940' in *Art in Britain 1930-1940 Centred Around Axis, Circle, Unit One* (exhibition catalogue) London, Marlborough Fine Art 1965, p.5.

5 Read, Herbert (Ed) (1936) *Surrealism* (London, Faber & Faber) p.20.

6 In 'A Nest of Gentle Artists' Read kaleidoscoped the early events of his friendship with Moore. He rightly recollects meeting the sculptor in 1928 and visiting his studio, but it was in fact not until April 1931 that he gathered photographs and published his *Listener* article.

7 Read, Herbert (1931) 'Henry Moore', *The Listener*, 22 April, p.689. See also Read, Herbert (1931) *The Meaning of Art* (London, Faber & Faber) pp.148-53.

8 Read, Herbert (1934) *Henry Moore Sculptor: an Appreciation* (London, A. Zwemmer) pp.12-13.

9 R. Fry (1939) *Last Lectures* Cambridge/London, p.45.

10 Read, Herbert (1945) *A Coat of Many Colours* (London, George Routledge & Sons) pp.282-91.

11 Read, Herbert (1935) 'What is Revolutionary Art?', in: Rea, Betty (Ed) (1935) *5 on Revolutionary Art* (London, Wishart) pp.11-22.

12 Read, Herbert (1936) 'Introduction', catalogue of *The International Surrealist Exhibition* (London, New Burlington Galleries).

13 Read (n.5) p.59.

14 *Ibid.* p.81.

15 *Ibid.* pp.87-8.

16 Read, Herbert (1931) *The Meaning of Art* (London, Faber & Faber) p.83.

17 Read (n.10) pp.190-5.

18 Read, Herbert (1938) 'Discussion between Realists and Surrealists', *London Gallery Bulletin* no.1, April, p.20.

19 A. Blunt, 'The New Realism in Sculpture', *Granta* xlvi, 21 April 1937, p.346.

20 A. Blunt, 'Art in Paris', *Spectator*, 6 Aug 1937, p.241.

21 A. Blunt, 'Picasso Unfrocked', *Spectator*, 8 Oct 1937, p.585.

22 Read, Herbert (1936) 'The Triumph of Picasso', *The Listener*, vol.xv, pp.1023-4.

23 Shewring, Walter (Ed) (1947) *Letters of Eric Gill* (London, Jonathan Cape) pp.245, 256, 262-3, 266-7. See also Collins, Judith (1992) *Eric Gill: Sculpture* (London, Barbican Art Gallery) cat. nos 82-90.

24 Gill, Eric (1933) letter to Graham Carey, 7 Oct, published in Shewring (n.24) pp.280-1.

25 Read, Herbert (1965) 'British Art 1930-1940', in (1965) *Art in Britain 1930-40 Centred Around Axis, Circle, Unit One* (London, Marlborough Fine Art Ltd.) p.5.

26 *Ibid.* p.6.

81 Joan Miró
Composition 1934.
Private collection*
(cat.no.136)

82 Max Ernst *La Ville
Petrifiée* 1933.
Manchester City Art
Galleries (cat.no.75)

83 Yves Tanguy *Untitled
c.*1936. Private
collection. Courtesy
Mayor Gallery
(cat.no.196)

81

82

83

from **Preface to** *The Philosophy of Modern Art,* 1951

The Philosophy of Modern Art is perhaps a grandiloquent title for a collection of essays written on various occasions over a period of fifteen years. I cannot claim that I had a coherent plan in mind all this time, and different purposes have required different styles of address. To mention one particular anomaly : the reader is bound to be disconcerted by the way I shift with little or no warning from the position of the spectator *ab extra* to that of the creative artist.

But what, if not philosophic, is this activity I have indulged in, not only in this book, but for the best part of a lifetime? It is not critical, for I have never pretended to assess the value of particular works of art, or to arrange artists in an hierarchy of worth. It is not historical, for though I am conscious of connections, and eager to trace the re-emergence of traditions, I am not systematic enough to give the complete picture of a period, nor confident enough to define a school or classify a generation. The method I adopt may be called philosophic because it is the affirmation of a value-judgment. To be precise : I believe that among the agents or instruments of human evolution, art is supremely important. I believe that the aesthetic faculty has been the means of man first acquiring, and then refining, consciousness. Form, the progessive organization of elements otherwise chaotic, is given in perception. It is present in all skills – skill is the instinct for form revealed in action. Beyond this physiological and instinctive level, any further progress in human evolution has always been dependent on a realization of formal values.

The realization of formal values is the aesthetic activity. Aesthetic activity is biological in its nature and functions ; and human evolution in particular, and by exception, is differentiated from animal evolution by the possession of this faculty.

The evidence for this belief is not presented systematically in this book, but the nature of this book is determined by this belief. There is no phase of art, from the palaeolithic cave-paintings to the latest developments of constructivism, that does not seem to me to be an illustration of the biological and teleological significance of the aesthetic activity in man. Such is the hypothesis that underlies these essays, and gives them whatever logical coherence they may possess.

84-89 Original illustrations from *The Philosophy of Modern Art* (1952)

84 Pablo Picasso *Girl Reading* 1934 (ill.2)

85 Paul Nash *Siren* 1930 (ill.10)

84

85

86

88

87

89

86 Paul Klee *A Girl Possessed* 1924 (ill.9)

87 Barbara Hepworth *Turning Forms* 1950 (ill.13)

88 Ben Nicholson *Project* 1946 (ill.5)

89 Henry Moore *Three Standing Figures* 1947-8 (ill.12)

Herbert Read's Paradigm: A British Vision of Modernism

David Thistlewood

90 Herbert Read
Aeroplane Landing 1917.
Private collection*

Herbert Read's writings on the avant-garde art of his time constitute a sensitive, contemporaneous response to Modernism. He witnessed early manifestations of Abstract Expressionism and extreme non-figuration just before the First World War; and forty years later he documented corresponding phenomena on their cyclic return. In the interval he mediated Constructivism and Surrealism – for him the great vitalising forces of Modernism – in all their varieties; and at each extreme of his working life he drew into his critique a movement he thought devitalising, Cubism and Pop. Central to his art criticism was a dual purpose – to interpret European (and, later, American) Modernism to a British audience and to cultivate a specifically British Modernism in continuation of a vital cultural tradition. He became known as an (occasionally reckless) defender of the emergent, ready to put into words what had barely been apprehended in avant-garde enterprise. He cultivated a considerable public for contemporary creativity, helping to moderate its reception as it gradually became evident in public collections. In a real sense he may be regarded as a great and influential (though unattached) curator of modern art.[1]

Read's original intention, however, was to be a critic of letters: his early diaries and autobiographies reveal little ambition towards the plastic arts comparable to his devotion to poetry and literature. The 1920s was the high point of his life as a literary scholar, culminating in his Clark Lectureship at Cambridge University and the study of Wordsworth that this realised. In this decade he edited the manuscripts of the classicist T. E. Hulme,[2] began an assimilation of romanticism to the Hulmean position,[3] and published other important works on literary theory and criticism besides his study of Wordsworth,[4] but to those interested in the origins of Read's art criticism this period appears characterised by avoidance. Given that he previously entertained notions of being an avant-garde painter, and that his critical exemplar, Thomas Ernest Hulme, had positively celebrated the achievements of Vorticism, a paucity of early writings on the plastic arts is difficult to explain.

But there are clues as to why Read may have been initially reluctant to annex modern painting and sculpture to an aesthetic theory of the literary arts. In the preface to his short collection of wartime poetry and prose, *Naked Warriors*, Read assumed to speak for the generation which had been compelled to participate in 'ghastliness and horror', 'inhumanity and negation', demanding a collective resolve to live with a 'cleaner and more direct realisation of natural values'. 'Then, as the reflex of such

90

stern activity, may we strive to create a beauty where hitherto it has no absolute existence ... In that way we may so progress that our ethical rage give us duly an aesthetic sanction'.[5] Intense percipience towards a 'natural' order of beauty; disciplined application of a resulting, clearly defined code of aesthetic values; this code to stand as a normal critique of the unacceptable in human conduct – expressed in 1919 this composite of intentions inspired the rest of Read's life's work.

In matters of art criticism Read's mentor was Frank Rutter, his coeditor of *Art and Letters*. Rutter's view on Modernism, with which it may be fairly assumed Read concurred, was quite explicit: in all its varieties since Post-Impressionism – namely, Cubism, Expressionism, Futurism, and Vorticism – it had had a single common quality in *violence*.[6] Rutter was neutral in this observation. For example, he found it intensely significant that a painting Wassily Kandinsky sent to Michael Sadler (shown to Rutter, Read and other members of the Leeds Arts Club in the winter of 1913) had clearly encoded premonitions of war. It was significant to Rutter also that the best war paintings had been Cubist and Futurist in spirit and formal organisation.[7] Modern art was to be regarded as ritualised aggression, and therefore, by Read, as the embodiment of those worst characteristics of present-day society that were to be sanctioned in rejection.

Those interested in the origins of Read's art criticism, then, must come to terms with a fairly unpromising decade in the 1920s when – after being on the fringes of Vorticism and counting Wyndham Lewis as a friendly collaborator – he nevertheless avoided critical interaction with modern painting and sculpture because of its 'inorganic' brutalism. This was not involuntary avoidance; nor was it total. His work at the Victoria and Albert Museum took him to Germany. With Max Sauerlandt, Director of the Hamburg Museum für Kunst und Gewerbe, he planned an exhibition of post-war German art for London, and through this involvement became aware of the Bauhaus, renewing acquaintance with Kandinsky's work and initiating a lifelong respect for Paul Klee. Read's disinclination to publish art criticism in the 1920s, then, is evidence of dislike for a 'mechanical' aesthetic to which German Expressionism and Klee's gentle abstractions were honourable exceptions. The latter especially gave hope for a Modernist idiom he could honestly support, and also confirmed in retrospect his efforts to secure a usable theory of originating creativity applicable to more than poetry.

This had consisted in his interpretation and enlargement of ideas recognised in Hulme's papers. Hulme had been an erratic theorist, intermixing principles selectively received from Bergson and Worringer, and Read genuinely added value to his work by editorial reduction. The result was a theory of creative origination which may be drastically summarised[8] as follows. The artist delves into the unconscious stream of experience and 'surfaces' having grasped some vague notion of a significant form. The essential irregularity of this form is gradually polished away, resulting in an abstract percept that symbolises both its origins in irrationality and its destination in rational contemplation. It is both timeless and of immediate significance, offering analogous relationship to religiosity. Modern abstraction is thus of the highest order within a system of human constructs (aesthetics) that is comparable to morality. Read himself only differed with Hulme's belief that perfected abstractions would necessarily be mechanical.

Read may therefore be considered as possessing, in the late 1920s, an incipient critique of modern art featuring a criterion of abstraction. This was an abstraction distinct from the mechanical, serving a 'cleaner and more direct realisation of natural values' – a construct virtually untested in the realm of plastic art for only Paul Klee seemed to fulfil its criteria in significant images and creative strategies. Read the Clark Lecturer on Wordsworth may yet have been unaware of his role in waiting, but in retrospect it is clear that he was prepared to celebrate intentionality similar to Klee's wherever it became apparent. When evidence materialised it was unexpectedly close to home. It was recognised in the work of Henry Moore, an artist who shared three things with Read – London exile from a Yorkshire homeland, a grounding in the aesthetic ambience of the Leeds Arts Club,[9] and devotion to an organic abstraction – initiating a celebrated forty-year reciprocation of Read's criticism and Moore's creativity.

In 1928 Read began a series of radio broadcasts on art which were transcribed in the BBC's weekly, *The Listener*, from the following year. His first major book on art – a wide-ranging, historical survey entitled *The Meaning of Art*[10] – was an enlarged collection of his *Listener* writings. It confirmed Read's determination to be taken seriously as a critic of the avant-garde by culminating in appreciations of Paul Klee and Henry Moore as artists making profound contributions to an advanced culture while at the same time defying classification by movements. Klee confirmed the validity of an abstraction violent neither in its inspiration nor its form. To Read he seemed to be evoking an 'alternative' nature, a world of imagery materialising from the shallow unconscious, an emergent formlessness given shape only in the moment when 'the pencil moves and the line dreams'.[11] This was a ready-made outcome of Read's provisional critique, endowing Klee's art with poetic equivalence.

Moore, however, provided the means of locating Read's critique specifically in the realm of the plastic arts. Moore appeared motivated by intimate understanding of his natural materials – stone, wood, clay – and the forms they *inevitably* had to assume in order to accommodate interpretations of the artist's subject-matter. He would imagine 'what a reclining woman would look like if flesh and blood were translated into the stone before him – the stone which has its own principles of form and structure … Sculpture, therefore, is not a *reduplication* of form and feature; it is rather the *translation of meaning* from one material into another …'

This necessitated an act of manifold empathy which, once recognised in the work of Henry Moore, remained central to Read's critique for the rest of his life. In order to be a *paragon* Modernist the artist had to empathise (i) with subject-matter (whether phenomenal or noumenal), (ii) with the nature of materials (respecting their legitimate form), and (iii) with organic nature (permitting creative concepts to evolve naturally rather than constraining them with a false aesthetic). Moore's creativity was thus perceived as

a four-dimensional process growing out of a conception which inheres in the mass itself. Form is then an intuition of surface made by the sculptor imaginatively situated at the centre of gravity of the block before him. Under the guidance of this intuition, the stone is slowly educated from an arbitrary into an ideal state of existence ... the primary aim of every artistic activity.[12]

It is significant that at this stage Read was noticeably less appreciative of Picasso. He damned him with faint praise: Picasso was directly or indirectly associated with all recognised Modernist movements, and the abounding energy he revealed in all these idiomatic changes was evidence of genius. But between Read's lines was an inability to admit the initiator of Cubism to an evolutionary critique. Klee, on the other hand, had to be 'dissociated from all modern art movements, and particularly from such labels as Cubist, Expressionist or Futurist'. His closest affinities were with Surrealism but it seemed clear to Read that the Surrealists were more indebted to Klee than he to them.[13]

Read's highly speculative discourse on Modernism in *The Meaning of Art* is in effect a postscript to a fairly conventional general history.[14] One of its tangible results was to indicate areas of Read's ignorance which he was quick to address. Only two years later he published, in *Art Now*,[15] an extensive account of Modernism intended to be definitive, and two things are evident in this – one partially acknowledged and the other tacit. The first attendant matter is Read's cited dependence on Douglas Cooper for many of the unprecedented array of illustrations accompanying this text. Cooper was a close friend of such as Picasso, Braque and Léger; and Read's now more reasonable discussion of Picasso's intentionality, and specifically of his relations with Cubism, are attributable to this source. Here the notion of Cubism as a denaturalised response to a violent age is abandoned. Instead Cubism – an attempt to rid the object of sentimental associations – is an idiom that denies the painter opportunities to 'mask his own lack of personality in the personality of things' and therefore exhibits universal form and individual peculiarities of gesture and expression in counterpoint. A distinction is made between different Cubists – 'tough-minded' and 'tender-minded'. The latter include Braque and Gris, who 'seem to carry their abstractions towards a decorative end' and convey 'some suggestion of the organic world'. The former, including Léger, Metzinger, Jeanneret and Feininger, on the other hand, inhabit a world of 'inorganic', 'mechanic' sensibility: their work has 'an undertone of the machine: the dynamo, the rock-drill, the hydraulic pump. Because of this relation, this aspect of cubism is sometimes given a special label: constructivism.'[16]

Under Cooper's guidance Read seems to have moderated his prejudice and, while still locating one side of Cubism within the critique inherited from Rutter, claimed the other for organic abstraction. But he associated Picasso with neither aspect. Picasso's fertile genius refused to be confined by the idiom he had invented. What fascinated Read now were accounts of Picasso's unpremeditated stylistic changes – he was possessed to paint images and make forms he could not foresee before their materialisation, and the only consistency perceptible

in all his idiomatic variety was an involuntary manifestation of recognisable symbolism.[17] Beyond noting that a reflex 'subjective idealism' seemed to be both a legitimate goal and a prime distinguishing feature of modern art, Read was disinclined to categorise Picasso further. Significantly, in the context of Read's belief in 1933 that, for the majority of Modernists, idiomatic adoption was a matter of conscious choice,[18] Picasso joined Klee in manifesting *involuntary* intentionality.

The second attendant matter is the paradigmatic nature of *Art Now*,[19] designed not merely to map Modernism but to reveal avant-garde aesthetic 'intentions'. Read's inclination to report on intentionality obliged him to abandon the portmanteau concept of a geometric and necessarily violent abstraction if only because he realised that the most violent artistic endeavours were associated with the informality of Dada. He saw it as the critic's responsibility to model intentionality in whatever form it became apparent, and in his case to attend equally to Constructivism and Surrealism. He therefore celebrated formal precision, harmony and elegant proportion, and he also provided a defence of the irrational and the imprecise. At a time when Modernism was split along such ideological lines this gave rise to accusations that he was hedging his bets.

But he made this into a dialectic virtue, seeking opposing tendencies – within the community of artists and within individual creativity alike – that could be counterposed in explanation. Thus in *Art Now* two tendencies (symbolism and expressionism) were explored in detail but set aside as not specifically Modernist,[20] while two more (abstract formalism and subjective idealism) were proposed as belonging uniquely to the avant-garde. There was an attempt to demonstrate their interrelatedness but this led to the rather lame identification of a 'common element' residing in the artists' skill, in both tendencies alike, in transposing 'mental images into linear signs' – their abilities to express personality.[21]

It is clear that here in his early critiques of Modernism Read employed a distinct methodology: he would identify intentionality and fractionalise it in order to appreciate its fullest extent. Klee's painting could be fractionalised into constructive and organic strategies. So too could Moore's sculpture: in Read's first dedicated critique of Moore he identified a comparable, though unequal, divergence:

In one direction the artist tends to create a work whose whole aesthetic significance resides in formal relations and in qualities of texture; in the other direction the artist combines these relations and qualities with a reflection or representation of qualities typical of living things or, at least, qualities due to natural processes. The first type of artist is a purist, and makes no kind of compromise with any world outside the ideal world of subjective creation; he merely gives outer and solid form to conceptions that are as abstract as any conceived by the mathematician ... The second kind of artist does not wish to limit his function in this way. He feels that if he can link his formal conceptions with

91

91 Henry Moore
Composition (Carving in Cumberland Alabaster)
1931. Repr. *Art Now*,
1933, pl.53

the vital rhythms everywhere present in natural forms, that then he will give them a force altogether more dynamic than the force of abstract conceptions. Henry Moore, though he does not exclude exercises in the abstract mode, and, indeed, finds such exercises a considerable aid to his development, belongs essentially to this second type.[22]

Read's conception of what a modern artist *did* was substantially shaped by this fractionalisation of Moore's creativity. Read's prototype paradigm featured precisely this periodic alternation: outwardly addressing nature (creating natural equivalents); inwardly addressing self-ordered preferences (exploring abstract relationships in a spirit of play or nervous replenishment). This model had applications beyond the individual artist: it explained the Modernist project. All contributors to Modernism were negotiating this axis, and their individual differences were explicable in terms of that part of the route they travelled most often.

It was in exactly these terms that Read announced the existence of an English Modernism in 1934 on behalf of the group of artists and architects that had formed with Paul Nash as their leader and Douglas Cooper as their secretary – *Unit One*.[23] In order to elicit information about individual objectives and working methods Read prepared a questionnaire and edited members' responses. This confirmed the usefulness of his 'shuttle' explanation, and also required its extension to incorporate a more complete introspection as a result of Ben Nicholson's revelation of an almost exclusively metaphysical creativity accommodating a minimum of reference to nature.[24]

Within three years the group had ceased to operate as a cohort, having become vastly enlarged by the gravitation of European emigrant Modernists. Within this greater community the parochial references to an organic creativity, and the mental map that served it, tended to be outshone by the heroic imported causes of Constructivism and Surrealism. They were evangelical and began to claim the loyalty of individuals[25] – each in fact attracting Read's support. As they were mutually antagonistic, the sense of beneficial interaction between the different poles of creativity was in danger of being lost. Read was determined to preserve this principle while at the same time explaining to his constituency its sudden saturation with the European avant-garde. The shaping of his paradigmatic critique, which may be seen developing in his work

Pages 80 and 81

92 Portocarrero *Head*
1967. Private
collection* (cat.no.180)

93 Ben Nicholson
September '53 – Aztec
1953. Private collection
(cat.no.165)

80   A British Vision of Modernism

93

94

94 Victor Pasmore
*Abstract in White, Black
and Green* 1955. Private
collection* (cat.no.175)

the work of those irrationalists who had been loosely grouped within Dada and Surrealism. So while celebrating that Britain was a haven for both Constructivism and Surrealism, Read momentarily abandoned critical neutrality and called himself a Surrealist.[28] It was in this climate, in 1936, that Read published his paradigm partly in order to defend his own position, and in his urgency he published it prematurely and incomplete.[29]

It was also slightly confusing in its unconventional terminology. In order to avoid giving prominence to *movements* Read emphasised *intentionality* to the extent of replacing 'Constructivism' and 'Surrealism' with 'Abstraction' and 'Superrealism' – terms signifying problematics rather than group-interests. In 1936 he was confident to maintain the equal prominence of Abstract and Superrealist intentionality. The former embraced the work of such painters as Mondrian, Hélion, Nicholson and Moholy-Nagy and sculptors including Brancusi, Gabo and Hepworth, and was essentially formalist. The latter was less essentially formalist and represented by such painters as Ernst, Dali, Miró and Tanguy and a sculptor, Hans Arp. 'The first tendency', Read had written a year earlier: 'is plastic, objective and ostensibly non-political. The second group is literary (even in paint), subjective and actively Communist.'[30] Consistent with his politicised critique, Read suggested that Superrealism had an immediate, dynamic, negative purpose in attacking and breaking down bourgeois values – it was the art of a transitional period. The revolutionary task of Abstraction, however, was passive yet constructive: its role was to remain 'inviolate, until such time as society will once more be ready to make use of them, the universal qualities of art – those elements which survive all changes and revolutions' when it would be instrumental in building a new, classless society.[31]

These brief quotations demonstrate Read's preoccupation with avant-garde creativity as an agent of beneficial change and as resistant to malignant sociopolitical forces. As his model gradually featured more centrally the work of the British avant-garde, it became heavily loaded with implications that the 'Cultural International' had moved from Paris to London, requiring only the presence of Picasso, perhaps, for its completeness. The model contained Abstraction (having largely undergone a process of revolution) and Superrealism (now occupying a revolutionary phase). These were tending to diverge, but certain individual artists, responsible for the profoundest creative achievements, were holding its centre:

Though at their extremes – a Mondrian against a Dali – these two movements have nothing in common, yet the space between them is occupied by an unbroken series, in the middle of which we find artists like Picasso and Henry Moore whom we cannot assign confidently to either school. Significantly, these intermediate artists are among those most evidently in possession of a fertile and powerful genius ...[32]

Read felt compelled to represent the extremes of his theory to opposing audiences. In the first of such efforts

throughout the 1930s, is therefore complicated with political contextualisation.

He knew well the victimisation of creatives and intellectuals that was taking place in fascist Germany. Even before the exodus had properly begun he had attempted to establish a 'Bauhaus' in Britain,[26] and his planned exhibition of modern German art had been made impossible by much of its proposed content having been declared 'degenerate'.[27] In addition he was made aware, by Russian artists and designers now in London after having earlier sought refuge in Germany, that Soviet Communism had also stamped on the avant-garde. His conclusion was that contemporary art had to become active rather than contemplative, partisan rather than disinterested, and subliminal rather than super-evident. In other words, artists and theorists had to adopt a militancy of a sort that was at this time most apparent in

– a contribution to the *International Survey of Constructive Art* of 1937 in which he pressed the claims of Superrealism – he suggested that Abstraction and Superrealism were different aspects of a single enterprise. This involved superimposing a model of the creative mentality on that of the broad front of plastic creativity. Just as Superrealism could be said to engage a latent imagery *below* the level of the conscious mind, Abstraction could be said to address imagery *beyond* the range of conscious attention.[33]

In an article in *The London Bulletin*, organ of the English Surrealist Group, Read elaborated the Abstractionist position and in so doing revived his pre-paradigm preoccupation with the organic. Abstraction took an interest in:

certain proportions and rhythms which are inherent in the structure of the universe, and which govern organic growth, including the growth of the human body. Attuned to these rhythms and proportions, the abstract artist can create microcosms which reflect the macrocosm ... [through] access to the archetypal forms which underlie all the casual variations presented by the natural world.[34]

Read made a further observation which was in effect a statement of philosophical intent: 'Just as surrealism makes use of, or rather proceeds on the assumption of, the knowledge embodied in psycho-analysis, so abstract art makes use of, or proceeds on the basis of, the abstract concepts of physics and dynamics, geometry and mathematics'.[35] A *latent* revolutionary Abstraction acknowledging the physical sciences; an *immediately*-revolutionary Superrealism informed by psychoanalysis; Abstraction and Superrealism themselves dialectically opposed: from the late 1930s onwards Read used these coordinates to defend the various types of intentionality of the avant-garde.

For a confusing period the developing model was a hybrid of at least three notional axes – linking metaphysical introspection and percipience towards organic nature; bridging the subconscious and the supra-conscious; conjoining Superrealism and Abstraction. For a brief and only time in Read's critical theorising Picasso exemplified his ideal. Not only was Picasso centralised within these notional axes (establishing his importance to the Modernist project), he provided evidence of Modernism as a normal extension of Western culture rather than an aberration. Picasso's depiction of the violated horse, infuriated bull and lamp of Truth in *Guernica* was evidence of an ability to create, in his trance-like way of working, symbols at once conventional ('banal') and immediately potent. This persuaded Read temporarily to entertain a distinction between an artist's abilities to equilibrate Abstraction and Superrealism (to be attuned to the 'now'), and to generate symbols of timeless significance (to surpass the 'now'). Picasso's images were to be regarded as universal in this special sense, for 'it is only when the widest commonplace is infused with the intensest passion that a great work of art, transcending all

95

schools and categories, is born; and being born, lives immortally'.[36]

Read began to interrogate the work of other Modernists for evidence of centric potency – some mediation between idiomatic or psychological axial extremes – such as he had perceived in the work of Picasso and Moore. He wrote of the need for an integral culture, in which the different modes of Modernism would command equal respect; and of the necessity for comparable integration as the basis of a system of education dedicated to cultivating individual mental personality and the external world of sensory experience in symbiotic harmony.[37] He devoted much of the Second World war years to a study of child art, during which he discovered an astonishing consistency, in paintings by the very young, of images that corresponded with Jung's archetypes – recognisable symbols of personality projection, and mother and earth dependency, besides ancient and cross-cultural abstractions of psychic unity, such as mandalas.[38] The 'normal' presence of the latter in children's experience was only

95 Pablo Picasso
Abstraction 1929. Repr.
Art Now, 1933, pl.107

96

96 Congo *Split Fan Pattern. Private collection* (cat.no.46)*

97 James Lloyd *Children at the Edge of a Wood* 1957. *Private collection* (cat.no.129)*

explicable in terms of a reservoir of inborn, collective experience.

It took Read another four or five years to say openly what he must have realised in 1943 – that authentic avant-garde creativity ought to be regarded as symbolic reclamation of infant vision. But it is significant that he immediately abandoned the classification of artists by *fixed* location along the Abstraction-Superrealism axis, and became sensitive to characteristic acts of integration or necessary preludes to integration. This enabled him to celebrate as a virtue what had been regarded by diehard Constructivists and Surrealists as a weakness – the resistance of British Modernists to exclusive factional identification.[39] He realised that Henry Moore, Ben Nicholson, Barbara Hepworth and Paul Nash could not be positioned precisely along the axis (as for example, Piet Mondrian and Max Ernst had been) for they periodically tended to shift their ground. Nicholson, for example,

seemed to combine the geometrical and the impression-istic in differing proportions; while Hepworth's work ranged from uncompromising abstraction to an intense and dramatic realism. In a letter to Read she had written: 'Working realistically replenishes one's *love* for life, humanity and the earth. Working abstractly seems to release one's personality and sharpen the perceptions ...'[40] and she thus reinforced his idea of a mutually-nourishing alternation. Nicholson and Hepworth would now respect the outer world of perceptions, now engage the inner world of structured Abstraction; and Paul Nash, it became clear to Read, would also cover this ground while occasionally giving expression to the Superreal.

In certain cases [Read wrote of Nicholson] it seems possible for an individual to alternate between the extremes represented by this polarity – to tend in one psychological phase towards an affirmation of the world which results in a naturalistic style, and

David Thistlewood 85

98

98 Barbara Hepworth
Concourse 1948. Private
collection* (cat.no.108)

99 Henry Moore
*Maquette for UNESCO
Reclining Figure* 1957.
Leeds City Art Galleries
(cat.no.149)

of the complete dialectical process ...'[44] while the work of
Hepworth, Nicholson and Nash demonstrated the neces-
sary preconditions of such resolution in their eclecticism.
Their various types of apprehension could be:

... arranged along a polar axis, with transcendental metaphysics
at one end and an intense self-awareness of physical vitality at
the other end. It is along the same axis that we can place
Abstraction and [Super]realism in art. But ... choice is not
imposed on the individual artist. The axis exists *within* the individual artist if only he [or she] can become aware of it.[45]

These last quotations suggest both the originality of the
model that occupied Read's attention during the 1940s
and the inherent feature that postponed its authoritative
publication. The model contained polarities of Modernism fundamentally attracted yet fundamentally opposed.
Hepworth, Nicholson and Nash had precipitated the
resolution of these opposites in acts of creative *integration*,
while Moore had directly achieved their *synthesis* in a condition of art Read now termed 'organic vitalism':

... obviously the whole scope of art is altered if you make it,
instead of the more or less sensuous symbolization of intellectual
ideals, the direct expression of an organic vitalism. No doubt
intellectual elements will enter into the choice and elaboration
of the [forms of this expression just as sensuous elements enter
into the] images which the intellect selects to represent its ideals
...[46]

Other artists drawn to the London International could be
afforded roles within this notional system. For example,
Naum Gabo seemed to have brought from Russia the
fruits of accomplished revolution in Abstraction, but as a
result of a long correspondence (and ironically after Gabo
had left Britain to reside in the USA) Read was persuaded of the fundamentally organic nature of his constructions.[47] Gabo was attempting to create natural
equivalents and therefore merited comparability to Moore.
The work of another refugee in London, Piet Mondrian,
however, though apparently similar to Gabo's in conception, had been anchored at the Abstraction extremity and
– because it was positively *locatable* – had memorialised
the previous revolution. A prerequisite of avant-garde
authenticity was an artist's resistance to *exclusive* association with idioms or movements. Had Picasso come to
London – even in spirit – he would have joined Moore
and Gabo in a formidable cohort of the avant-garde.

Read's dialectic development of the paradigm was
never fully articulated, though most of his preparatory
work was published, as a random sequence, in *The Philosophy of Modern Art* in 1952. Read was almost sixty now,
and had clearly desired this book to be definitive. However, his concern to persuade artists of an axis existent
within themselves, and the nagging belief that his model
had to accommodate Picasso as paragon Modernist, were
the distracting features of his work that postponed its
satisfactory completeness. The notion of the 'interior axis'
was built upon guesswork about the creative subconscious, which in the 1940s Read had sought to explain

in another psychological phase towards a rejection of that
world, which results in an abstract style of art.[41]

And by an extension of this this argument to accommodate Nash Read acknowledged a periodic tracking
back and forth across the entire ground between Abstraction and Superrealism.[42]

Thus many of the artists who informed Read's model
as it matured had produced works that traced their passage across all or parts of the spectrum of specifically-
modern art. There were exceptions to this principle, however. Moore's best work did not exhibit a range of distinct
idiomatic identities but rather fused the Abstract and the
Superreal. Whereas the works of Hepworth, Nicholson
and Nash seemed to indicate a willingness to *integrate*
Abstract and Superreal intentionality, Moore's appeared
to exemplify a *synthetic resolution* of the polarities.

The various versions of Read's argument that followed
the premature publication of 1936 were stages in the construction of exactly this sort of dialectic. He rehearsed
Moore's commitment to natural forms – stones, shells,
bones, weathered timbers – as providing insights into the
shapes his materials ought 'naturally' to adopt. *Material*
development was sustained with this acute observation
while *thematic* content was sustained with Moore's
idealised recollections of his mother, the landscape of his
youth, and the labyrinth (coal mine) that had been the
workplace of his ancestors. It seemed highly characteristic
of this artist's work that: '... a given form is broken down,
allowed to suggest associative forms and phantasies. If the
first process may be called *crystallization*, this might be
called *improvisation*. It is another aspect of the opposition
between constructivism and superrealism which [Moore]
is always seeking to synthetise.'[43]

Moore demonstrated that it was possible to envisage:
'... an inclusive ambivalent attitude, a taking-into-oneself

with an ill-fitting mixture of Freudian and Jungian principles. This was a system of coordinates in which horizontal factors were the various Jungian mental types, ranging from introversion to extroversion, and vertical factors the several layers of a Freudian subconscious (but incorporating a Jungian collective unconscious and Read's own idea of the supraconscious, an accessible field beyond the range of consciousness).

It is clear from Read's development of this model, as a succession of experimental diagrams leading to the published version in *Education through Art* (1943) that he had combined Freudian and Jungian principles with considerable licence. This tendency pervaded the essays he combined in his *Philosophy of Modern Art*, resulting in an unsatisfactory shifting between Freudian and Jungian interpretations that was only really perceptible when the collection was assembled. However, Read's subsequent adoption of a predominantly-Jungian rationale of the unconscious was not simply a matter of editing for clarity. He realised that Freud had been chiefly valuable as an explicator of the 'mannered' automatism of Surrealism and Picasso's idiomatic promiscuity. As Picasso became less relevant to Read's theory of the avant-garde the Freudian prop became correspondingly redundant.

This crucial change was initiated by Read's re-evaluation of *Guernica* and realisation that he had too eagerly accepted contemporary accounts of Picasso's tranced or involuntary 'intentionality'. In the 1950s Read was much less inclined (than he had been as a Surrealist) to accept that the genuine materialisation of images from the unknown – images unanticipated before the specific act of painting or making – would result in conventionally recognisable symbols accessible to scholarly interpretation. Now that evidence was available of Picasso's systematic refinement, in sketches and preparatory studies of *preselected* symbols – horse, bull, light-bearer, woman with dead child – and of the introduction and discarding of others – for example, a Pegasus – the myth of spontaneous emission was discredited. This in turn licensed the dis-

covery of Picasso's rehearsal in earlier works of the range of symbols previously considered to have materialised uniquely out of his rage before fascism. What was redeemable was an explanation much less interesting to Read: Picasso began with images laden with literal or historical significance, which he gradually reduced and replaced with new significance deriving from his own powers of formal distortion and exaggerated expression.[48] Read expressed an undisguised sense of betrayal:

It is not inconceivable ... that the traditional symbols [Picasso] uses are used with deliberate intention. But as Jung has said, 'a symbol loses its magical power ... as soon as its dissolubility is recognized. An effective symbol, therefore, must have a nature that is unimpeachable ... its form must be sufficiently remote from comprehension as to frustrate every attempt of the critical intellect to give any satisfactory account of it; and, finally, its aesthetic appearance must have such a convincing appeal that no sort of argument can be raised against it on that score.'[49]

While Picasso could not be faulted 'on that score' he could be taken to task for rewarding with a reservoir of dead symbolism the penetration of his surface genius.

As Read had intoned Jung in this judgment he sent him a copy of his published text. Jung concurred[50] while delivering a more devastating critique of Picasso than Read had hazarded. This was an absolutely decisive exchange, for it not only suggested that Picasso had evaded avant-garde responsibilities: it confirmed a coupling of avant-garde intentionality and purpose that, when filled out with specific references to the emergent art of the 1960s, perfected Read's paradigm in the last years of his life. Jung defined the modern artist as an individual able to dream the future by attending to the images and forms emitting from the unconscious, accepting responsibility to reveal them *without modification*, avoiding temptation to make them conform to the familiar. The creative act was to be regarded as an event *visited upon* the artist[51] by virtue of an ability to tap the collective unconscious. The resulting symbols (unwelcome guests) would be embodiments of primordial experience condensing as reality. 'Who is the awe inspiring guest who knocks at our door portentously? Fear precedes him, showing that ultimate values already flow towards him. Our hitherto believed values decay accordingly and our only certainty is that the new world will be something very different from what we were used to.'[52]

While apparently possessing the potential ability and creative strength to materialise reality (in forms that would initially be disliked because of a general fear of the unknown), Picasso had abdicated this responsibility by *modifying* the results of unconscious formation in order to make them more acceptable by dilution and fragmentation. 'By this regrettable digression he shows how little he understands the primordial urge, which does not mean a field of ever so alluring shards, but a new world, after the old one has crumpled up'.[53]

To Jung the negative aspect of modern art was its pandering to a general prejudice against the future –

99

100 Graham Sutherland
Thorn Trees 1945-6. The
British Council
(cat.no.195)

'which we obstinately want to be as we expect it'. This confirmed to Read that Picasso had avoided engagement with the real – by distracting the Modernist audience with formal and idiomatic variety, by offering visions of modernity that, however scandalising, were popularly *preferable* to the real, and by moderating the real with historical and literary allusion. It was a tribute to Picasso that a painting like *Guernica* nevertheless communicated profoundly in spite of the artist's strategies for evasion, but what it communicated was due to Picasso's extraordinary ability aesthetically to revivify the cliché, rather than to *generate symbolism in living form*.[54]

It was this more vital ability, finally, that distinguished Henry Moore. He worked with very few motifs – most often a coalescence of the female form, the landform and the labyrinth – to reveal essential truths about interlocked systems of human existence, mutual dependence and natural sustentation (not especially welcome in an age of technological optimism).

The modern sculptor proceeds from form to image – he discovers (or we discover for him) the significance of his forms *after* he has created them. What we must admire, in the modern artist, is the confidence with which he accepts as a gift from the unconscious, forms of whose significance he is not, at the creative moment, precisely aware.[55]

Picasso *almost* matched this creative enterprise but wilfully handicapped himself with preordained symbolism and (according to Jung) with fostering a popular myth of the modern artist's fragmented vision. Popularism, even in this perverse form, was anathema to an avant-garde project dedicated to revealing Jung's unwelcome guests. Moore's direct expression of organic vitalism, though, was the apotheosis of this project, justifying the preliminary stages of idiomatic traversion. Symbiotically, it justified also those consistent factional cross-representations (evidence of philosophical 'inconsistency' to those who knew no better) that had constituted Read's development of his paradigm over a quarter of a century.

The slow evolution of the paradigm was the reason it was never published definitively. Read devoted a lifetime to its development and left little time for application.[56] At last perfectly tuned to British Modernism, it had become retrospective – its dedicated avant-garde was an old guard. Archetypes evinced by this older generation conformed to Jungian staples – symbols of motherhood and the earth, growth and harvest, alternative personalities, mutual aid – in images and forms of relatively clear focus, strong specificity and timeless relevance. Emulation of this generation's achievements required empathy with biological formation.[57] A Cold War generation, however, materialised ingrained preoccupations that were equally pressing, less specifically organic, but insistently related to prevailing conditions of human existence. While sustaining the *established* revolution by perfecting a critique of Moore and comparable artists, then, Read accepted the achievements of a younger generation of British sculptors

as signalling a dialectic advance of art *beyond* Moore's achievement.

The new sculpture *respected* the organic but not as an exclusive priority. It expressed materialising forces – earth, air, fire, water – and harnessed them to a collective psychic anxiety in the presence of the atomic threat, creating restless, linear symbols of energetic nervousness, or casting in the solid state the visual characteristics of molten liquidity. The sculptor – generally a blacksmith rather than carver or modeller – would exercise 'uncontrol' in rescuing, from the formless flux of molten materials, solidified moments of intense significance.[58] The gentle organic archetypes of the generation that had matured in the 1930s receded before archetypes shot through with anxiety – the tensed animal; the scuttling insect; the watcher; the stranger flexed for flight – symbolising a 'geometry of fear'.[59]

Read recognised the most significant contemporary movement in painting – variously termed Abstract Expressionism, Tachisme, Action Painting – as a genuinely international phenomenon.[60] He accepted that the triumph of European Modernism had been to condense in an American climate a most profound aesthetic expression of the condition of contemporary existence; and he gradually became aware of identical achievement in a younger generation of Europeans in spite of its loss of leaders to the USA. The new existential painting already had many variants. Sufficient of these agreed with Read's paradigm to ensure that in its last phase his model, de-parochialised, was fulfilled as a British vision of Modernism.

The existential painter – Read had in mind such artists as Sam Francis, Mark Tobey and Jackson Pollock – would proceed by reflex actions that were nevertheless geared to the purpose of materialising an image of inexplicable, yet obviously true and vital, necessity.[61] Others – Henri Michaux, Jean Fautrier, Jean Dubuffet – in their scrapings and pourings would conjure states of 'sudden glory' out of amorphousness.[62] Observers were given sensational contact with compulsive 'graphs of uncertainty'. Such images were informal, in the minor sense of being relatively unfocused and unspecific, but more significantly in symbolising the chaos reigning beneath and

---

The artist is not a mere discoverer ... but an interpreter. His forms are aesthetic, which means that he uses the power he takes from living things to give vitality to the creatures of his imagination. Sutherland ... has entered another philosophical climate, and though his relations to a Heidegger or a Sartre may be as remote as Turner's was to Schelling or Novalis, the growing fearsomeness of the symbols reflects the now prevailing cosmic anxiety.

The Tenth Muse, pp.311-12

100

101

101 Lynn Chadwick *The Stranger* 1954. Collection of the artist (cat.no.39)

The great achievements of Moore, the lesser achievements of Picasso, together with those of their generation who had not quite matched them but had nevertheless been part of the collective enterprise, now constituted the *established* revolution. The current achievements of such as Alan Davie, Patrick Heron, Reg Butler, Kenneth Armitage and Lynn Chadwick constituted the actual revolution under way. There was no mediation between these extremes – no middle ground or *compromise* in Naturalism – and therefore even clearer evidence of a dialectic in operation than there had been in Moore's day.

The pattern did appear to be repeating: Read had perceived in his lifetime a series of revolutions and dialectic advances comprising the initial achievements of Abstraction in the first two decades of the century; the Superrealist response in the 1930s, the resolution of these mutually antagonistic tendencies in the Organicism typified by Moore, and now the emergence of a new antithesis in Existentialist painting and sculpture of a rising generation. Read accepted two remaining responsibilities – to continue sustaining the established revolution by perfecting a critique of Moore and comparable artists; and to strengthen the current revolution as his part in the fusion of Organic and Existential polarities he could foretell but probably would not see.

In the realm of painting he predicted a reaffirmation of the concrete image, for he believed that in a Francis or a Tobey the limits of iconic informality had been reached. To reflect indefinitely on an existential chaos or nothingness – an act of utmost value in the present moment – would be to abdicate proactive responsibilities.

The modern painter has reached the end of his voyage of discovery, and stares into the unknown, the unnamed. To render back to others that sense of vacuity is not to create a work of art, which everywhere and at all times has depended on the presentation of a concrete image ...
Our images must be at once universal and concrete, as were the images of past myth and legend ... the images of a new mythology, but it must be the mythology of a vision that has explored the physical nature of the universe ...[65]

Read adopted a definition that, in the choice of words, ultimately reveals his paradigm to have been – in its final mutation and perhaps always – essentially a paradigm of sculpture: 'the fully concrete work of art should combine the individuality of representation with the universality of abstraction in a unity made possible through the exploration of spatial occupancy.'[66] Painting has reached an unsurpassable automatism; *prolonged* reflection on the void of uncertainty is evasion of responsibility; a new symbolism, the product of 'a vision that has explored the physical nature of the universe' will combine universal and individual principles (finite concreteness and infinite resonance) 'through the exploration of spatial occupancy' – these thoughts may indeed be interpreted as predicting the resolution of the mutual contradictions of, say, a Mark Tobey and a Lynn Chadwick *in the realm of sculpture*.

beyond consciousness. Compared to their *genuine* automatism, that of Surrealism now seemed mannered or overlaid with conventionalised interpretation, like the effort involved in remembering a dream. Thus Read exorcised his mid-life lapse into factionalism.[63]

The new art was instinctive, reflex and (closing a circle by evoking Kandinsky) formed in moments of 'internal necessity': practitioners delivered themselves not so much to the unconscious force of the imagination as to a liberating 'irresponsibility'.[64] The process seemed close to Kandinsky's slowly formed inner feeling, worked over by non-directed purpose. It was something Jung had commented on, attributing it to creative elaboration within the unconscious mind. Jung's advice had been to cultivate precisely the sort of 'irresponsibility' that now was evident – an objective yet disinterested process of watching the development of fragments of fantasy.

Does this mean that Read at the last abandoned painting? On the contrary, he thought that in its post-Existentialist manifestations painting had abandoned the Modernist project. It is necessary to consider this in the context of Read's belief in the *temporary* validity of gestural abstraction. There would be retreat from extremes of informality or formlessness, and a more concerted engagement of images of archetypal potency – images shunning academic, historical or literary conventions and avoiding the self-consciousness of Surrealism, but nevertheless replete with deep-seated, social meaning. This is what his paradigm heralded. When he witnessed other emergent tendencies – particularly Pop – he assumed critical responsibility for a false advance. Painters had gazed into the formless void but on readdressing the concrete they had settled for a debased formal currency. When he commented bitterly on this Read was in effect lamenting a failure of critique. It is in the nature of paradigms that they are temporary: they illuminate, collapse and ultimately fail. Read believed that in its moment of completeness his paradigm had failed in its ultimate purpose of guiding the next avant-garde.

It seems clear that in this he sustained two main regrets: that he had not dealt earlier with the problem of Picasso, and that he had overemphasised the Superreal. The Pop artists' preoccupation with a specific imagery was comparable to Picasso's engagement of the 'banal': if revitalising the conventional had largely defeated him it would also defeat those who worked with an even lower order of symbolism. The Superreal had been interpreted in terms of the symbolic fantasies of the cinema, science fiction and consumerist advertising. Read found it barely acceptable that artists had taken the typical imagery of this 'popular culture' (he considered this term misleading since, largely associated with advertising, it was exploitative) and modified it with some respect for facture, interpretation and transformation – though he doubted whether such remnants of an aesthetic conscience would really redeem it from incoherence and thus irrelevance.[67] He could not tolerate, however, and was compelled to condemn, what he saw as the casual re-presentation of arbitrary forms, a mindless repetition of the clichés of an imposed pictorial regime, a reversal of culture.

Art, he said, would have no history but for the individual artist's efforts to invent new, significant forms in response to some unique, originating intentionality. Culture is a dialectic moving forward, annexing and occupying new experience, an organic event unfolding. As he wrote when he perceived Moore's work as having surpassed idiomatic alternation, and as synthetic in its direct, organic vitalism:

A synthesis is merely the meeting place of two ideas, and from this conjunction arises a new idea. But each new idea is in its turn a thesis which merges into an endless dialectical chain, and the only finality is something we agree to call the Truth, which seems to recede with every step we take towards it.

Notes

1 Comparable in all other respects to Alfred Barr, whose direction of the Museum of Modern Art, New York, provided the principal alternative source of intelligence in the medium of English.
2 Read, Herbert (Ed) (1924) *Speculations by T.E.Hulme: Essays on Humanism and the Philosophy of Art* (London, Kegan Paul, Trench, Trubner & Co).
3 Read, Herbert (1926) *Reason and Romanticism: Essays in Literary Criticism* (London, Faber & Gwyer).
4 Read, Herbert (1928) *English Prose Style* (London, G. Bell & Sons Ltd); Read, Herbert (1928) *Phases of English Poetry* (London, Hogarth Press); Read, Herbert (1929) *The Sense of Glory: Essays in Criticism* (Cambridge, Cambridge University Press); Read, Herbert (1930) *Wordsworth: the Clark Lectures 1929-30* (London, Jonathan Cape).
5 Read, Herbert (1919) *Naked Warriors* (London, Art & Letters) p.5.
6 Rutter, Frank (1926) *Evolution in Modern Art: a Study of Modern Painting 1870-1925* (London, George G. Harrap & Co) p.114.
7 *Ibid.* pp.115-17 and Plate 28, fac.p.116 (*Composition* by Wassily Kandinsky).
8 For more extensive discussions of all principal parts of this essay see Thistlewood, David (1984) *Herbert Read: Formlessness and Form: an introduction to his Aesthetics* (London, Routledge & Kegan Paul).
9 There is no evidence that Moore attended or was aware of the Leeds Arts Club, but Tom Steele has argued persuasively that, studying at the Leeds Art School, Moore could not have avoided immersion in its principles. See Steele, Tom (1990) *Alfred Orage and the Leeds Arts Club* (Aldershot, Scolar Press) esp. 'Herbert Read, Henry Moore and Barbara Hepworth: a Postscript' (pp.231-9).
10 Read, Herbert (1931) *The Meaning of Art* (London, Faber & Faber).
11 *Ibid.* pp.145-8.
12 *Ibid.* pp.148-53.
13 *Ibid.* p.145.
14 It is ironic that *The Meaning of Art* has enjoyed the longest currency of all Read's writings, having been some sixty years in print.
15 Read, Herbert (1933) *Art Now: an Introduction to the Theory of Modern Painting and Sculpture* (London, Faber & Faber).
16 *Ibid.* pp.108-10.
17 *Ibid.* pp.121-7.
18 *Ibid*, p.121. Read referred to 'the dilemma of the typical modern artist, the artist who has renounced the reproduction of the visible appearance of the object as an aim in art, and who then hesitates between abstraction and free subjective form'.
19 Read must already have been aware of Alfred Barr's intention to map Modernism as a succession of movements. Barr had consulted Wyndham Lewis in 1926 before making a 'grand tour' of European avant-garde artists following an order suggested by the proposal that all the great aesthetic advances of the previous twenty-five years had emanated from Cubism. Read is certain to have been aware of this through friendship with Lewis and also because of Barr's subsequent, systematic research in every part of the European arena in which Read was active. Though they seem not to have met at this time, Read and Barr must constantly have encountered traces of one another as they explored the same territory. On Barr's 'grand tour' see Sandler, Irving and Newman, Amy (Eds) (1986) *Defining Modern Art: Selected Writings of Alfred H.Barr, Jr* (New York, Harry N.Abrams Inc.) p.103. See also Lynes, Russell (1973) *Good Old Modern: an Intimate Portrait of the Museum of Modern Art* (New York, Atheneum) p.27.
20 In a sympathetic and appreciative letter to Read dated 18 Nov 1933 (in response to Read's gift of a copy of *Art Now*) Wassily Kandinsky attempted to correct Read's view that Expressionism was not specifically-modern, asserting that his own book *Über das Geistige in der Kunst* (1912) and the periodical he published jointly with Franz Marc before the First World War, *Der Blaue Reiter*, had subsequently influenced all 'interesting' developments in German art: 'die Entwicklung der deutschen Kunst ausübte und

102 Karel Appel *Portrait of Sir Herbert Read* 1962. The Montreal Museum of Fine Arts Collection, Purchase Horsley and Annie Townsend Fund (cat.no.7)

noch heute jedem kunstinteressierten Deutschen …' 48/73 Read Archive, University of Victoria, British Columbia.

21 *Art Now* (n.15) p.144. In subsequent editions 'linear signs' was changed to 'plastic forms'.

22 Read, Herbert (1934) *Henry Moore, Sculptor : an Appreciation* (London, Zwemmer) pp.10-11.

23 Read, Herbert (1934) *Unit One : the Modern Movement in English Architecture, Painting and Sculpture* (London, Cassell & Co) The group comprised (sculptors) Barbara Hepworth and Henry Moore; (painters) John Armstrong, John Bigge, Edward Burra, Tristram Hillier, Paul Nash, Ben Nicholson and Edward Wadsworth; (architects) Wells Coates and Colin Lucas.

24 *Ibid.* 'Introduction', esp. pp.14-16.

25 Read, Herbert (1965) 'British Art 1930-1940', catalogue of the exhibition *Art in Britain 1930-40 centred around Axis, Circle, Unit One* (London, Marlborough Fine Art) pp.5-6.

26 In an open 'Proposal for a Scottish Philanthropist', undated [1932], he had sought funds to establish a Bauhaus in Edinburgh. 37/55, Read Archive, University of Victoria, British Columbia. His contacts with such as Walter Gropius, Wassily Kandinsky and László Moholy-Nagy and his knowledge of the approaching crisis in Dessau would certainly have led to their being, at the very least, consulted on its formation.

27 Tangible outcomes of this plan were Read's leading role in bringing the Third Reich exhibition of '*Degenerate' German Art* to the New Burlington Gallery, London, 1938, and his support in publishing a defence against 'degeneracy' in: Thoene, Peter (1938) *Modern German Art* (Harmondsworth, Penguin Books): see Read's 'Introduction', pp.7-11.

28 See Read, Herbert (1937) 'Why I am a Surrealist', *New English Weekly*, vol.10, March, pp.413-14. For an extensive account of Read's involvement with Surrealism and his use of the term 'Superrealism' see Ray, Paul, C. (1971) *The Surrealist Movement in England* (Ithaca and London, Cornell University Press) pp.108-32.

29 Read and Barr both issued their paradigms in 1936 – Read's in a postscript to the second edition of *Art Now* (1936) ; Barr's in Barr, Alfred H. Jr (1936) *Cubism and Abstract Art* (New York, Museum of Modern Art) on the occasion of the exhibition of the same title. It is tempting to detect competition: each would have been aware of the other's project in outline through their common network of artists, dealers, picture agencies and other sources of information. Read would have known the priority Barr afforded Cubism and (since both Read and Barr had simultaneously completed major studies of Surrealism and also shared sources in this specific arena) he would have been aware of the dependency on Cubism that Barr attributed even to Surrealism. See Read, Herbert (Ed) (1936) *Surrealism* (London, Faber & Faber) ; Barr, Alfred H. Jr (1936) *Fantastic Art, Dada and Surrealism* (New York, Museum of Modern Art). But competition with Barr was less urgent than the need to express solidarity with the Europeans. The fact that Read called himself a Surrealist in order to accomplish this weakened the reception of his ideas. In comparison, Barr's control over exhibition interpretation at the Museum of Modern Art enabled him to rehearse his model in all the museum's publications, conventionalising the proposal that Modernist authenticity descended from Cubism.

30 Read, Herbert (1935) 'What is Revolutionary Art?' in: *Five on Revolutionary Art* (London, Wishart) p.19.

31 *Ibid.* pp.20-1.

32 Read, Herbert (1936) *Art Now* (2nd rev. ed.) (London, Faber & Faber) p.146.

33 Read, Herbert (1937) 'The faculty of abstraction', in: Martin, J.L.; Nicholson, B. and Gabo, N. (Eds) *Circle : International Survey of Constructive Art* (London, Faber & Faber) p.64.

34 Read, Herbert (1939) 'An art of pure form', *The London Bulletin*, no.14, pp.6-9. This was a republication of a passage in Read, Herbert (1937) *Art and Society* (London, Heinemann) pp.259-60.

35 'Faculty of abstraction' (n.33) p.66.

36 Read, Herbert (1938) 'Guernica', *The London Bulletin*, no.6, p.6.

37 See Read, Herbert (1943) *Education through Art* (London, Faber

& Faber) esp. 'Modern art' (pp.97-100) and 'Unconscious processes of integration' pp.186-203.

38 For an extended discussion of the significance of Jungian archetypes to Read's socio-political and educational theorising, see: Thistlewood, David (1986) 'Creativity and political identification in the work of Herbert Read', *British Journal of Aesthetics*, vol.26, no.4, Autumn, pp.345-56.

39 For example, Paul Nash had been encouraged to resign, then effectively expelled, from the English Surrealist Group, for exhibiting surrealist, naturalist and abstract works side by side. Letter Nash to Read dated 21 Jan 1939; 48/99 Read Archive, University of Victoria, British Columbia.

40 Letter Hepworth to Read dated 15 May 1944; 48/61 Read Archive, University of Victoria, British Columbia. See also references to this correspondence in: Read, Herbert (1948) 'Barbara Hepworth; a new phase', *The Listener*, vol.XXXIX, p.592; and Read, Herbert (1948) 'Realism and Abstraction in modern art', republished as Chapter 5 of Read, Herbert (1952) *The Philosophy of Modern Art* (London, Faber & Faber) pp.88-104 (p.98).

41 Read, Herbert (1948) 'Ben Nicholson', republished as Chapter 12, *Philosophy of Modern Art* (n.40) pp.216-25 (p.220).

42 An eclecticism noted in various writings between 1944 and 1949, correlated in the celebratory essay Read, Herbert (1952) 'Paul Nash', Chapter 10, *Philosophy of Modern Art* (n.40) pp.174-94 (esp. pp.179-82, 185-88).

43 Read, Herbert (1944) 'Henry Moore', republished as Chapter 11, *Philosophy of Modern Art* (n.40) pp.195-215 (p.209).

44 Read : 'Realism and Abstraction in modern art' (n.40) p.104.

45 *Ibid.* p.97. The bracketed addition to this quotation, changing 'realism' to 'superrealism', is intended to clarify Read's meaning. In the same essay he stated : '… realism will include, not only the attempt to reproduce with fidelity the images given in normal perception, but also those distorted or selected images due to exceptional states of awareness which we call idealism, expressionism, superrealism, etc. In the same way, abstraction will include any form of expression which dispenses with the phenomenal image, and relies on elements of expression that are conceptual, metaphysical, abstruse, and absolute …' *Ibid.* p.88.

46 Read, 'Henry Moore' (n.43) p.207. The bracketed words are present in Read's handwritten draft of this essay (Blue Notebook 13/2/3, Read Archive, University of Victoria, British Columbia) but appear to have been missed in typesetting, causing ambiguity in the published version.

47 A flavour of their exchange may be indicated in Read's observation to Gabo as follows: 'The ambition to "create reality" seems to me a little self-deceptive. It is an extreme of ego-centrism which I am willing to entertain … but what is essentially a subjective attitude, you turn into a positive activity, and in some sense detach yourself from existence to create essence …' Letter Read to Gabo dated 5 Oct 1947 (Gabo Archive, Yale University Library). For a summary of the Read-Gabo exchange see 'Appendix to the essay on Constructivism, Chapter 13a, Read : *Philosophy of Modern Art* (n.40). For an extended discussion, including correspondence omitted from this source, see Thistlewood: *Formlessness and Form* (n.8) pp.85-94.

48 Read, Herbert (1960) 'The created form', Chapter 4 of *The forms of things unknown* (London, Faber & Faber) pp.64-75 (pp.65-9).

49 *Ibid.* p.69.

Someone objects because he has seen a face in the blazing vortex ; and does not the artist himself suggest that he has painted a portrait of Mr X or Miss Y ? nevertheless he has taken no notice of their public faces, but has represented their private ecstasies.

Preface to *Paintings Karel Appel* London, ICA, 1957

102

50 Letter C. G. Jung to Read dated 2 Sept 1960 (48/72, Read Archive, University of Victoria, British Columbia) in response to Read's gift of a copy of *The forms of things unknown*.

51 A 'thing that happens to you'; Jung letter p.3.

52 *Ibid*. pp.2a-3.

53 'Picasso is ruthless strength, seizing the unconscious urge and voicing it resoundingly, even using it for monetary reasons'. *Ibid*. p.2a.

54 Read, 'Created form' (n.48) p.70.

55 *Ibid*. pp.74-5.

56 It received two specific applications in books dedicated to individual artists: Read, Herbert (1965) *Henry Moore; a study of his life and work* (London, Thames & Hudson); and Read, Herbert (1968) *Arp* (London, Thames & Hudson).

57 In this remaining phase of his life Read was able to present his ideas in an arena other than his writings. From 1947 he was founding President of the Institute of Contemporary Arts, London, one of the purposes of which was to rehearse in exhibitions, publications and debates his antithetical principles in order to inform the next avant-garde advance. See Thistlewood, David (1989) 'The MOMA and the ICA: a common philosophy of modern art'; *British Journal of Aesthetics*, vol.29, no.4. Autumn, pp.316-28. The ICA embraced all aspects of relevant intentionality, including Abstraction, Superrealism, and every shade or tendency between them, but biological formation was a special devotion in recognition of its importance to Moore's generation. It is instructive to sample a little of what the ICA membership would have debated. Good form is perceptible in all manner of natural organisms at microscopic, normal and macroscopic scales, and exhibits such attributes as structural order, elegance, harmony, economy, and dynamic equilibrium. Objectified in art-making, such properties suggest the comparability of growth in nature and composition in art. See Thistlewood, David (1982) 'Organic art and the popularization of a scientific philosophy', *British Journal of Aesthetics*, vol.22, no.4, Autumn, pp.311-21.

58 See Read, Herbert (1958) 'Great Britain', in: Brion, M. (Ed) (1958) *Art since 1945* (London, Thames & Hudson) pp.221-50.

59 See Read, Herbert (1958) 'Lynn Chadwick', in Read, Herbert (1962) *A letter to a young painter* [and other essays] (London, Thames & Hudson) pp.101-3 (p.101).

60 Read, Herbert (1962) 'The limits of painting' in: Read, Herbert (1967) *Art and Alienation: the role of the artist in society* (London, Thames & Hudson) pp.52-3.

61 Read, Herbert (1956) 'An art of internal necessity', *Quadrum One*, Brussels, pp.7-22 (p.22).

62 Read, Herbert (1960) holographed notes on typescript of 'The informal image in modern art', Read's communication to the IV International Congress of Aesthetics, Technical University of Athens, 1-6 Sep; verso p.10. 35/7 Read Archive, University of Victoria, British Columbia.

63 Surrealism 'which seemed for so long to offer the possibility of a new art, an art "in the service of revolution", was finally to break up, and now, in retrospect, in comparison with the art that has actually been revolutionary in our time, it seems to have been entirely academic. I hope I shall not be misunderstood at this point: I supported the Surrealist movement in the 'thirties and I would support it again were the circumstances still the same. But we have learned from experience – our aesthetic no less than our social experience – and we have moved towards a more revolutionary art precisely because Surrealism as a philosophy of art was not adequate for a new situation.' Read, 'Limits of painting' (n.60), p.46.

64 Read, Herbert (1955) 'Blot on the scutcheon', *Encounter*, vol.v, no.1, July, pp.54-7.

65 *Ibid*. p.55.

66 Read, 'Limits of painting' (n.60), quoting Feibelman, James K. (1962) 'Concreteness in painting, Abstract Expressionism and after', *The Personalist*, vol.43, no.1 (University of Southern California Press).

67 Read, Herbert (1964) 'The disintegration of form in modern art', in Read, Herbert (1965) *The origins of form in art* (London, Thames & Hudson) pp.174-87 (p.183).

Herbert Read: A New Vision of Art and Industry

David Thistlewood

Herbert Read's *Art and Industry: the Principles of Industrial Design*,[1] written in a very short time after his return from Edinburgh and published in 1934, is a seminal pre-war study of the Modern Movement in design.[2] Between 1944 and 1956 it was revised three times and reprinted on a further three occasions: this suggests a strong implication of this essay – that *Art and Industry* substantially informed the design culture surrounding the *Festival of Britain* in 1951. As the *FoB* has rightly been excluded from the strict canon of the International Style[3] on account of its idiosyncratic romanticism, it will be inferred that Read, too, avoided this fateful cul-de-sac. In this sense his work anticipated the efforts of historians and theorists who would attempt, from the late 1960s onwards, to establish some sense of continuity in design stemming from 'heroic' early Modernism and offering hope of continuing aesthetic renewal and development in place of International Style stagnation.[4]

Unlike his theories of art, Read's principles of design crystallised virtually instantaneously, resulting from brilliant insight and requiring little subsequent revision. After the collapse of his future as a Professor of Fine Art he sampled a variety of alternative roles – broadcasting, writing, editing – including re-establishing himself as an authority on made artefacts. He had already published scholarly histories of ceramics and stained glass in his former occupation at the Victoria and Albert Museum. He had tried to establish a 'Bauhaus' in Edinburgh, and he was in contact with Walter Gropius and László Moholy-Nagy. His friend Paul Nash, a member of the Council for Art and Industry, involved him in the formation of Unit One, and here he met the architect-engineer Wells Coates and, through Coates, a circle which included Frank Pick of the Design and Industries Association and Coates's colleagues who were designing and equipping new offices and studios for the BBC. In addition, he had already appreciated the work of the Museum of Modern Art, New York, and this institution's interest in improving the standards of American product design.

Uniquely, therefore, Read had grasp on a number of significant contemporary issues, the fusion of which created the essence of his book. He appreciated Arts and Crafts idealism, but knew sufficient of the history of craft industries (and indeed had boyhood memories of forge and smithy) to regard machine production as a practical necessity. He realised that an age of crude machining, characterised by soulless attempts to copy handwork, was a distant past and that it was now legitimate to conceive of forms of beauty *specific* to machine processes. He understood German product design to be geared to appropriate formal ideals of geometric purity, but he was beginning to think also in terms of a specifically north-European ingenuity in the expressive use of new materials such as plastics and plywood, and of old materials in novel forms, for example, glass. He was a devotee of Moholy-Nagy's writings, which were sufficiently distanced from 'orthodox' Bauhaus principles to indicate that Read was not entirely uncritical of Gropius. And he was himself a broadcaster – a specifically twentieth-century phenomenon – with an insider's perception of the communications industry in its great pioneering phase; and he believed implicitly in the medium's power to propagate good taste, to provide appropriate techno-aesthetic exemplars, and to be the engine of the modern economy.

Among the several individuals (Wells Coates, Serge Chermayeff, Raymond McGrath, P. Morton Shand) and institutions (BBC, MOMA) Read acknowledged for helpful contributions to *Art and Industry*, two people, Gropius and Moholy-Nagy, were singled out for special recognition. Gropius was cited for his influence on the quality of manufactured goods in countries respondent to the Bauhaus idea, and for his inspirational leadership of all who possessed 'the new vision in industrial design'. However, Moholy-Nagy was acknowledged as having written the book *The New Vision*[5] that had provided Read with the impetus to write his own. This is really very significant: the tribute to Gropius is in effect a politeness towards the leader Read believed had established standards of form and of design education; that to Moholy-Nagy is recognition of a programme for the future that would be more congenial than the strict exactitudes of Gropius's classical aesthetic. Read chose the *romantic* path (which he probably would have discounted had he written his book five or six years earlier) and it led to a future shaped by Moholy-Nagy's techno-artistry, his cinematic and filmic consciousness, and fascination for phenomena the Bauhaus had relatively disregarded: electricity and light. Read's identification with Moholy-Nagy's eccentric text suggests that one possible future he was considering for himself was as producer and disseminator of design 'intelligence' via the radio and the fledgling television service, chairing 'brains trusts' and reporting on good taste, and creating propaganda out of appealing contradictions – the pure science and gadgetry – that sustained the new medium.

Consider first, then, the benchmark principles of formal design that Read attributed to a 'classic' Bauhaus influence. It is important to note that these were intrinsically aesthetic, for he distrusted functionalism as a generator of *necessarily* beautiful or appealing form.

One false theory assumes that if the object in question performs its function in the most efficient way possible, it will *ipso facto* possess the necessary aesthetic qualities. To this argument we must reply that an object which functions perfectly may, and probably will, possess aesthetic qualities, but that the connection is not a necessary one. Aesthetic values are absolute or universal values to which an object, restricted by its function to a particular form, may approach; but by very reason of its particularity, cannot inevitably assume. In other words, art implies values more various than those determined by practical necessity.[6]

In *The Meaning of Art* Read had generalised about a cyclic reinterpretation of principles of harmony and order constituting the universals of art. He had suggested that the characteristics of distinct cultural styles and historic movements resulted from the reinvigoration of universal principles with symbolism unique to each new circumstance. The uniqueness of the present design culture arose from the availability of new materials, construction techniques and methods of fabrication – conditions that afforded almost limitless scope for the creation of objects in diversities of shape and scale. Notions of 'functional economy' and celebration of a range of forms peculiar to machine processes would serve to regulate this potential chaos, discounting for example, gratuitous embellishment and imitation of the styles of other periods. However, Gropius's great contribution to industrial design as typified in his Bauhaus courses at Weimar and Dessau (as Read understood them) was to have realised that a peculiarly-contemporary aesthetic would not result from principles of machine application and functional efficiency alone, but would only distil in conjunction with dedicated artistic research as exemplified in the best of modern abstraction.

Thus Read already distanced himself from the MOMA interpretation of Bauhaus design[7] that would, for a considerable time, become standard – that a contemporary aesthetic was to be revealed in the forms made possible by modern machine processes such as cutting, planing, turning, extruding, plating and so forth, when executed with precision in the exact fulfilment of functional needs. While accepting that this might indeed produce results of generalised beauty, Read maintained that the most profound aesthetic was revealable only in art, and that it was the designer's responsibility to effect its permeation of designed artefacts.

To demonstrate the universality of this principle Read compared two earthenware vessels, an Attic vase or drinking cup of *c*.530 BC and a Chinese vase of the Sung dynasty. Each was perfectly suited to its purpose as a container of liquid, each was unadorned with superfluous decoration, and each was of geometric typology. But the Chinese vase exhibited slight formal imperfections Read found pleasing, suggesting to him that an aesthetic principle had prevailed in its formation – that the designer-maker had *avoided the precision imperative* for the sake of a higher order of formal significance.[8] He recognised categories of manufactured goods that would not tolerate

imperfection, for example, electrical components and precision instrumentation, and he proposed the characteristic properties of such artefacts as these – their 'appeal of lines and masses harmoniously organised'[9] – as intrinsically symbolic of the age. However, he cast a critical eye on certain objects the MOMA had endowed with significance for their precision engineering – stainless-steel drinking tumblers – because to Read there was no cause for pretending that such goods required either sophisticated manufacture or absolute uniformity of production. 'Good proportions, perfect precision, beauty of "finish" – in what essential qualities [he asked] do these ordinary examples of machine art differ from the Attic vase ...?'[10] This backhanded compliment to MOMA typology betrays a difference with what was to become conventional wisdom, and indicates Read's early recognition of a tendency steering British design clear of International Style orthodoxy and towards the invigorated modernism of the *FoB*.

For to invest faith in the aestheticising properties of machine processes *per se* was ultimately to accept the formal *standardisation* of industrially produced goods. This was true whether machinery was applied to ever greater degrees of precision *excluding* considerations of harmonics and chromatics, or whether these were *included* in the manufacturing process as a codified regime. The only way satisfactorily to imbue design with appropriate aesthetic qualities was to cultivate an 'intuitional abstraction' comparable to that of a small number of avant-garde artists – indeed the future role of the abstractionist would be to design for industry rather more than producing unique objects and images for sale. Society had to:

... recognise the abstract nature of the essential element in art, and as a consequence ... that design is a function of the abstract artist ... the artist must design in the actual materials of the factory, and in the full stream of the process of production. His power must be absolute in all matters of design, and within the limits of functional efficiency, the factory must adapt itself to the artist, not the artist to the factory.[11]

This artist-designer's touchstone would be the sort of 'intuitional abstraction' typified by the work of Ben Nicholson, Piet Mondrian and (singled out by Read for illustration) Jean Hélion, ensuring that industry's aesthetic research enterprise would be sensitive to the idiosyncratic and the vital. The appropriate theoretical referents and contextual knowledge that would be brought to such designing would be those provided by Moholy-Nagy. There are obvious stylistic similarities between Moholy-Nagy's *The New Vision* and Read's *Art and Industry* – for example, both invest in the compelling modernity of radio towers and images of connoted and actual technics. However, the real continuity of the two texts consists in Read's acceptance of Moholy-Nagy's socio-cultural defence of abstract designing as a basis for his own extrapolation, particularly the claim that Constructivism was to satisfy the perceptual, as well as utilitarian, needs of the twentieth-century citizen.

Moholy-Nagy's credentials were impeccable. He had been the last of the painters appointed by Gropius to teach Form at the Bauhaus. He had shared the editorship of the Bauhausbücher, and he had been instrumental in efforts to internationalise Constructivism in the mid-1920s. His book summarised his experiences of working alongside Johannes Itten, Paul Klee, Wassily Kandinsky, and Oskar Schlemmer, and his collaboration with such as Naum Gabo and El Lissitsky. His original interpretation of the Modern Movement identified a general, peculiarly heightened condition of modern perceptual awareness and the consequent need to design urban environments expressly to cater for this intensification of vision.

He argued that the illusionistic space-representation of the Renaissance had given way to an art in which the *surface* of painting – its area-division, its chromatic properties, and in particular its balancement of two-dimensional forces – had become paramount. He argued that sculpture had passed through comparable stages of development – from the dominance of form to that of space – until it too had realised a condition he called *equipoise*, a balancement of three-dimensional forces. This was informing perceptual trends within the population at large, and so it seemed possible, using the avant-garde aesthetic principles as a guide and projecting forward their likely development, to predict the characteristics of environmental qualities future generations would find stimulating and fulfilling. He thought that painting (in the form of light-projection) and sculpture (as kinetic equipoise) would become largely de-materialised. Artistic expression of all kinds would consist in systems of elements held in dynamic equilibrium: only architecture would have tangible substance; and within its ambience there would be light projections and kinetic features as a matter of course.

Crucially for Read, Moholy-Nagy argued that specifically-modern perceptual capabilities included the reading of virtual volumes, by which he meant an ability to construct a mental image of a volume, and a feeling for its true scale, out of essentially linear information – for example in a photograph of the skeletal form of a dirigible under construction. To Read this suggested a widespread ability to apprehend linear symbolism (marking a significant difference from the more orthodox Bauhaus preoccupation with shape and surface) and provided an opportunity to fill out Moholy-Nagy's argument with less esoteric references. Read celebrated an endemic linearity in traditional English spindle furniture and wrought-iron work; but more significantly he proclaimed a deep-seated, essentially north-European, virtuosity of linear expression[12] that licensed a legitimate preoccupation for contemporary designers. The emergence of an Anglo-Scandinavian 'school'[13] of plywood and tubular-steel furniture design, exhibiting greater convolution than more strictly-geometric Bauhaus counterparts, was proof of the validity of this goal. The evident linearity of furniture design later associated with the *FoB* (coinciding

103

103 Jean Hélion *Abstract Painting* 1934. Repr. *Art and Industry*, 1934, ed. p.38

with the emergence of the linear idiom Read recognised as a profound development in sculpture) further justified this objective and was annexed to revised editions of *Art and Industry*.

A further crucial concept provided by Moholy-Nagy was *perceptual equipoise*, signifying abilities to perceive an event frozen by photographic or filmic technology, and to 'reconstruct' a detailed account of events that had preceded it and followed it – taking hold, so to speak, of a perception in a state of dynamic equipoise between a past and a future. Read's modification of this concept took two variations. The earlier, which characterised *Art and Industry* in all its editions, featured empathetic appreciation of design – the ability to apprehend a designed artefact as both a 'register' of the designer's creative intentionality, and an expression of the future values it was intended to serve. In this sense everyone was to be regarded as a designer in actuality or in empathy.

The later variation was expressed by Read in retrospect when in 1960 he indulged in one of his very few post-*Art and Industry* dissertations on design. Here, in an essay entitled 'Form in architecture', he wrote of an empathetic identification with design (architecture) as: 'an equilibrium of forces, a state of arrested movement, of tension – *not as the expression of intellectual clarity*'.[14] This discussion offers the briefest of insights into something about which he wrote little, and certainly made no claims – the vindication of his pre-war views on design in contradistinction to the post-war failings of the International Style. It is legitimate to interrogate this late argument and to apply it retrospectively to *Art and Industry* as Read himself might have done in moments of reflection.

The most obvious feature of this argument is a persist-

104 The Radio Tower at Königswusterhausen (293 metres high). Repr. L. Moholy-Nagy, *The New Vision*, 1932, p.122

105 Wrought-iron grille. English, 13th century. Collection Victoria and Albert Museum. Repr. *Art and Industry*, 1934 ed. p.60

106 British Broadcasting Corporation. 500 foot mast, West Regional Transmitting Station. Repr. *Art and Industry*, 1934 ed. p.16

107 Skeleton of a dirigible. Repr. J. Moholy-Nagy, *The New Vision*, 1932, p.101

108 László Moholy-Nagy *Nickel Sculpture* 1921. Repr. L. Moholy-Nagy, *The New Vision*, 1932, p.103

109 British Broadcasting Corporation. A coupling coil used in the modulated amplifier unit, Empire Broadcasting Station, Daventry. Repr. *Art and Industry*, 1934 ed. p.20

110 State Porcelain Works, Berlin. Distilling vessels and mortar. Repr. *Art and Industry*, 1934 ed. p.49

111 Robert Maillart. Salginatobel Bridge in the Engadine. 1929-30 (90 metre span). Repr. *Art and Industry*, 1934 ed. p.28

112 Raymond McGrath. Moving coil microphone suspended in universal bronze frame. Repr. *Art and Industry*, 1934 ed. p.22

104

106

105

107

108

111

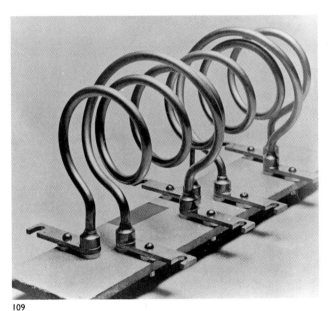

109

112

110

ing Moholy-Nagian essence, though it is an essence now assimilated to Read's general theory of organic vitalism by means of the familiar technique of dialectical opposition. There is a comparison of two distinct Modernist positions, each claiming priority, each claiming organicism, and each found by Read to be wanting in this latter respect. One of these is based on the achievements of Ludwig Mies van der Rohe, who like Gropius had directed the Bauhaus (Dessau and Berlin phases) and by this time, too, had migrated to the USA and had been instrumental in fulfilling the International Style programme initiated by the MOMA at more or less the moment Read wrote *Art and Industry*. The other is the position of Frank Lloyd Wright, the native American Modernist whom the MOMA never quite afforded (in his lifetime) the cachet reserved for immigrant Europeans.

The Miesian position Read understood to be this. The modern architect had accepted a discipline of form inherent in available materials and the inevitability of their standardised production. Rational order, clarity, economy were the designer's guiding principles, ensuring that all types of problematic would resolve towards, and all scales of production would express, an underlying formal consistency. Thus the aesthetic was to be regarded as sustained by a code of conduct towards materials, entirely rejecting designers' preconceptions. 'Form', Mies van der Rohe had said in 1923: 'is not the aim of our work, but only the result. Form, by itself, does not exist. Form as an aim is formalism; and that we reject'.[15] Later he had modified his position to accommodate an indefinable sense of genius that strict materiality seemed to exclude. The designer of significant architectural form was one who respected materiality, rejected formalism, but nevertheless composed in a sense of accord with the 'spirit of the time'. Sensitivity to the 'needs' of materials, moderated by the 'demands' of the Zeitgeist, for Mies van der Rohe constituted the great achievement of the 'organic' sensibility.[16] To Read this was worthy of note, compatible with his own theory, but unacceptably biased towards materiality.

The second position on organicism was the Wrightian. Wright's architecture had embodied a love of natural materials, intrinsic rather than artificial finishes, life close to the land (even in suburban settings) and utopian alternatives to ubiquitous twentieth-century urbanism. Like Mies van der Rohe's, Wright's responsibility to society in general had been to ensure perfection in each particular instance of designing; but in fundamental difference he had stressed the paramountcy of private invention as opposed to a collective strategy (his utopianism, too, was reactionary, but to Read this was a less important point). In conventional appreciation of Modernism (underlying the MOMA's promotion of the International Style) these two tendencies had been assimilable only by default: the inspirational exception had proved the collective rule.

What Read – characteristically – sought in 'Form in architecture' was: '... some formula that would combine

113

114

individual initiative with universal values, and that combination would give us a truly organic form'.[17] In other words, he required in modernity celebration and emulation of the ancient Chinese designer-maker's combination of utmost respect for universal forms and narrow avoidance of their slavish deployment. Equally characteristically, Read gave credit to another writer for supplying him (in 1959) with the decisive concept that had in fact been obviously present in all editions of *Art and Industry* from first publication:

A very perceptive American critic, Roger Shattuck, has recently suggested that what distinguishes the modern movement in the arts is the rejection of the principle of unity. The modern sensibility, at the turn of the century, 'began to proceed not so much by untrammelled expansion of the unities as by a violent dislocation of them in order to test the possibility of a new coherence … a work of art began to coordinate as equally present a variety of time and places and states of consciousness. The process, because it seeks to hold these elements in meaningful relationship, relinquishes both classic unity and also the quality of self-forgetfulness which characterizes romanticism.' *Juxtaposition* is the key-word of this new sensibility; setting one thing beside the other without connective. The twentieth century has addressed itself to arts of juxtaposition as opposed to earlier arts of transition.[18]

This signified the rejection of Miesian classic and Wrightian romantic unities but required their simultaneous presence as contrasting and mutually-enhancing alternatives.

Now Shattuck's theory related specifically to Cubism, that unprecedented mixture of geometric simplification and romantic re-complication of form, Renaissance, pre-Renaissance and non-Western cultural influences, notorious individualism and collective enterprise that (according to MOMA convention) was the essential condenser of the dominant Modernist aesthetic. Read did not subscribe to this interpretation, but in endorsing Shattuck he ignored such philosophical difference for the sake of the illuminating concept: juxtaposition, setting things in discontinuous relationship. Shattuck's own application of the concept to architecture had been rather lame: one of its most successful manifestations had been in functional architecture which exhibited all its parts as if they constituted its 'subconscious'. Read admitted this would serve to describe the 'brutalism' of the late International Style persisting as he wrote.[19] But such limited application did not do justice to a concept which – though he found the telling phrase in someone else's writing – had consistently characterised Read's own design philosophy: Design as the equal presence of different conditions of time, place and consciousness; the factory adapting to the creative artist whose efforts ranged between Constructivism and Superrealism; industry accepting the fruits of 'intuitional abstraction' in all their variety and vitality.

Now the very interesting game may be played of interrogating Read's seminal text for an eclecticism that preceded Postmodernism by a quarter of a century. His

world of designed artefacts comprised realisations of the *functionalist imperative predominant yet transgressed* – examples of strict utility outshone by dynamic equipoise in a Maillart bridge or a McGrath suspended microphone; the functional efficiency of laboratory vessels decontextualised with reference to tableware;[20] the 'mechanical handicraft' of machine-produced lace; besides the 'Bauhaus' austerity-with-comfort as exemplified in plywood furniture. It is not unreasonable to propose that Read's disruption of the functionalist programme both conditioned the outlook of the rising generation of designers who would substantially shape the *FoB*, and resulted in the Festival's inherent 'austerity-binge' conundrum that for the popular audience was among its most appealing features. This at least is the opinion of one of the *FoB*'s principal contributors;[21] but it should be stressed that the record is bereft of Read's own views. It is perhaps unfortunate that *Art and Industry* was so strongly imbued with a 'radio culture' that soon passed, and in this sense became time-cast. However, one of Read's illustrations – Serge Chermayeff's *Ecko Model 74* radio receiver not only became an icon of its age but may still be regarded as an effective symbol of Read's values. Made of bakelite, it harboured no material conventions; functional, it brought the romance of technology into the home; culturally-neutral, it provided intimate connection with countless states of time, place and consciousness around the world. It was industry and art, functionalism transcended by delight.

Notes

1 Read, Herbert (1934) *Art and Industry: the Principles of Industrial Design* (London, Faber & Faber); new and revised editions 1944, 1953, 1956.

2 Surpassing in enduring relevance comparable publications such as Gloag, John (1934) *Industrial Art Explained* (London, Allen & Unwin) – the revised edition (1946) contains a critique of Read's book, pp.135-9 – and Pevsner, Nikolaus (1937) *An Enquiry into Industrial Art in England* (Cambridge, Cambridge University Press).

3 As defined *eg* by Russell-Hitchcock, H. and Johnson, P. (1932) *The International Style* (New York, Museum of Modern Art); applied to industrial design in MOMA exhibitions eg: *Objects 1900 and Today* (1932) and *Machine Art* (1934).

4 *Eg* Heinrich Klotz, who proposes a history of successive 'fiction-alisations' of a basic aesthetic established by 1920, in relation to which the strict principles of the International Style are to be regarded as a temporary and non-creative distraction. See Klotz, H. (1984; trans. 1988) *The History of Postmodern Architecture* (Cambridge Mass., MIT Press).

5 Moholy-Nagy, Lázló (1929) *Von Material zu Architektur* (Munich, A. Langen) trans. Hoffman, D. M. (1932) *The New Vision: from Material to Architecture* (New York, Brewer, Warren & Putnam).

6 Read (n.1) p.2.

7 As exemplified in the exhibition *Machine Art*, Museum of Modern Art, New York, 1934.

8 Read (n.1) pp.21, 24-5.

9 *Ibid.* p.100.

10 *Ibid.* pp.67-8.

11 *Ibid.* p.39.

12 *Ibid.* p.115.

13 Consisting of furniture designed, for the most part, by Scandin-avians (Alvar Aalto) or immigrants (Serge Chermayeff, Marcel Breuer) but afforded recognition and promotion by the *Architectural Review* and emulated by British designers such as Gordon Russell.

14 Read, Herbert (1960) 'Form in architecture', *Architectural Association Journal*, vol. LXXV, no.842; reprinted in Read, Herbert (1965) *The Origins of Form in Art* (London, Thames & Hudson) (pp. 97-112) p.112. My italics.

15 Mies van der Rohe, Ludwig (1923) re-quoted by Read (n.14; p.107) from Johnson, Philip C. (2nd ed. 1953) *Mies van der Rohe* (New York, Museum of Modern Art) p.189.

16 Read (n.14) pp.107-8.

17 *Ibid.* p.110.

18 *Ibid.* p.111, Read quoting Shattuck, Roger (1955) *The Banquet Years: the Arts in France, 1885-1918* (New York; 2nd ed. London, Faber & Faber) pp.256-7.

19 *Ibid.* pp.111-12.

20 Products of the Berlin State Porcelain Works compared to Wedgwood 'Queensware' tableware. Read (n.1) pp.48-9.

21 Drew, Jane (Architect of the *FoB* Regatta Restaurant), interviewed by the author, Aug 1993.

Herbert Read on Sculpture

Terry Friedman

In 1921 – just as a new young generation of radical British sculptors, later to be championed by Herbert Read, was first finding its feet – the American sculptor Lorado Taft published his six Scammon Lectures, delivered in 1917 at the Art Institute of Chicago under the title *Modern Tendencies in Sculpture*. Starting with Rodin, then turning to work by a large number of artists in France, Germany and other European countries, including Britain, and ending with Augustus Saint-Gaudens and the American scene, they offered what was at the time probably the most comprehensive survey of recent trends in Western sculpture. Taft, trained at the Ecole des Beaux-Arts in Paris, was a confirmed realist and by far the majority of his examples were taken from the prevailing academic figure tradition. Modernist (abstract) sculpture was summarily dismissed as an aberration outside this mainstream. The 'notorious painter' Matisse's *Young Girl*, 1906, was a 'foolish caricature of a woman', Brancusi's *Mlle Pogany*, 1913, a 'startling abortion'; even Maillol's *Crouching Woman*, 1902-5, was an instance of 'simple studies well begun which have been arrested in their development', their primitiveness, their 'pronounced ... reaction against highly finished and realistic work' specimens of an 'an absurd naiveté'. Taft warned against the 'misguided activities of a Matisse or an Archipenko', Lehmbruck's perversions, Gaudier-Brzeska's 'inflated monsters', the 'crudities of Epstein': 'there are always some who like their meat raw!' And he concluded that from 'mischief or through sheer imbecility many unsuccessful sculptors turned to this form of prostitution'.[1]

Thirty-three years later, in 1954, when Read delivered his six A.W. Mellon Lectures in the Fine Arts at the National Gallery of Art in Washington DC (subsequently published as *The Art of Sculpture* in 1956) he offered an elaborate dissertation in which sculpture of the past was brought to the service of the present, but a past expurged of undesirable academic elements and a present exclusively Modernist in outlook, and moreover in which the world of sculpture criticism had been redirected to laud and heroize the previously ridiculed and condemned. Read repeated the well-known passage by Henry Moore about Brancusi's 'special mission to get rid of this outgrowth [that is, 'all sorts of surface excrescences which completely concealed shape'], and to make us once more shape-conscious' by concentrating on 'very simple direct shapes'. Maillol's achievement, according to Read, was 'to represent plastic form in its essential massiveness, to allow it to stand resolutely and assertively in space'.[2] In Read's final assessment of the subject, *A Concise History of Modern Sculpture*, 1964, published four years before his

115

death, Matisse's sculpture was shown to have captured the 'unique quality of wholeness [rather] than to get lost in the study of detail', while that 'great artist' Brancusi's work 'embodies more precisely and perhaps more deliberately than any of the pioneers of modern sculpture the universal element of spirituality'. Moreover it was 'through Brancusi that a further characteristic of modern

115 Constantin Brancusi *Mlle Pogany* 1913. Museum of Modern Art, New York. Repr. *The Art of Sculpture*, 1956 pl.195

116 Jacob Epstein
Female Figure in Flenite
1913. Tate Gallery,
London

117 Eric Gill, Working
model for *Prospero and
Ariel* 1931. Tate Gallery,
London (cat.no.93)

sculpture was established – respect for the nature of materials ... This mystique of material, and of the correspondence of form and content, has had a widespread influence on the development of modern sculpture.'[3]

When precisely Read first introduced the subject-matter of sculpture in his writing is still unclear. *The Crucifix*, one of a group of poems entitled 'The Scene of War' published in the collection *Naked Warriors* in 1919, suggests the image of some deeply moving mediaeval carving and a recognition of the potency of sculpture to convey the horrors of the battlefield:

> His body is smashed
> through the belly and chest
> the head hangs lopsided
> from one nail'd hand.
> Emblem of agony
> we have smashed you!

But lines from another poem, *My Company*, from the same collection:

> My men, my modern Christs
> your bloody agony confronts the world[4]

show that he was thinking in terms not of stone but of living flesh.

Read did not get into his stride as an active supporter of the cause of sculpture until the early 1930s but the seed was sown during and immediately after the First World War. He had been introduced to abstract art soon after entering Leeds University as an undergraduate in 1912, visiting both the private art collection of the Vice-Chancellor, Michael Sadler, which included work by Gauguin and Van Gogh, and Leeds City Art Gallery, whose Curator from 1912 to 1917 was Frank Rutter, author of *Revolutionary Art*, 1910 and founder of the Allied Artists Association in London in 1908 as a platform for promoting Modernism. Read also joined the Leeds Arts Club, which had been founded in 1903 by A. R. Orage but who was then editor of the London avant-garde periodical *The New Age*, of which Read was a voracious reader.[5] During this period academic sculpture still represented the mainstream. Modernist sculpture was on the fringe, hardly at all understood by either conservative critics or the general public. But though little was yet to be seen in any British public collection it was exhibited regularly in certain advanced London commercial galleries. Some was the brunt of vituperative public controversy (Epstein's *Risen Christ*, 1917-19, first shown at the Leicester Galleries in 1920, when it was reviled for having 'the appearance of an Asiatic-American or Hun-Jew', is perhaps the most notorious example[6]) but Modernist sculpture also attracted serious critical appraisal which Read would have known.

The English philosopher T. E. Hulme, who was killed on the Western Front in 1917, had championed the abstract sculpture of Epstein, stressing its 'archaic elements' and reliance on 'African and Polynesian work' in

116

an article published in 1913 in *The New Age*.[7] The virtues of 'primitivism' were also the theme of three important essays by Roger Fry published in *Vision and Design* in 1920.[8] In the following year Read assumed the editorship of Hulme's private manuscripts, which appeared in 1924 as *Speculations*, with a foreword by Epstein. Ezra Pound was also writing about Epstein in the mid-1910s and the American poet's pioneering book *Gaudier Brzeska A Memoir*, which appeared in 1916 (the year after the twenty-four-year old sculptor had been killed on the Front) surely would not have gone unnoticed. Gaudier had published his powerful Vortex announcement 'Sculpture energy is the mountain' in Wyndham Lewis's Vorticist manifesto *BLAST* in 1914,[9] and a second Vortex statement 'Written from the Trenches' appeared posthumously in the July 1915 War Number, which included a photograph of his *Hieratic Head of Pound*.[10] Read had already joined the army and was to fight at Ypres in November of 1915. The central importance accorded the radical work of Gaudier and Epstein in the avant-garde pantheon nevertheless remained peripheral to Read's own interests in sculpture. His Modernist taste, once it finally emerged, was differently directed and altogether more complicated. This brief essay examines two significant episodes: Read's vital pioneering promotion of individual Modernist sculptors during the early 1930s and his world view of sculpture as it matured during the 1950s, towards the end of his life.

It was not until 1929 that Read found himself probably for the first time directly involved with a major Modernist sculptor. As a contributor to the BBC's weekly literary magazine *The Listener* (beginning with the 25 September 1929 issue) he recommended Eric Gill to execute carvings on the BBC's new headquarters in Portland Place. Though critically acclaimed, the figure style was too conservative for Read.[11] Like Gaudier and Epstein, Gill did not fit into his Modernist aesthetic.[12] This was a false start but another effort through the BBC proved remarkably fruitful.

In 1928 or 1929 Read's boss at the Victoria and Albert Museum, Eric Maclagan, had introduced him to Henry Moore, and following a visit to the studio in Hampstead Read published the first seriously considered general article on the sculptor's work, in *The Listener* in 1931.[13] The foundation of Moore's great reputation had begun to be laid in 1928 by other sympathetic critics.[14] In 1931 Epstein spoke in glowing terms of his younger colleague: 'For the future of sculpture in England Henry Moore is vitally important', a prophetic if self-deprecating statement.[15] Nineteen thirty-one was the seminal year in which Epstein lost ground to Moore as the leader of Modernist sculpture in Britain in the popular imagination: 'Epstein's rival has arrived' (*The Sheffield Mail*, 13 April), 'Epstein out-Epsteined' (*The Daily Herald*, 23 May). It was then that Read pounced.[16]

The Listener article of 22 April 1931, covering just over one page and illustrating two recent major carvings, is given distinctive power by its intentionally controversial opening statement:

Since the fifteenth century sculpture has been a lost art in England. Perhaps it has been a lost art in Europe generally, for it is possible to argue that the whole Renaissance conception of sculpture was a false one [because] the sculptor of the Renaissance sedulously copied its [the classical art of ancient Greece and Rome] external appearances.[17] We may say without exaggeration that the art of sculpture has been dead in England for four centuries; equally without exaggeration I think we may say that it is reborn in the work of Henry Moore.

Acknowledging the achievements particularly of Epstein, Gill, Brancusi and Zadkine, Read maintained that Moore nevertheless 'in virtue of his sureness and consistency, springs straight to the head of the modern movement in England'. There it is: brazenly stated. Moore has been jockeyed into position – though a position not reserved exclusively for him at this time. Read's introduction to the catalogue of a joint Hepworth/Nicholson exhibition at Arthur Tooth's Gallery in November 1932, in which he makes an early and important attempt to place the twenty-nine-year old sculptor's achievement, also claimed that:

the decadence of European sculpture during the last three or four centuries has been due above all to an increasing separation between the artist and his material ... To this revival [of the 'vital connection' between them] England is making a vigorous and original contribution [in which] Hepworth occupies a leading position. In her work ... stone and wood yield their essence to give form a concrete significance ... [such] modern artists ... step boldly in a new venture which may succeed in redeeming art from its present triviality and insignificance.[18]

This became, as we shall see, a ritual phrase Read repeated most frequently in the context of Moore's art. This repetition may have been Read's way of responding to an annoying attack on Moore's Leicester Galleries exhibition in 1931, published a few days after the *Listener* article, by Adrian Bury, who stated that 'such sculpture is trying to lead us away from civilisation [and] is far too easy to do, giving an arrogant contempt for European tradition'.[19]

In Read's *Listener* article sculpture is narrowly defined as 'the art of carving or cutting a material of relative hardness', such as stone, rather than some more pliable material. Realism – 'the appearance of the object', the foundation of Western academic sculpture – is rejected in favour of the 'structure' of material, stone: 'its degree of hardness, the ways it reacts to his [the sculptor's] chisel ... how this stone has reacted to natural forces like wind and water ... what form he can best realise in the particular block of stone he has before him.' Taking 'the reclining figure of a woman' (Read is almost certainly describing the physical creation of the 1929 Leeds carving), the sculptor imagines the image of flesh and blood

translated into the stone ... which has its own principles of form and structure. The woman's body might then ... take on the appearance of a range of hills. Sculpture, therefore, is not a reduplication of form and feature; it is rather the translation of meaning from one material into another material ... it is the only key that is needed for the understanding of sculpture like this of ... Moore's.

Moore's 'greatest success, distinguishing him from most of his contemporaries' lay in his grasp of the principle that in this translating process

you must create that form from the inside outwards ... a four-dimensional process growing out of a concept which inheres in the mass itself. Form is then an intuition of surface made by the sculptor imaginatively situated at the centre of gravity of the block before him. Under the guidance of this intuition, the stone is slowly educated from an arbitrary into an ideal state of existence.

This text was reprinted virtually without changes in *The Meaning of Art*, published in August 1931.[20] And when Moore spoke to Arnold Haskell in 1932 he also stressed 'the power a work gets naturally from the resistance offered by a hard material' and that 'Sculpture in stone should look like stone, hard and concentrated'.[21]

In April 1933 Read gave up the post of Watson Gordon Professor of Fine Art at Edinburgh University and returned to London, took up the editorship of *The Burlington Magazine* and moved briefly into Henry Moore's house at No.11a Parkhill Road, Hampstead and then to nearby No.3 The Mall Studios, where he and his wife lived until

just before the outbreak of war. At first their neighbours included the Moores, Hepworth and Nicholson (at No.7 The Mall Studios) and the Yorkshire painter John Cecil Stephenson. During the next few years (up to 1939) they were joined in Parkhill Road and the nearby streets by Marcel Breuer, Wells Coates, Naum Gabo, Walter Gropius, László Moholy-Nagy, Piet Mondrian, Adrian Stokes, F. E. McWilliam, Paul Nash, Roland Penrose and others.[22] This was then the major avant-garde art community in Britain, the core of Read's assessment of Modernism and the platform upon which he promoted the Modern Movement first in Britain, then in Europe and America, and in which sculpture played an increasingly prominent role. Above all these were the years Read most closely identified himself with Moore.

The ideas first tested in 1931 were refined further in the book *Unit One: The Modern Movement in English Architecture, Painting and Sculpture*, published in 1934 and edited by Read. His introduction identified the new group formed in the previous year (Hepworth, Moore, the painters John Armstrong, John Bigge, Edward Burra, Tristram Hillier, Paul Nash, Ben Nicholson and Edward Wadsworth, and the architects Wells Coates and Colin Lucas) as standing for 'the expression of a truly contemporary spirit' with the aim 'to form a point in the forward thrust of modernism'.[23] The book was a manifesto, in presentation distinct from the topical exhibition review, in which the sculptor's ideas could be powerfully and decisively stated. The oft-quoted series of terse observations authored by Moore were in fact composed jointly by him and Read:[24]

Truth to material. Every material has its own individual qualities. It is only when the sculptor works direct, when there is an active relationship with his material, that the material can take its part in the shaping of an idea. Stone, for example, is hard and concentrated and should not be falsified to look like soft flesh – it should not be forced beyond its constructive build to a point of weakness. It should keep its hard tense stoniness.
Full three-dimensional realisation. Complete sculptural expression is form in its full spatial reality.
Only to make relief shapes on the surface of the block is to forego the full power of expression in sculpture.
Observation of Natural Objects. The observation of nature is part of an artist's life, it enlarges his form-knowledge, keeps him fresh and from working only by formula, and feeds inspiration.
The human figure is what interests me most deeply, but I have found principles of form and rhythm from the study of natural objects ...
Pebbles and rocks show Nature's way of working stone. Smooth, sea-worn pebbles show the wearing away, rubbed treatment of stone and principles of asymmetry.
Rocks show the hacked, hewn treatment of stone, and have a jagged nervous block rhythm.
Bones have marvellous structural strength and hard tenseness of form ...
Shells show Nature's hard but hollow form ... and have a wonderful completeness of single shape ...[25]

It is interesting to compare the poignant final passage,

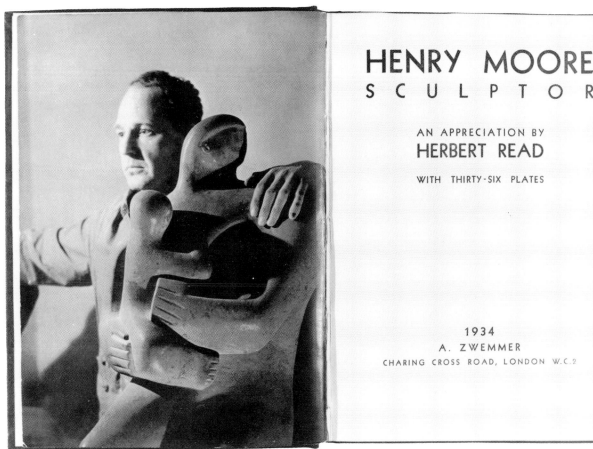

HENRY MOORE
S C U L P T O R

AN APPRECIATION BY
HERBERT READ

WITH THIRTY-SIX PLATES

1934
A. ZWEMMER
CHARING CROSS ROAD, LONDON W.C.2

118

Ruskinian in both flavour and origin, with the beautiful evocation of the pleasures of limestone washed by water and worked by man employed by Adrian Stokes in *Stones of Rimini*, his study of the work of the Renaissance sculptor Agostino di Duccio in the Tempio Malatestiano:

Stone is the earth's crust. There is a condition in one's appreciation of sculpture when for deeper understanding one must look at the lands, at mountains and valleys ...
The weathering of stone is omnipresent. Pavement, no less than pebbles, are polished and shifted ...
Earth is decomposed rock. The 'stoniness' of stone is but one aspect of its impression ...[26]

Stokes then lived a short distance from Moore and Read in Parkhill Road and *Stones of Rimini*, published in January 1934, suggests that a new language to describe new ideas about sculpture, ancient and modern, might have been a topic of mutual discussion among members of the Hampstead circle.

Undoubtedly by 1934 Read felt fully confident in issuing a more extended and fuller analytical assessment which would secure once and for all Moore's unrivalled leadership of British Modernism: this was effected in the monograph *Henry Moore Sculptor An Appreciation*, comprising 39 photographs and Read's longest text on sculpture to date (10 pages) and designed in an up-to-date Modernist layout. With a dramatic frontispiece portrait of the young artist standing next to the green Hornton

stone *Mother and Child* of 1932 (then as now in Robert Sainsbury's collection), there is a representative selection of 'masterpieces' from the sculptor's early years – masks, heads, half-figures, full figures reclining, seated, flying, mother and child groups and abstract compositions with holes – executed in a variety of unconventional materials: Cumberland alabaster, Hornton stone, African Wonder stone, ebony, reinforced and carved concrete, etc. Some of the works are from the private collections of Epstein, Gill and Sadler.

The 'iconic' brown Hornton stone *Reclining Figure* of 1929, now in Leeds City Art Galleries and Eric Gregory's grey and white-veined Armenian marble *Woman (or Half-figure)* of 1932, now in the Tate, each represented by two illustrations, are the most monumental demonstrations of Moore's concerns to achieve the stoniness of stone in carving and to make figures which are both human and geological (landscape-like), which is one of Moore's most original ideas.[27]

The text of *An Appreciation* covers some of the same ground as the earlier essay and also expands on it. Moore's vital historic reviving role occurs at the end of a long period, beginning in the Middle Ages, during which the 'practice and appreciation of sculpture in England has been virtually dormant, if not dead'.[28] The fundamental distinction is made between carving and modelling, in which Read quotes from *Stones of Rimini* and develops Stoke's definition to include the notion of the sculptor responding not only to the 'stoniness of stone' but to the 'demands of an abstract and immaterial imagination' where the 'point of departure, the genesis of the sculptor's conception, is surely within his mind, more particularly the subconscious levels of the mind.' This process is common to both carving and modelling but in the former the sculptor encounters 'a different degree of resistance' and in the case of stone an 'altogether greater ... tension'. 'If the idea demands compactness, the greatest possible degree of centripetal coherence, then stone will be the appropriate material, and carving the appropriate technique', as in Moore's case, whereas if 'the idea demands the greatest degree of centrifugal expansion, an open form, then the appropriate material will be clay, and modelling the appropriate technique', so that ultimately the distinction 'depends on an ethical injunction, which might be expressed in three words: truth to material'.[29]

Related to this is a distinction between the sculptor as abstract 'purist' – say Brancusi – and Moore with his ability to 'link his formal [abstract] conceptions with the vital rhythms everywhere present in natural forms' which he derives from 'close observation and study'. Here Read paraphrases the *Unit One* text:

Pebbles and rocks show nature's way of treating stone ... Stone is not an even mass, and symmetry is foreign to its nature ... Rocks show stone torn and hacked by cataclysmic forces, or eroded and polished by wind and rain ... Bones combine great structural strength with extreme lightness; the result is a natural tenseness of form ...

There is yet a further distinction between the sculptor seeking the fidelity of real appearances reduced to an archetypal beauty, as in late classical sculpture, and Moore who seeks the 'kind of fidelity represented by archaic types' such as Egyptian, Greek, Etruscan and ancient Mexican sculpture and the Oriental tradition of the so-called 'Animal Style'.[30]

Read contrasted this with the taste for those realistic statuettes popularised by late Victorian and Edwardian Academicians ('boudoir' sculpture) which still prevailed and which he condemned as the products of 'only a very decadent sculptor'.[31] 'Representational figure sculpture can never be anything but a travesty of one material in another ... It is only in decadent periods [from the 16th to the 19th centuries, for instance] that the aim has persisted of trying to represent flesh in naked stone.'[32] This was, of course, also Moore's view. Read believed that: 'Only a sculptor who carves his own stone can know the capabilities and limitations of his material; only a sculptor who explores the natures of different stones can enlarge the possibilities of carved expression, can extend the range of his own plastic consciousness.'[33]

Read advocated a revival of 'monumental', 'communal', 'public' art, and he concluded that

like all great artists, he [Moore] is consumed by an endless curiosity – curiosity concerning the possibility of his material, curiosity concerning the nature of life ... The matter for wonder, in his case, is the consistency of his course, the gathering power, the increasing clearness of his intention ... There has been no compromise in the life of Henry Moore, and now, in the fullness of his powers, he offers us the perfected product of his genius.[34]

Few twentieth-century British sculptors before this moment had been treated in print to quite such adulation. After all, Moore was then only thirty-six, just entering mid-career, just becoming known to a general audience, and with as it happened a further fifty or so years of production. Nevertheless the fundamental ingredients of the Moore 'legend' were established in 1934 and in retrospect it may not be improper to believe that history's verdict, encouraged by Read's pioneering endeavours, may well be that the work of the late 1920s and early 1930s was his most brilliant achievement.

Of course Read continued to champion the work of Moore and Hepworth through the 1930s – for example, he was the first to draw attention in print to the cast lead and bronze *Reclining Figure* maquettes of 1938 purchased by the Museum of Modern Art in New York and Peggy Guggenheim.[35] (The contemporary bronze cast now in Leeds City Art Galleries is from the collection of Rudolph Mock, a Swiss Modernist architect then practising in New York). In 1944 Read wrote the Introduction to the first of the Lund Humphries monographs devoted to Moore, followed by studies of Hepworth in 1952, Gabo in 1957, and a book on Jean Arp in 1968.[36] In 1952 Read was a member of the panel which selected nine British sculptors – Robert Adams, Kenneth Armitage, Reg Butler, Lynn Chadwick, Geoffrey Clarke, Bernard Meadows, Moore, Eduardo Paolozzi and William Tucker – to represent Britain at the Venice *Biennale*, and he wrote the introduction to the catalogue 'Recent Aspects of British Sculpture'. Meanwhile Read co-chaired the Central Committee for the International Competition for a Monument to the Unknown Political Prisoner, launched in January 1952, and as President of the Institute of Contemporary Arts represented Britain on the International Jury. Out of some 3,500 entries from 57 countries, from which 140 maquettes were selected, triumphantly Butler was awarded the Grand Prize, Hepworth one of the second prizes and Chadwick an Honourable Mention. Gabo, representing the United States but encouraged by Read to enter, was also a prize winner.[37]

Read's *Concise History of Modern Sculpture*, 1964, grew out of his pre-war lectures delivered in London, Bangor and Newcastle-upon-Tyne. These were first set down in *Art Now: An Introduction to the Theory of Modern Painting and Sculpture*, which was first published in 1933 and dealt with work by Arp, Barlach, Calder, Giacometti, Gonzalez, Hepworth, Lipchitz, Laurens, Moore, Picasso, Schwitters and Zadkine. *Surrealism*, edited by Read and published in November 1936, was based on the International Surrealist Exhibition held in London earlier in that year, and included sculpture by Agar (Read was Agar's Angel of

119 Henry Moore
Reclining Figure 1929.
Leeds City Art Galleries
(cat.no.139)

119

Anarchy), Arp, Brancusi, Calder, Ernst, Giacometti, Moore, Nash, Picasso, Man Ray and others. As Read turned to writing two major surveys of sculpture in the post-war years, his world view of sculpture as presented in its most complete form as the 1954 Mellon Lectures and the book of the same title, *The Art of Sculpture*, 1956, also had its origins in his pre-war deliberations.

Two academic posts – Assistant Keeper in the Department of Ceramics at the Victoria and Albert Museum between 1922 and 1931, and the Watson Gordon Chair of Fine Art at Edinburgh University between 1931 and 1933, exposed him to a wide and astonishing historical, geographical and stylistic range of material. These experiences were expanded during the 1930s in his role as editor of *The Burlington Magazine*, the leading art history journal, and as a contributor to *The Listener*. In *The Meaning of Art*, 1931, a reworking of some of the early *Listener* articles in book form, the breadth of his interests is impressive. (Indeed, Gill was to report in 1933 that 'Herbert Read ... has a v. wide knowledge of ancient & modern art and an appreciation of the latter possessed by few').[38] Twenty of the 46 illustrations are devoted to sculpture (the rest to paintings) ranging from ancient Egyptian, Sarmatian

and Chinese objects through mediaeval Coptic, Viking, Hispano-Moresque, Spanish, German and English work, the Italian Renaissance (Agostino di Duccio) and Baroque (Bernini) to African tribal carving and, uniquely though not unexpectedly, Henry Moore. *Art and Society*, first published in 1937, examined prehistoric, Bushman, Negro and Scythian art. Some of the photographic juxtapositions are deliberately intriguing in their seeming incongruity – for example, the 'nearly equivalent ... formal values' of Riemenschneider's *Adam* and an Ivory Coast mask, though Read pointed out that 'in the change from the art of primitive man to the art of the civilised man, there has been no real change in the psychological workings of the artist's mind'.[39] The format of these books – thematic and analytical rather than chronological and nationalistic (as in the case of Taft) – became the basis of the approach used in *The Art of Sculpture*.

The Art of Sculpture began as the Ferens Fine Art Lectures delivered at the University of Hull during the fruitful season of 1951-2. These were 'recast' and expanded in 1954 into the Mellon Lectures. The book is dedicated to Gabo, Hepworth and Moore 'Sculptors and Friends in Gratitude' and it is as a Modernist that Read defines his

120 Ernst Barlach *Monks Reading* 1932; Ossip Zadkine *The Sculptor* 1933. Repr. *Art Now*, 1933, pl.56 & 57

121 Dragon of carved jade. Chinese (Chou dynasty) 12th-3rd century BC. Rutherston Collection. Repr. *The Meaning of Art*, 1931, fig.6

56. ERNST BARLACH (b. 1870)
Monks reading (Wood). 1932
Photo. Boehmer

57. OSSIP ZADKINE (b. 1890)
The Sculptor (Wood). 1933
Edward Wadsworth Collection

120

121

narrow limits of acceptable sculpture: abstract not representational or pictorial; static not active; fully three-dimensional not relief; carved not modelled. But the range of examples covers 27,000 years of human history in 123 pages of text and 240 illustrations. Its backbone is Read's belief that: 'Sculpture ... has always had difficulty in establishing its independence as an art, and this has been in some measure due to the lack of any clear formulation of the requisite autonomous laws'.

Having long submitted to 'the rule of architecture or the painter', Rodin had finally liberated it physically as an independent artistic force, 'a free sculpture' – its preferred state – from which had 'arisen what is virtually a new art – a concept of a piece of sculpture as a three-dimensional mass occupying space and only to be apprehended by senses that are alive to its volume and ponderability, as well as to its visual appearance.' The purpose of the lectures and book was to give this ideal 'historical support and theoretical extension', since Read saw 'the sculpture of the past as often approaching and even attaining this independent character, this ideal that only the sculptors of our time have fully realised'.[40]

The book is presented in the form of six chapters which carry the reader along Read's sculpture vision. The central premise of *The Monument and the Amulet* concerns the complex relationship between architecture and sculpture, which Read saw as evolving from 'an original unity' identified as the monument: 'a solid sculpture object' of monolithic form and monumental scale, such as the 'purely crystalline, abstract construct' of Egyptian pyramids (stone sarcophagi) or the 'enormous columnar images', phallic forms of ancient Indian temples, particularly those carved out of solid rock: 'elaborate constructions that are sculptured mountains'.[41] Independent of the monument in both origin and usage is the amulet: 'the small, portable charm worn on the person as a protection against evil, or as an insurance of fertility', which was 'gradually to merge with sculpture'. Read hints at the possibility that 'the specific art of sculpture … comes into existence somewhere between these two extremes – as a method of creating an object with the independence of the amulet and the effect of the monument'.[42]

When he deals with the proper method of treating sculpture on buildings, great reliance is placed on Ruskin's *The Stones of Venice* and *Lectures on Art*. 'One of the puzzles of architectural sculpture has always been to know from what distance the sculpture should be viewed. It is foolish, as Ruskin says, "to carve what is to be seen forty feet off with the delicacy which the eye demands within two yards"'.[43]

Ruskin's guiding principles for good architectural sculpture, which Read endorsed, are the 'right placing of masses' and that they give 'life by flexure of surface, not by quantity of detail', and he quotes Ruskin's demand for a homogeneity between the forms of organic sculpture and the geometry of architecture:

You must not cut out a branch of hawthorn as it grows, and rule a triangle round it [rather] the spirit of triangle must be put into the hawthorn. It must suck in isoscelesism with its sap. Thorn and blossom, leaf and spray, must grow with an awful sense of triangular necessity upon them, for the guidance of which they are to be thankful, and to grow all the stronger and more glorious.[44]

Read then applied Ruskin's Victorian vision of Gothic to modern architectural sculpture: '[the] quality of formal "necessity" [described above, combined with the] virtues of simplicity and emphasis … dictated by another external consideration or limitation, that of distance, to sculpture conceived in the round – like an amulet, but an amulet enlarged to some convenient yet still portable size'.

The example he offers is Moore's Portland stone *Screen*, 1952-3, carefully sited on the lower of the two terrace levels of the new Time-Life Building in Bond Street, London, where on the street façade itself 'an uncompromisingly geometrical expression of its administrative functions, offered no foothold for sculpture of any kind'. When submitting his maquette to the architect Michael Rosenauer, Read relates, the sculptor explained: '… it seems to me that a portrayal of some pictorial scene … would have no connection with your building and would only seem like hanging up a stone picture there, like using the position as a hoarding for sticking up a stone poster'. Moore's solution was a sequence of four independent enframed abstract carvings, each monumental amulets, hung onto a wall, Read rightly observing that the 'sculpture is suspended in the prime, architectural plane and thus is completely integrated'.[45]

In 'The Image of Man' Read described how the 'limitations and essential qualities of … the art of sculpture … are determined by the manageable dimensions and direct tactility of the amulet'.[46] Throughout history the human body has dominated the subject-matter of sculpture and the earliest surviving examples are amulets or fertility figures of women dating from prehistory: the most famous example being the Willendorf 'Venus'. In ancient Egyptian figure sculpture

the form is frozen … into a rigid convention; all vitalistic impulses are subordinated to symbolic values, to the metaphysical idea … [but here] for the first time in the history of art there emerges a clear and contemporaneous distinction between the geometric and the naturalistic in art [combining] … a tendency to abstract harmony [and] a tendency to naturalistic vitality.

The massive hieratic hard-stone carvings of public religious imagery with their rigid formality and 'immense concentration of power' are contrasted with the greater naturalism found in intimate domestic wood carvings with their concern for exquisite delicacy (what Wilhelm Worringer in his book *Egyptian Art*, 1928, in just the sort of cultural jump which appealed to Read, described as 'of an absolutely Japanese lightness').[47]

In the next stage of evolution, Greek figure sculpture, even in late archaic examples and more especially in later examples, the body is anatomically realistic, striding free of the block, and the facial features are expressive.

Thenceforth the way was open to all the refinements of realism … The body image had been fully realised as an anatomical structure, had been detached in space from the welter of other sense impressions, and had become a symbol of human self-sufficiency, of human self-satisfaction.[48]

This, Read might have added, was the state in which

122

Western figure sculpture had become suspended up to his own time. He recognised another separate tradition in the magic or religious art of so-called primitive societies. Other English writers had noted the importance of these non-Western traditions (Roger Fry as early as 1920 in *Vision and Design*); Read was able to make a connection between the 'grotesque distortions' of their figure sculptures with distortions found in Greek cult objects such as Cycladic amulets.[49] He then made a giant though inevitable leap into Modernist sculpture, again selecting the work of Moore as exemplary.[50] In his soaring (2.21m

122 Henry Moore Working model for *Time/Life Screen* 1952. The Henry Moore Foundation (cat.no.147)

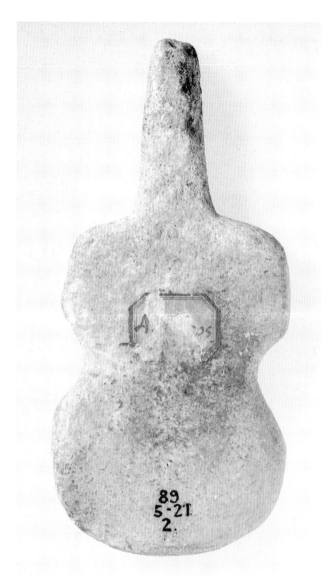

123

into space came late in the history of art. In ancient civilisations a sense of sculpture space was virtually unknown. Egyptian sculptors were reluctant 'to isolate the human figure in space, to dissociate it from its niche or socket';[55] even less rigid small-scale examples carved in wood still belonged to the architectural geometry from which they had emerged. Likewise, a 'law of frontality' governed Greek sculpture and despite its glorious achievement of 'a completely realistic rendering of the human body image ... this narcissistic form of projection, this re-creation of the self, Greek sculpture remained either bound to architecture ... or anchored in some way to the earth'.[56]

Only with the secularisation of art and the emancipation of the artist during the Italian Renaissance which resulted in the 'growth of a sense and of a philosophy of individualism' was the object finally detached and

high) bronze – technically even more breathtaking in the marble version: 'all the elements of the human form are present but completely dislocated ... and recomposed into a formal structure only remotely suggested by or suggestive of the original motif. Formally and aesthetically this figure is not far removed from ... Cycladic figures.'[51] This is particularly true in its exaggeration of the female sexual parts of breasts and hips rather than of the head, which may be likened to the 'violin' form of many Cycladic amulets,[52] and to a characteristic elongation of the neck as an expression of the fundamental *haptic* (derived from the Greek *haptikos* meaning 'able to lay hold of') sensation of swallowing.[53] This is perceptive because it excludes the possibility of Moore's amazing structural sculpture being merely virtuosic carving, a quality Read deplored.[54]

The Discovery of Space distinguished between the illusion of space created in painting and the creation of a three-dimensional object in space, which is characteristic of, and essential to, sculpture. The liberation of sculpture

124

125

126

125 Giovanni Lorenzo
Bernini *Ecstasy of Saint
Teresa*. In Santa Maria
della Vittoria, Rome
1645-52. Repr. *The Art
of Sculpture*, 1956, pl.118

126 *The Victory of
Samothrace*. Greek, end
of IV century BC (or II
century BC?) Louvre,
Paris. Repr. *The Art of
Sculpture*, 1956, pl.181

isolated : 'for the first time artists are found contemplating pieces of sculpture – monuments, not amulets – as *detached works of art*, are found collecting them [ancient Greek and Roman sculptures] and appreciating them irrespective of the architectural function for which they were originally conceived and executed'. This new freedom manifested itself in a 'transportable' sculpture 'set ... on its own isolated pedestal'.[57]

Read thought that the unique quality of sculpture is 'its realisation of an integral mass in actual space' which has 'nothing in common with ... the visual impression of a three-dimensional form on a two-dimensional plane'.[58] It is 'precisely when this preference ... to tactile [over visual] sensation ... is clearly stated that sculpture attains its highest and its unique aesthetic values'.[59] Modelling 'tends not only to looseness and imprecision of form but also to a preoccupation with surface effects to the detriment of mass. Cutting tends to monolithic rigidity, to a fear of freedom'.[60] For these reasons he rejected much of the sculpture produced in the West between the Renaissance and the end of the nineteenth century, dominated as it was by 'the painterly conception of sculpture [which] was based on a false aesthetic'.[61] Bernini's *Ecstasy of St Teresa* is seen as an example of the sculptor aiming 'to create a pictorial illusion in which the ponderability of the material was etherealised'.[62] The notion of a progressive degeneration of the art which 'led with logical inevitability to the horrors of academic sculpture at its worst' had been one important means by which Modernist sculptors of the early twentieth century, and the critics

who supported them, were able to disassociate themselves from their immediate predecessors. For Read, even in the 1950s, the nineteenth century was one in which 'virtually no sculpture of any permanent value was to be created anywhere in the civilised world'.[63] He argued that 'the greatest sculpture always has a certain compactness', 'irrefragability', quoting Michelangelo's dictum that good sculpture is only that which could be rolled from the top to the bottom of a mountain without breaking.[64]

In *The Realization of Mass* he gives examples, all stone carvings, from a number of historical periods: a Mexican mask admirable in its 'complete plastic integrity;[65] the work of the fourteenth-century Italian carvers Arnolfo di Cambio, Giovanni Pisano, Tino di Camaino and their circle, growing out of the organic Gothic tradition with a new feeling for 'the compactness of mass and the ponderability of the figure';[66] Aristide Maillol, whose achievement was 'to represent plastic form in its essential massiveness, to allow it to stand resolutely and assertively in space', 'a palpable reality [in which] our sensations ... are sensations of thrust, of weight, of solid existence'.[67] In selecting mottled or striated stone and leaving rougher surfaces, chisel and hammer marks (rather than the universal academic choice of white marble, where the surface is 'monotonous and dead' and where the 'object seems to be to produce the visual impression of a plane surface shaded like white paper'), as Moore had done with the Leeds *Reclining Figures*, is to 'call attention to mass'.[68] 'There is, in the full scale of plastic sensibility, a power attaching to ponderability and mass, to the

127 Aristide Maillol
Bather. Private
collection* (cat.no.131)

128 *Adam* Detail of the
stone figure by Tilman
Riemenschneider from
the Marienkirche,
Würzburg, German;
1491-3. Carved wooden
mask from the Ivory
Coast, Africa. Repr. *The
Meaning of Art*, 1931 figs
18 & 19

gestated and palpable volume of a solid creation, that cannot be experienced in any other manner, by any other means'.[69]

Having rejected pictorial illusion as a legitimate sculptural virtue Read found no contradiction between sculpture and *The Illusion of Movement* through the use of rhythm and linear sequences – for example, the *Winged Victory of Samothrace*, 'where an invisible wind, against which the figure is poised for flight, whips the drapery into ripples and fluttering folds that induce in the spectator an acute consciousness of movement', or the *Panathenaic Procession* from the Parthenon frieze, with its 'repetition of parallel folds of drapery ... gently kicked forward by the movement of the feet, the projection of the knees, and the swaying of the fringe of the upper garment'.[70] In addition, there is actual or kinetic movement as in the mobiles of Alexander Calder. In a French ivory *Virgin and Child* dating from the fourteenth century the line is 'a contour tracing the volume beneath, very much like the contours of a map'.[71] The long delicate maternal Gothic grace and sway of the figures results from the sculptor following the natural curve of the elephant's tusk out of which the group has been fashioned. Yet Read believed that subsequent attempts to create the appearance of movement in the human figure by depicting it 'engaged in some more or less violent action, especially at some moment of tension or strain', where the 'eye is ... inevitably caught into the movement of the composition' and where 'we identify ourselves with the dynamic action', found especially in Baroque sculpture (such as J. T. Stammel's boxwood carving of a figure symbolising *Fear*) was 'one of the causes of the decline of the art of sculpture: the agitation, the de-composition of the material, destroys all sense of ponderability, all possible appeal to a tactile sensibility'.[72]

In Rodin's *St John the Baptist* the sequence of movements from the left foot pressing the ground balanced by the glance of the figure to the right, with the right foot advancing to grasp the ground and the raised left shoulder restoring the weight of the body to that side to help the trailing leg forward (Read is here paraphrasing Rodin's own analysis) 'gives a powerful impression of actual movement ... both the movement that has been completed and the movement that is just beginning'.[73] Read recognised this as a 'way to represent the movement of the body without recourse to such rhetorical violence' as employed in the Baroque, but he regarded Rodin's approach as 'an impressionistic trick'.[74]

He accepted with reservations the Modernist 'creation of a dynamic interplay of plane surfaces' where the 'planes with their arrowlike points strike in all directions and create a machinelike kinetic rhythm'.[75] Its origins are found in the 'cubist' paintings of Cézanne and in African Negro sculpture. This produced on the one hand an 'illusion' of movement as in Russian Constructivism, where sculpture exists in both space and time, its forms – tensile arcs, conical cylinders, zig-zags – and the inclusion of

127

reflecting and refracting material like plastic suggest movement (Read saw such experiments as a return to the 'principle inherent in Gothic and the pre-Gothic sculpture of the North: the expression of movement by abstract linear means'); and on the other hand the 'actuality' of movement as in Calder's mobiles which are 'like Gregorian chant and repeat their graceful movement endlessly. We contemplate the movement as such – movement with a defined configuration of space'.[76]

Cézanne, says Read, 'striving to realise the cubic volume and tactile surfaces of the objects he painted, was rightly horrified by [the] rhetorical devices' where light distorts 'the actual form of an object', to fall with 'obliterating force on those prominent points that it meets and from which it is reflected, and to throw into insignificant shade all parts of an object that lie outside the

Photo. Gundermann.

18. Adam. Detail of the stone figure by Tilman Riemenschneider from the Marienkirche, Würzburg. German; 1491-1493.

46

19. Carved wooden mask from the Ivory Coast, Africa. From *Les Arts Sauvages—Afrique*, by A. Portier and F. Poncetton.

47

128

immediate area of impact', resulting in a chiaroscuro. He avoided such 'arbitrary light effects' by rendering colours in their purity in an evenly distributed light. From this Read observed:

If this evasion of arbitrary light effects is essential for the painter in his rendering of three-dimensional form on the two-dimensional surface of his canvas, it is obviously still more important for the sculptor who is striving to create three-dimensional forms of direct sensational appeal [and to achieve this end the sculptor will even] endeavour to anticipate the impact of light and to modify his forms to receive it.[77]

This final chapter is appropriately entitled 'The Impact of Light'.

Rodin the 'impressionist' and Brancusi in his polished forms 'deliberately exploited light' by their choice of material: bronze, with its reflective power. Gabo, in selecting plastic (Lucite and Perspex), 'a material of crystal purity', 'seems to create his forms in light itself'.[78] Moore discovered that instead of creating 'areas of high-light' by directing 'the impact of light on the surface of an intentionally solid mass' which could result in 'a disin-tegrating effect on the static tension of the mass', if light were

admitted through the mass at such a point of impact, a subtle

counterpoint of volume and void would ... be brought about. For each convexity a corresponding concavity is created, and the result is an expressive rhythm of forms far superior to the rhythm of the form from which light is too crudely reflected. [Light is] ... no longer in opposition to the solidity of the object but is an integral part of the total sculptural effect. Space invades the object, and the object invades space, with the one plastic rhythm.

Moore was 'the supreme master of this device'.[79] In returning to Moore again and again in *The Art of Sculpture* Read reaffirmed his belief in the special achievement of Modernism in the history of art.

In the closing pages of the book Read reasserted his conviction that the art of sculpture

achieves its maximum and most distinctive effect when the sculptor proceeds almost blindly to the statement of tactile values, values of the palpable, the ponderable, the assessable mass. Integral volume, not apparent to the eye alone, but given by every direct or imaginable sensation of touch and pressure – such is the unique sculptural emotion.[80]

The 'monuments' of sculpture, 'monoliths' along a four hundred century path, are 'milestones' of man's spiritual odyssey without which he would be 'like a child lost in the night'.[81]

129

129 Auguste Rodin *The Walking Man* 1877-8. The Trustees of the Irina Moore Grandchildren's Settlement (cat.no.189)

130 Naum Gabo *Linear Construction No.2* 1970-1. Version of a work formerly in the collection of Herbert Read. Tate Gallery, London. Presented by the Artist through the American Federation of Arts in memory of Sir Herbert Read 1971

Notes

1 Taft, Lorado (1921) *Modern Tendencies in Sculpture* (Chicago, University of Chicago Press) pp.27-8, 40-1, 63-4, 80, 118, pls 51 (*Standing Nude*), 55-9, 120 (*La Méditerranée*).

2 Read, Herbert (1956) *The Art of Sculpture* (London, Faber & Faber) pp.75, 87.

3 Read, Herbert (1964) *A Concise History of Modern Sculpture* (1983 ed., London, Thames & Hudson) pp.42, 191-2.

4 Read, Herbert (1966) *Collected Poems* (London, Faber & Faber) pp.34, 39.

5 See Steele, Tom (1990) *Alfred Orage and the Leeds Arts Club 1893-1923* (Aldershot, Scolar Press).

6 *The Graphic*, 14 Feb 1920, quoted in Epstein, Jacob (1942) *Let There Be Sculpture The Autobiography of Jacob Epstein* (London, Michael Joseph) p.107.

7 Hulme, Thomas Ernest (1913) in: *The New Age*, 25 Dec. Hulme owned one of Epstein's most blatantly abstract figure carvings, *Female Figure in Flenite*,1913, now in the Tate Gallery, and sat for his portrait in 1916. See Silber, Evelyn (1986) *The Sculpture of Epstein with a complete catalogue* (Oxford, Phaidon) cat.nos 45, 69).

8 'The Art of the Bushmen', 'Negro Sculpture' ('The sculptors seem to have no difficulty in getting away from the two-dimensional plane ... So far from clinging to two dimensions, as we tend to do, he actually underlines ... the three-dimensionalness of his forms. It is in some such way ... that he manages to give to his forms their disconcerting vitality, the suggestion that they make of being not mere echoes of actual figures, but of possessing an inner life of their own') and 'Ancient American Art' in Fry, Roger (1920) *Vision and Design* (London, Chatto & Windus) pp.56-75.

9 Lewis, Wyndham (Ed) (1914) BLAST 1, p.155.

10 'MY VIEWS ON SCULPTURE REMAIN ABSOLUTELY THE SAME ... I SHALL DERIVE MY EMOTIONS SOLELY FROM THE ARRANGEMENT OF SURFACES ... MY DESIGN got its effect (just as the gun had) FROM A VERY SIMPLE COMPOSITION OF LINES AND PLANES'. Lewis, Wyndham (Ed) (1915) BLAST 2 (July 1915) pp.33-4, 84.

11 Collins, Judith (1992) *Eric Gill: Sculpture* (London, Barbican Art Gallery) cat. nos 82-90. Shewring, Walter (Ed) (1947) *Letters of Eric Gill* (London, Jonathan Cape) pp.245, 344-9, 455-6, 464-5.

12 King, James (1990) *The Last Modern: A Life of Herbert Read* (London, Weidenfeld & Nicolson) pp.95-6.

13 Moore recalled the event, in King (n.12) pp.95-6.

14 P.G. Konody recognised his 'sympathies [being] entirely with the extreme modernists' (*The Observer*, 20 Jan 1928); R.H. Wilenski his 'monumental vision', 'Foreword' to (1930) *Drawings and Sculpture by Some Contemporary Sculptors* (London, Zwemmer Gallery) but subsequently, in 'Ruminations on sculpture and the work of Henry Moore', *Apollo*, Dec 1930, pp.409-13, and (1932) *The Meaning of Modern Sculpture*, pp.136, 161, failed to grasp Moore's special qualities or the direction in which he was heading. For a full chronological listing of writings on Moore see Davis, Alexander (1992) *Henry Moore Bibliography* (Perry Green, The Henry Moore Foundation) vol.1, 1898-1970.

15 Epstein, Jacob (1931) 'Foreword', *Catalogue of an Exhibition of Sculpture and Drawings by Henry Moore* (London, Leicester Galleries). Also in 1931 Epstein said: 'What is so clearly expressed is a vision rich in sculptural invention, avoiding the banalities of abstraction and concentrating upon those enduring elements that constitute great sculpture ... Even the smallest works of ... Moore have an impressive and remote grandeur'. Epstein, Jacob and Haskell, Arnold L. (1931) *The Sculptor Speaks: Jacob Epstein to Arnold L. Haskell, a series of conversations on art* (London, Heinemann) pp.135-6.

16 This shift in fame is discussed in Friedman, Terry (1987) 'Epsteinism', in Friedman, Terry and Silber, Evelyn (Eds) (1987) *Jacob Epstein Sculpture and Drawings* (Leeds City Art Galleries and Whitechapel Art Gallery, London) pp.35-43.

17 Moore had written as early as 1924 condemning Donatello as 'a modeller, and it seems to me that it is modelling [with its reliance on anti-sculptural pictorial effects] that has sapped the manhood out of Western sculpture'. James, Philip (Ed) (1966) *Henry Moore on Sculpture* (London, Macdonald) p.37.

18 The Foreword is reprinted in Hepworth, Barbara (1970) *Barbara Hepworth A Pictorial Autobiography* (London, Adams & Dart) p.21.

19 Bury, Adrian (1931) 'Art notes: painting and sculpture', *Saturday Review*, 25 April.

20 Read, Herbert (1931) *The Meaning of Art* (London, Faber & Faber) pp.148-53. The text, extensively quoted in Underwood, Eric G. (1933) *A Short History of English Sculpture* (London, Faber & Faber) pp.167-71, is dismissed as being 'fantastic claims'.

21 Moore, Henry (1932) 'On carving: a conversation', *New English Weekly*, 5 May, pp.65-6.

22 Read, Herbert (1962) 'A Nest of Gentle Artists', *Apollo*, Sep, pp.536-40, reprinted with additional material in (1965) *Art in Britain 1930-40 centred around Axis, Circle, Unit One* (London, Marlborough Fine Art).

23 Read, Herbert (Ed) (1934) *Unit One: The Modern Movement in English Architecture, Painting and Sculpture* (London, Cassell) pp.10, 12.

24 'One of the most personal and eloquent statements made by a sculptor is the short text, The Sculptor's Aims, which Henry Moore contributed to Unit One in 1934. It is almost too eloquent, and not entirely characteristic of Moore's other writings. Knowing that Herbert Read was editor of Unit One, I once asked Read if he had had a hand in writing it. He smiled and wanted to know why I had asked this question. I told him that I had observed a painter friend describing his work in the words that I had used in writing of his art. Read agreed that this happened all the time: yes, he and Moore had written The Sculptor's Aims together.' Bowness, Alan (1989) *The Conditions of Success: How the Modern Artist Rises to Fame* (London, Thames & Hudson) pp.21, 23.

25 Read, *Unit One* (n.23) pp.29-30.

26 Stokes, Adrian (1934) *Stones of Rimini* (London, Faber & Faber) p.27.

27 These points are discussed in Friedman, Terry (1991) 'The Young Henry Moore in London, Paris and Florence', *Leeds Arts Calendar*, no.109, pp.14-15.

28 Read, Herbert (1934) *Henry Moore, Sculptor: An Appreciation by Herbert Read with Thirty-Six Plates* (London, Zwemmer) p.7.

29 *Ibid.* pp.8-10.

30 *Ibid.* pp.11-15.

31 *Ibid.* p.7.

32 *Ibid.* p.15.

33 *Ibid.* p.10. Read is attacking the academic carving practice of manual execution by studio assistants and the almost exclusive use of white marble.

34 *Ibid.* p.16. Compare this commitment with R.H. Wilenski's hesitancy: 'I personally feel confident that we are about to witness the creation of sculptural masterpieces … and one of the artists who, I believe, may produce them is Henry Moore. Perhaps Moore has already produced such masterpieces, though we do not yet recognise them as such.' ('Ruminations on Sculpture and the work of Henry Moore', *Apollo*, Dec 1930, p.413). Among the seven illustrations in this article is the 1929 *Reclining Figure* in brown Hornton stone, now in Leeds City Art Galleries.

35 Read, Herbert (1939) 'Three English Sculptors', *XXe Siècle*, IIᵉ année, no.1, repr.p.23: 'since the Middle Ages we seem to have lost that particular kind of plastic sensibility. It may be that we are returning to it, after such a long fallow period, with renewed vigour and original conceptions.' The three sculptors are Moore, Hepworth and Ben Nicholson represented by his relief paintings. Rudenstein, Angelica Zander (1985) *Peggy Guggenheim Collection, Venice* (New York, Harry N. Abrams) cat.no.125.

36 Read, Herbert (1944) *Henry Moore: Sculpture and Drawings* (London, Lund Humphries / Zwemmer); (1952) *Barbara Hepworth: Carvings and Drawings* (London, Lund Humphries); (1957) with J.L. Martin *Gabo: Constructions Sculpture Paintings Drawings Engravings* (London, Lund Humphries); (1968) *Arp* (London, Thames & Hudson).

37 Catalogue for the *International Sculpture Competition: The Unknown Political Prisoner* sponsored by the Institute of Contemporary Arts, Tate Gallery, London, 14 March – 30 April 1953, with a Foreword by Herbert Read; Nash, Steven A. and Merkert, Jörn (1985) *Naum Gabo: Sixty Years of Constructivism* (Munich, Prestel-Verlag) cat. nos 61-61.2.

38 Shewring (n.11) pp.280-81.

39 Read, *Meaning of Art* (n.20) p.45, pls.18-19.

40 Read, *Art of Sculpture* (n.2) pp.ix-x.

41 *Ibid.* pp.5-7. One is reminded of Gaudier-Brzeska's dictum 'Sculpture energy is the mountain'.

42 *Ibid.* p.5.

43 *Ibid.* p.14.

44 *Ibid.* pp.16-17.

45 *Ibid.* pp.22-3.

46 *Ibid.* p.24.

47 *Ibid.* pp.36-7.

48 *Ibid.* pp.39-40.

49 *Ibid.* p.41.

50 The bronze version of *Double Standing Figure*, 1950, illustrated as pl.209, was selected by Read for the Venice *Biennale* in 1952.

51 *Ibid.* p.42.

52 *Ibid.* p.35.

53 *Ibid.* pp.30-1.

54 He observed: 'there is an exceptional type of artist whose only purpose is to display his technical skill; with him the means becomes the end. We call him a virtuoso, and he is apt to be a very inferior kind of artist'. *Ibid.* p.33.

55 *Ibid.* pp.53-4.

56 *Ibid.* p.55.

57 *Ibid.* pp.58-60.

58 *Ibid.* p.71.

59 *Ibid.* pp.69-70.

60 *Ibid.* p.77.

61 *Ibid.* p.82.

62 *Ibid.* p.84.

63 *Ibid.* p.44.

64 *Ibid.* p.75.

65 *Ibid.* p.76.

66 *Ibid.* pp.80-1.

67 *Ibid.* p.87.

68 *Ibid.* p.72.

69 *Ibid.* p.86.

70 *Ibid.* pp.90-1.

71 *Ibid.* p.96.

72 *Ibid.* pp.91-2.

73 *Ibid.* p.92.

74 *Ibid.* pp.92, 97.

75 *Ibid.* pp.97-8.

76 *Ibid.* p.101.

77 *Ibid.* pp.105-6.

78 *Ibid.* pp.109-10.

79 *Ibid.* p.113.

80 *Ibid.* p.117.

81 *Ibid.* pp.122-3.

The Geometry of Fear: Herbert Read and British Modern Sculpture after the Second World War

Robert Burstow

These new images belong to the iconography of despair, or of defiance; and the more innocent the artist, the more effectively he transmits the collective guilt. Here are images of flight, of ragged claws 'scuttling across the floors of silent seas', of excoriated flesh, frustrated sex, the geometry of fear.[1]

It has become customary to invoke this metaphorical and allusive passage of Herbert Read's when discussing post-war British sculpture.[2] The passage appears in a brief catalogue essay which introduced the influential, cosmopolitan visitors attending the 1952 Venice *Biennale* to eight 'young' male sculptors (they were all under forty): Robert Adams, Kenneth Armitage, Reg Butler, Lynn Chadwick, Geoffrey Clarke, Bernard Meadows, Eduardo Paolozzi and William Turnbull. Read's catalogue essay presented them as sharing to some extent a common identity and their skeletal metal sculpture as expressing a post-war sense of violence, despair, impotence and guilt. If not cited in full, then at least Read's culminating phrase is usually given as evidence that this sculpture somehow represented the political anxieties of the Cold War.[3] Read's evocative phrase was taken up in contemporary journalism and has since become so associated with these artists that it has been used as a shorthand to identify them as 'the geometry of fear sculptors', or even 'school'.[4] In one sense then, Read has a special claim on these sculptors although any discussion of his relation to sculpture in Britain after the war needs also to take account of his continued support for Barbara Hepworth and Henry Moore.

Herbert Read's international status as a commentator on the visual arts was extremely high by 1952. The painter and critic, Patrick Heron, who was especially well informed on the Anglo-American scene, identified Read in that year as 'the most important writer on art in English now living'.[5] There can be no doubt that Read had a particular enthusiasm for sculpture, that his opinion of *British* sculpture was extremely high,[6] and that among the artists he was closest to, three were sculptors. He had long supported Naum Gabo, Barbara Hepworth and Henry Moore, the three to whom he dedicated his 1956 book *The Art of Sculpture*,[7] but his expanding taste, signalled in Venice, immediately gave great prestige to these new and little-known sculptors.[8] Although he later approved of other British sculptors, some of whom had studied under those exhibiting in Venice, his original eight remained central to what Read identified in his writings and lectures as 'the renaissance of sculpture in England'.[9]

By 1964, however, Read's influence was evidently in

131

decline: that year's *Biennale* was the last to include any of his favoured British sculptors and the *Documenta* contained none.[10] That this year marked an end to Read's powerful position is perhaps further suggested by his adoption of a more retrospective stance with the publication of his popular book *A Concise History of Modern Sculpture* where he laments 'the general tendency to abandon carving and even modelling in favour of various methods of assemblage'.[11] Read no doubt had in mind a still younger generation of sculptors, associated with Anthony Caro, Phillip King and the St Martin's School of Art, who had propagated a more formalist and reductivist aesthetic, and stolen the critical acclaim.[12] The champion theorist of this movement, American critic Clement Greenberg, had mounted an attack on Read a year or so earlier, asserting that Read's criticism had gone 'astray' because 'modernist painting and sculpture have outrun the common categories of art criticism, invalidating them not only for the present or future but also for the past'.[13] However, for nearly twenty years after the Second World War, Read's influence had been pervasive; he had both established the canon of British sculptors and the dominant view of their work.[14]

Read promoted modern sculpture on several fronts. The post-war development of state-funded organisations supporting British culture created new professional roles for expert advisers. Despite his anarchist philosophy which favoured devolvement of political power away

131 Naum Gabo, Henry Moore and Barbara Hepworth at a memorial presentation for Sir Herbert Read at the Tate Gallery, London 1970

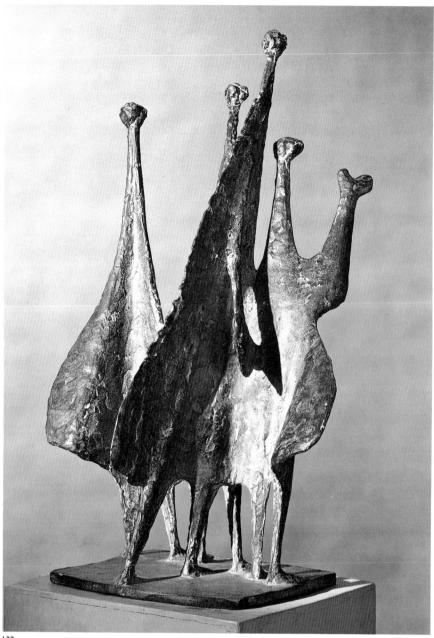

132

132 Kenneth Armitage
People in a Wind 1950.
Exhibited Venice
Biennale 1952. Tate
Gallery, London

133 Reg Butler *Woman*
1949. Exhibited Venice
Biennale 1952. Tate
Gallery, London

prominence to the exhibitors.[19] Although Read was realistic about the political purposes of the Council, he was quite prepared to take advantage of its influence: 'It was founded by an imperialist (Lord Lloyd) and its aims are undoubtedly politely chauvinistic. But I have not the slightest doubt that through its agency the position (prestige) of our artists throughout the world has been immensely enhanced ...'[20] By 1964 the work of these sculptor-emissaries had been exhibited in fifty cities worldwide, to enormous acclaim, and the British Council had established its own collection of sculpture consisting exclusively of works by these same sculptors.[21]

Herbert Read's presence was also felt within the newly founded Arts Council: he served on its Art Panel from 1947 until 1953. During this time the Arts Council was active in support of modern sculpture, both acquiring works for its own collection and in its programme of

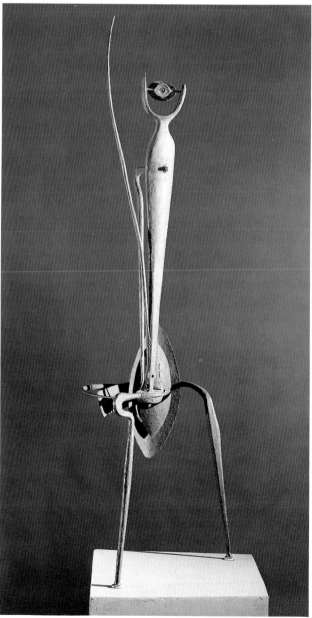

from centralised government, Read participated energetically in these new cultural bureaucracies, and was an indefatigable member of numerous committees, panels and juries. As a member of the British Council's Fine Arts Committee – if not its 'chief advisor on art' as some perceived him[15] – Read exercised considerable influence.[16] From 1948 until 1964, an unbroken succession of his preferred sculptors were accepted by the Committee to represent Britain at the *Biennales* in Venice and São Paulo, where they frequently won prizes awarded by international juries for which Read was often the British representative.[17] The British Council also organised a steady flow of exhibitions of Hepworth, Moore and various permutations of *Young British Sculptors* which toured Europe, North and South America, and still further afield[18] while Read's catalogue essays gave further

133

exhibitions.[22] It co-organised a series of open-air sculpture exhibitions in London parks which endeavoured to promote a popular audience for contemporary sculpture while a series of *Sculpture in the Home* exhibitions tried to encourage private patronage from the middle-classes.[23] For the 1951 *Festival of Britain* extravaganza, the Arts Council commissioned works from twelve sculptors, including Hepworth, Moore and five of those shown in Venice the following year.[24]

Another newly formed arts organisation of considerable significance to British sculpture, where Read exerted still greater influence, was the Institute of Contemporary Arts in London. As Read's brainchild it was originally conceived idealistically as a microcosm of an anarchistic society[25] but while endeavouring to exist independently of state subsidy it remained dependent on private philanthropy, Read accepting $2,500 from John D. Rockefeller on one occasion.[26] During the early years of Read's presidency, the ICA mounted several exhibitions which featured contemporary British sculpture, such as *Young Sculptors* of 1951-2. Some of these exhibitions, such as *40,000 Years of Modern Art* in 1948-9, polemicised modern sculpture's affinities with the prehistoric and the 'primitive'[27] – Read's own 1953 lectures on 'The Aesthetics of Sculpture' suggested a similar timeless universality for this art.[28] During 1952-3 the Institute organised the largest-ever international sculpture competition which took the theme of 'The Unknown Political Prisoner'.[29] Read served as the British representative on the International Jury which awarded most of the top prizes to Constructivist and Expressionist entries and more prizes to Great Britain than any other country: minor prizes were awarded to nine British entrants, including Frink, Hutchinson, McWilliam and Paolozzi, major prizes to Chadwick and Hepworth, and the Grand Prize to Reg Butler.[30]

Butler, as the holder of a Gregory Fellowship at Leeds University (which paid a generous annual stipend), had been able to concentrate single-mindedly on the Competition. Herbert Read's friendship with E. C. Gregory, joint director of the Bradford publishing firm Percy Lund Humphries and Company Limited, proved to be extremely fortuitous in more ways than one for British sculpture. Read described Gregory as Henry Moore's 'first patron, and always his best friend'.[31] In 1934, Gregory's firm had printed the first small book on Moore with an essay by Read.[32] From then on, Lund Humphries (as the firm became) issued books on British sculpture regularly, including (eventually) a six-volume catalogue raisonné of Moore's sculpture and substantial monographs on Barbara Hepworth.[33] Under both Read's and Moore's encouragement, Gregory's patronage also extended towards younger sculptors. Of the eight Gregory Fellowships offered to painters, sculptors, poets or musicians by Leeds University between 1950 and 1964 (Read, as a trustee, helped select these) four were conferred upon sculptors: Butler was followed by Armitage, Hubert Dalwood and Austin Wright.[34]

134

134 Bernard Meadows *Black Crab* 1953. Private collection (cat.no.133)

It is as a writer and lecturer that we might expect Read to have influenced British sculpture most profoundly. After the war he produced a great number of books and articles on sculpture, and lectured on the subject in Europe, the United States and beyond.[35] Read wrote on art mainly for the middle-class intellectual readership of small circulation politico-cultural journals, such as *Encounter*, *Horizon* and the *New Statesman & Nation*, rather than for the professionally-defined, specialist subscribers to art, art historical and architectural journals, or the mass readerships of newspapers. He was able to assume a degree of familiarity in his readers with the ideas he borrowed eclectically from Bergson, Freud, Jung, Kropotkin, Langer, Nietzsche and others. In fact, Read published relatively little which explicitly discussed the younger generation of British sculptors despite the fact that he is so strongly identified with them. He wrote mainly short catalogue or book introductions, occasional exhibition reviews (the bulk of these were on Hepworth and Moore) and essays or books which surveyed the history of modern sculpture.[36] His catalogue and review essays tended to be written in a very generalised manner. Indeed, one of Read's admirers, Patrick Heron, criticised him for his lack of specificity. Heron felt that Read could simultaneously show 'an undeniable insight into a given painting or sculpture *and* an equally undeniable aloofness from it'. From Heron's highly formalist standpoint, one problem of Read's criticism was that 'his main passion was not for the picture itself as much as for the meaning of the picture'; on these grounds he characterised Read as 'a philosopher rather than a critic'.[37] But Read would have been perfectly content with this appellation, as Heron must have realised, recognising his own tendency to write generally and admitting in 1956 that this had been his approach to Moore. He seems to have worried that giving a *critical* appreciation of an artist's work might have dampened his enthusiasm.[38]

In consequence, perhaps, Read always retained his great admiration for Henry Moore, who remained one of his closest friends and the subject of several essays, two monographs and one of only two biographies Read wrote on artists.[39] Read had undoubtedly enhanced Moore's international reputation and, once this was secured after the war, Moore's glory reflected back onto his greatest apologist.[40] In the 1930s, Moore's sculpture had achieved for Read a new aesthetic synthesis, an advance in what he conceived of as the dialectic between Abstraction and 'Superrealism'.[41] With Read's growing interest in Jungian psychology during the 1940s, he now found in Moore's massive and monumental sculpture the 'archetypal', 'biologically significant'[42] forms (part of the 'world language of form' as he referred to it) which he considered an indispensable component of all art. Following his early love of Ruskin, Read also commended a moral quality of 'truth-to-materials' in his carvings. Taking his cue partly from Moore's own statements, Read identified in his work an 'organic vitalism' and 'power of expression' which surpassed conventional beauty: where the latter merely pleased the senses, Read believed, the former had a deeper spiritual dimension.[43]

Read had also been a consistent supporter of Barbara Hepworth since 1932, contributing the introductory essay to the first major monograph on her twenty years later.[44] Sharing in the Yorkshire background of Read and several of his closest friends, she and Read sustained a lengthy friendship and correspondence. But Hepworth was only accorded the same prestigious honours, and the opportunity to establish an international reputation, some years after Moore.[45] The 'dialectic' between abstraction and naturalistic forms of realism, which especially preoccupied Read in the 1940s, was resolved successfully for him in both Moore's and Hepworth's work.[46] While he identified similar archetypal forms in Hepworth's work to those he had found in Moore's, he used the sculptors' own words to distinguish between their ideals. Hepworth's desire for 'a sense of mystery', 'loveliness' and 'some universal or abstract vision of beauty' Read valued less highly than Moore's desire for 'power' and 'vitality',[47] although he resisted any simple explanation of this in terms of their gender.[48] Read anticipated, and to some extent shared, the conventional attitudes of Hepworth's

135

136

1950s audience, explaining that she had 'remained a completely human person, not sacrificing either her social or her domestic instincts, her feminine graces or sympathies, to some hard notion of a career'.[49] Though Read evidently admired Hepworth's sculpture, he clearly regarded Moore as the 'father' of the younger generation of British sculptors and did not recognise Hepworth as a female parent, much to her indignation.[50]

Read's recognition of this younger generation was first occasioned, in fact, not by the 1952 Venice *Biennale* but by a commission in late 1950 to prepare for 'those purveyors of mass culture, Penguin Books', as he privately described it, 'a Pelican or King Penguin or some other bird-book, on Contemporary British Art'.[51] In what he regarded as a report on the most historically significant art 'in Great Britain at the mid-point of the Twentieth Century', having discussed the work of Moore and Hepworth at some length he had then briefly mentioned and illustrated work produced in the previous two years by six 'younger sculptors' (all of those subsequently shown in Venice except Armitage and Clarke).[52] His approval for their new type of 'linear' sculpture acknowledged the influence of Giacometti and Picasso (as well as Moore – two of them had been his assistants),[53] but Read viewed this as part of a reorientation in British art away from Paris and the Mediterranean. Instead, he related their 'outlining of space' and 'representation of rhythm' to a northern expressionist tradition which had revealed itself as much in the 'linear grace' of English Gothic art and architecture as in the anti-classicism of Turner and Constable. Some of their work was seen to bear affinities with Surrealism but Read believed that Surrealism had grown out of an essentially English tradition of romantic and fantastic art. Thus Read represented Moore and these younger British sculptors as part of 'a return to our Romantic tradition',[54] whereas Hepworth stood outside of this with her interest in abstraction, classical harmony and 'pure form'. Read's belief in geographically-defined cultural traditions determined by climate and soil, which had been encouraged by his reading of *Form in Gothic* by the German art historian, Wilhelm Worringer,[55] was in accord with the high nationalist sentiments of the year of the *Festival of Britain* and the ethos of the Neo-Romantic movement in literature and painting which had been gaining ground since the later 1930s.[56]

The following year when Read wrote his introduction to these same sculptors for the Venice *Biennale*, he stressed their difference of attitude and approach to that of his established sculptor friends, Gabo, Hepworth and Moore, but still accepted Moore as 'the parent of them all' as suggested by his recent *Double Standing Figure* placed symbolically outside the pavilion.[57] While emphasising that these sculptors were all individuals and 'not members of an organised group', he connected their work through its iconography (plants, insects, animals and humans), its materials ('metal in sheet, strip or wire'), its formal effects ('a linear, cursive quality' and an 'isomorphic

137

materiality') but, above all, its expressive qualities (of 'agony', 'despair' and 'frustration'). Borrowing metaphors from an old literary friend, Read was reminded by these modern 'iron waifs' of Eliot's 'Waste Land' peopled by 'Hollow Men'.

Although Read's notorious phrase, 'the geometry of fear', has assumed a definitive status, some writers have recently questioned its adequacy and appropriateness to the work of particular sculptors, although without any

138 Hubert Dalwood
Icon 1958. Leeds City
Art Galleries

139 Austin Wright *Moon*
c. 1962. Leeds City Art
Galleries (cat.no.223)

In the 1940s, Read used the Jungian concept of the 'collective unconscious' to give further credence to Worringer's psychologising. Jung believed that the external world had a 'tremendous affect on the psychic life of the individual' and gave a bleak diagnosis of that world: 'we are living in times of great disruption ... political passions are aflame, internal upheavals have brought nations to the brink of chaos, and the very foundations of our *Weltanschauung* are shattered'.[63]

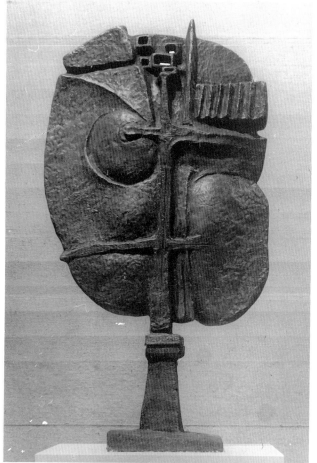

138

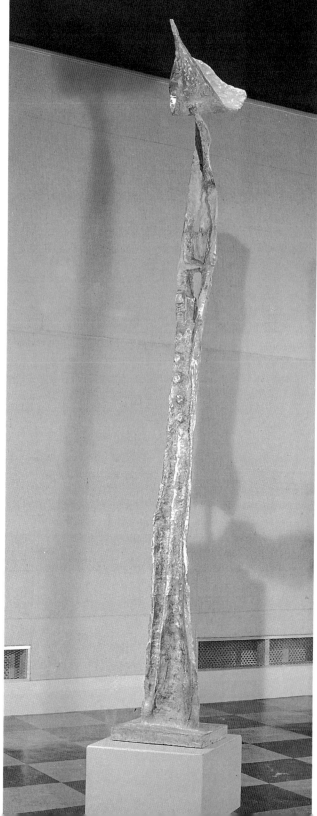

139

detailed consideration of what Read intended.[58] While this is difficult to establish, it is helped by returning to Worringer, to whom in this year Read dedicated his book *The Philosophy of Modern Art*, describing him as 'my esteemed master in the philosophy of art'. Worringer's *Abstraction and Empathy* was first translated into English at this time – not personally by Read (as *Form in Gothic* had been) but very likely at his instigation.[59] This 'epoch making thesis', as Read later described it, remained indispensable to his understanding of abstract art.[60] Worringer's book, first published in 1908 and subtitled *A Contribution to the Psychology of Style* attributed differences in the formal character of art to the collective psychological condition of its makers. Read summarised part of Worringer's argument as follows: '... the tendency to make art unnatural, geometric, abstract is a tendency found in periods when, or in climates where the environment is against man'.[61] When man enjoys a happy pantheistic relationship with nature there is an opposite tendency to make a vital, naturalistic art which produces an empathetic response in the observer. The 'tendency to abstraction' results from a fear of the outside world and produces a geometricised art, such as the Egyptian pyramids or Byzantine mosaics. In developed civilisations this fear may have a religious or metaphysical basis.[62]

By 1952, in the aftermath of world war and amidst the political antagonisms of the Cold War (rabid anticommunism in the West and military intervention in Asia), Read believed the 'collective unconscious' had been transformed by the shame of war-time atrocity, the helplessness of the individual in the face of global conflict and the hopelessness of life ever fearful of atomic war. Read's 'geometry of fear' linked Worringer's explanations of geometric abstraction to this modern collective anxiety. Believing that art was instrumental in the development of human consciousness[64] through giving concrete form to unconscious intuitions, Read wrote approvingly of the young British sculptors that they represented 'some general extension of consciousness'.[65]

However, Read recognised the limitations of crude Zeitgeist theories which could not explain how contrasting styles occur simultaneously within one culture, and even concurrently within one artist's work (such as Moore's or Hepworth's). As the Cold War thawed towards the end of the 1950s, and the credibility of a unified collective mental state receded, Read further adapted Worringer's thesis to allow that in the twentieth century, when the environment is rarely a life-threatening, hostile force, the tendency to either abstract geometry or realistic depiction is more likely to be determined by hereditary or psychological factors.[66] With his decisive conversion to Jungian ideas, and perhaps all too aware of the inadequacy of his 'frequently quoted' phrase as a sufficiently encompassing description of modern sculpture, Read attempted in 1958 to clarify it.[67] He now understood 'fear' as the 'anxiety' possessed by the individual artist, 'a demonic force pent in the unconscious' (Jung's 'Shadow'), but which he believed was 'the primary source of creative activity'. For Read, the artist only released this force directly when it was successfully transferred into an archetypal form and this determined the vitality of the work of art, exemplified for him by the prehistoric 'Venuses' of Lespugue and Laussel.

Read pondered his celebrated phrase again in 1964 but now related it to his Ruskin-like aversion to modern society, a recurrent theme in Read's later writing. 'It is temptingly easy to interpret the many diverse phenomena of modern art as expressions of an "Angst" or despair induced by the alienation prevailing in our technological civilisation – a "geometry of fear", as I once expressed it'.[68] Read noted that this view had become so dominant that an exhibition in Darmstadt the previous year had taken it as a theme: *Evidences of Anxiety in Modern Art*.[69] In an earlier lecture of 1956 on British sculpture he had already adopted similar language deriving from Heidegger and Sartre:

The whole modern movement in art and literature should be conceived as a reflection of this existentialist anxiety ... I wish only to justify this group of young sculptors in England who, without being even aware of these philosophical discussions, have penetrated into the heart of the specifically modern problem, and given us true symbols of our tragic fate.[70]

140 Henry Moore
Double Standing Figure
1950. Exhibited Venice
Biennale 1952

140

Elsewhere Read compared Armitage to Sartre, as an artist who revealed the truth about 'the disintegration of our civilisation'.[71] Wishing to reconcile existentialism with his aesthetic theories he had earlier suggested that Heidegger's *Angst*, or dread, corresponded with Worringer's *Raumscheu*, or 'space-shyness', only the former was a 'fear of nothingness' extended to 'cosmic dimensions'.[72] Now, in a more Jungian frame of mind, he could accept that not all artists would necessarily express this alienated condition. Geometric abstraction needed no longer to be a formal characteristic necessarily possessed by all advanced contemporary art, but became the dominant avant-garde tendency from which some artists might deviate permanently or temporarily depending on the artist's individual psychic state. Moore, for example, whose work Read regarded as deeply rooted in nature and the landscape, he did not consider an alienated artist.

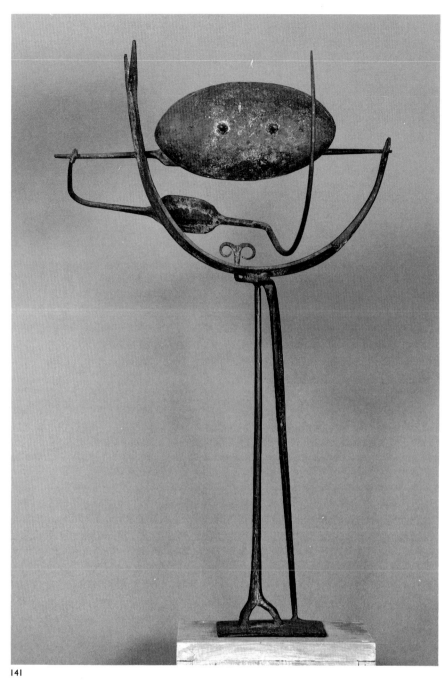

141

141 Reg Butler *Head*
1948-9. Private
collection* (cat.no.32)

hierarchy of materials: modelling clay and forging iron were unable to satisfy 'the full range of aesthetic sensibility' because they lacked 'that nostalgia which ever seeks ... perenniality in its monuments'.[76] Nevertheless, he valued Butler above the other 'young' sculptors, seeing his earlier work as closer to nature and his later work as 'humanistic'.[77] The vital, naturalistically-derived, symbolic forms of these three sculptors Read regarded as affirmative of life and, corresponding with Worringer's conception of the art of non-alienated civilisations, offering the promise of hope. Read declared that 'the artist projects the anxieties of his age, but he would have no creative energy if he were completely filled with despair.'[78]

While Read prized the independence of the artist from the state, he was always concerned with the nature of the relationship of the artist to society. In a 1952 conference address, 'The Sculptor in Modern Society', delivered by Moore but probably largely written by Read,[79] it was claimed that sculpture is 'a public art' and that in this fragmented, transitional society the sculptor must find a middle way between public and private patronage.[80] Sculptors should welcome new opportunities for public commissions but their freedom and independence must be protected. Read encouraged Moore to become involved with public art[81] and in 1952 regarded Hepworth's greatest achievements to date to be her *Vertical Forms*, commissioned for Hatfield Technical College, and her *Contrapuntal Forms*, commissioned for the *Festival of Britain* and destined for the new town of Harlow. Although Read recognised a gap between his own tastes and the public's, his utopian fantasies overcame his fear of contemporary realities:

... even more detrimental to any social acceptance of modern sculpture on a monumental scale is the almost complete atrophy of plastic sensibility in the public at large ... Harlow may be a 'new town' but it is not ready for the impact of a 'new reality'. All the more credit ... to those in authority who have had the courage to mount these monoliths as pointers to a new civilisation.[82]

Read's encouragement contributed importantly to the post-war resurgence of public art in Britain and works by many of his favoured sculptors were placed in public parks and other urban spaces until the modernist dream began to fade in the early 1960s. Even by 1955, after the furore surrounding the bias towards abstraction in the ICA's *Unknown Political Prisoner* competition, Read was in less optimistic mood: 'A controversy ensued in which the distance separating the artist from the public was once more revealed as infinite and apparently unbridgeable'.[83] He blamed the aesthetic apathy of the public who had apparently found all forms of 'modernistic' sculpture undifferentiated and similarly 'incomprehensible' but despised still more the 'ignorance and lack of vision' of individual critics.

The freedom allowed to the individual, and especially the artist, within society was a crucial aspect of Read's anarchist philosophy and his theory of the advancement

Increasingly Read regarded the purpose of modern sculpture as one of creating 'symbolic icons': 'a plastic symbol of the artist's inner sense of numinosity or mystery, or perhaps merely of the unknown dimensions of feeling and sensation'.[73] His admiration for British sculptors was bound to this achievement, and Dalwood, Hepworth and McWilliam all entitled sculptures with his privileged term *icon*. Read describes Hubert Dalwood as using 'primeval archetypes'[74] and implies that Chadwick's 'ossatures' (bone-like armatures) aspired to this symbolic state.[75] But Read's enduring admiration remained for Moore and Hepworth, not only because their discovery of archetypal imagery provided 'transcendental values' but also because of his belief in a 'natural'

of consciousness through art. In 1950 he attended the first meeting of the Congress for Cultural Freedom in Berlin and two years later the Congress's *International Exhibition of the Twentieth Century Arts* in Paris. In 1953 he presented the ICA's *Unknown Political Prisoner* competition as a celebration of the triumph of individualism over totalitarianism.[84] However, it is now known that the Congress was part of a covert propaganda offensive initiated by the American CIA to woo European intellectuals and artists away from communism.[85] Read was certainly suspicious of American political motives and dismissive of their cultural values.[86] But Read held no financial power within the Institute, unlike fellow managers, E. C. Gregory, Roland Penrose and Peter Watson, whose personal wealth frequently rescued it from debt, and who were more prepared to accept American money and influence.[87] While the likelihood of CIA involvement in the funding of the sculpture competition is also strong, it is almost certain that Read was unaware of this.[88] Nevertheless, his high valuation of individualism proved compatible with the strident anti-communism of a new post-war conservative liberalism and its attempts to co-opt modern art into the propaganda battle.

While Read's influence as an interpreter of modern sculpture during the 1950s was pervasive, it did not pass uncontested. The Marxist critic John Berger, for example, who supported Social Realism in art, regularly served up trenchant attacks on modern sculpture and what he regarded as mystifying bourgeois criticism.[89] He accused Hepworth of 'emptiness', over-idealising and ignoring social realities; Moore of failing to find vitality or a significant theme; and Armitage of gimmickry. His review of the 1952 *Biennale* ignored the British sculpture. By contrast, Berger regarded George Fullard (whom Read ignored) as the best young British sculptor because he observed and captured the detail of modern life.[90] But Read was also criticised by Modernist fellow travellers, like Greenberg and Heron, who adhered to a more formalist doctrine. Before Greenberg's direct personal attack on Read in the 1960s, he had reviewed one of Read's books uncomplimentarily[91] and had disparaged Moore's sculpture with some of the worst insults to any avant-gardist: Moore was 'tasteful' and 'traditional' – 'the sincere academic modern'.[92] But Greenberg praised the new anti-monolithic, 'draftsman's sculpture' in America (and Paris and London, as he understood it) because, unlike Read, he regarded this development as an assertion of sculpture's autonomy and purity.[93]

Read's identification with British sculpture in the 1950s has also tended to overshadow the importance of other critics who were supportive of it, such as J. P. Hodin, Robert Melville, and David Sylvester. Sylvester, for example, knew Moore's work well,[94] was in Paris in the later 1940s where he knew Dubuffet and Giacometti and young British sculptors who were visiting, such as Paolozzi and Turnbull.[95] He translated Kahnweiler's influential book on Picasso's sculptures, which included

142

many illustrations of his skeletal iron sculptures from the 1930s, disseminating knowledge of these works in Britain.[96] He wrote and broadcast on contemporary sculpture, describing Butler's sculptures in existentialist terms before Read,[97] and then selected the ICA's exhibition of sixteen *Young Sculptors* (which included Frink and two other women and, but for the presence of Chadwick, served as a kind of audition for the 1952 Venice *Biennale*).[98]

Herbert Read's promotion of this new group of British sculptors after the war was neither isolated nor oppositional. Although other critics had already shown interest in the work of a broader assembly, Read's essay for the *Biennale*, and the selection of sculptors, established the

142 George Fullard *Angry Woman* 1958. Sheffield City Art Galleries

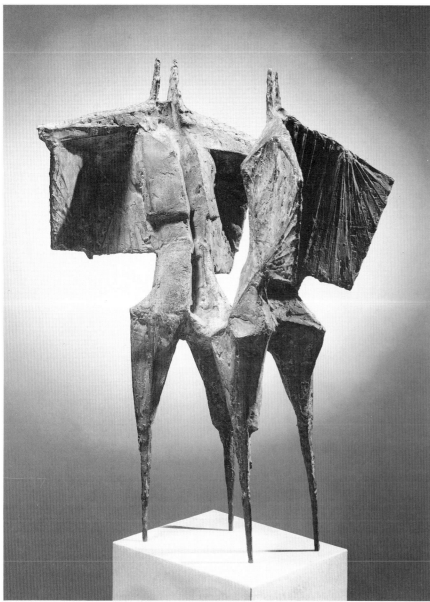

143

144

145

143 Lynn Chadwick
Winged Figures 1955.
Tate Gallery, London

144 John Warren Davis
*Double Figure c.*1960.
Private collection*
(cat.no.62)

145 Vojin Bakic *Torso*
*c.*1960. Private
collection* (cat.no.16)

enduring interpretation of their work and set the canon.
His re-interpretation of his own famous phrase shifted the
alleged meaning of this sculpture from being an expression of collective fear under the historical conditions of the
Cold War to the expression of an existentialist anxiety of
modern society, with a Jungian conception of that psychic
anxiety as the well-spring of creativity. However, Read
actually valued the work of this group of sculptors less
highly than others who made more affirmative symbolic
images.

Read's life is permeated with irony and contradiction.
In a less than reverential obituary, the *New York Times* art
critic, Hilton Kramer, observed that Read was a pacifist
who had held a military commission, an anarchist who
accepted a knighthood and an intellectual with an
exalted sense of vocation who at times produced populist
potboilers.[99] In relation to post-war art, it could be added
that Read was an opponent of centralised government

who tirelessly participated in state art institutions, a proponent of devolved forms of democratic rule who held the personal vision of the public artist sacrosanct, and an ardent advocate of artistic and intellectual freedom who became an unwitting instrument of American imperialism. When faced by the realities of popular taste or political power, the awkward contradictions between his anarchistic idealism and artistic vanguardism became acute. Casting the artist in the elevated role of society's saviour from 'the chaos of modern civilisation' while participating in the institutions of the state, led Read inevitably into personal compromise. And although Read had come to be dubbed 'the Pope of Modern Art', the criteria by which he judged post-war modern sculpture were at odds with a growing number of younger artists and critics. While Read had always rejected the Social Realists' premise that art must serve some higher political purpose, he now dissented from American-led polemic for the exclusion of overtly natural or human subjects from the Modernist aesthetic. Where the new criticism judged art by its formal purity, conceptual autonomy and stylistic internationalism, Read valued archetypal resonance, spiritual transcendence and national tradition. Read's liberal humanism produced a compassionate social conscience and a romanticising aesthetic.

146

ACKNOWLEDGMENT

I would like to thank Fred Orton for his comments on the manuscript and all the staff of the Herbert Read Archive in the McPherson Library, University of Victoria, British Columbia, for their kind assistance, especially Dietrich Bertz.

Notes

1 Read, Herbert (1952) 'New Aspects of British Sculpture' in British Council (1952) *The XXVI Venice Biennale, The British Pavilion* (London, Westminster Press), June-Oct; also included paintings by Graham Sutherland and Edward Wadsworth. Read quotes from T. S. Eliot's *The Lovesong of J. Alfred Prufrock*.

2 Two recent examples: Kent, Sarah (1984) 'A Bestiary of our Time' in Robertson, Bryan (Introduction) (1984) *Elisabeth Frink, Sculpture: Catalogue Raisonné* (Salisbury, Harpvale), p.51; and Farr, Dennis and Chadwick, Eva (1990) *Lynn Chadwick, Sculptor* (Oxford, Clarendon Press) p.8.

3 For a current, prominent example: the interpretative panel accompanying the display of 1950s British sculpture in Room 22 of the Tate Gallery, London, is entitled 'The Geometry of Fear' and quotes most of the cited passage.

4 For an early example, see Denvir, Bernard (1956) 'The geometry of fear', *Art*, 29 June, p.3 (review of Chadwick at the Venice Biennale); more recently, see Kent, Sarah (1985), 'Another View: The Sculpture of Elisabeth Frink' in Royal Academy of Arts, London (1985) *Elisabeth Frink, Sculpture and Drawings*, p.11.

5 Heron, Patrick (1952) 'The Philosophy of Herbert Read', *New Statesman & Nation*, 29 March; reprinted in Heron, Patrick (1955) *The Changing Forms of Art* (London, Routledge & Kegan Paul) pp.268-71. This judgment elevated Read above likely contenders, such as Clive Bell or Clement Greenberg; Heron was by no means unbiased – his book acknowledges Read's personal encouragement.

6 He advised his friend the German art historian, Will Grohmann that 'it would be little less than disastrous to present painting

147

separately from sculpture' in his contribution on British art to Grohmann's proposed book on art since 1945; see H. Read letter to W. Grohmann, 8 March 1958 (Read Archive, University of Victoria, British Columbia).

7 Read, Herbert (1956) *The Art of Sculpture* (London, Faber & Faber); dedicated to 'sculptors and friends in gratitude'.

8 Their works were bought by museums and private collectors in Germany, Italy and the United States, including Peggy Guggenheim and Alfred H. Barr (for the Museum of Modern Art, New York and other American collectors).

9 Hubert Dalwood (student of Armitage), Elisabeth Frink (student of Meadows), John Hoskin (student of Chadwick), Bryan Kneale, Kenneth Martin, Victor Pasmore, Leslie Thornton and Austin Wright; see, for example, his 1956 lecture 'Henry Moore and the Renaissance of Sculpture in England', typescript pp.17-22; or his 1960 lecture 'The Ambiguity of

146 John Hoskin *Insect* c. 1960. Private collection* (cat.no.115)

147 Eduardo Paolozzi *Forms on a Bow* 1950. Exhibited Venice Biennale 1952. Tate Gallery, London. Presented by the Contemporary Art Society 1958 (cat.no.171)

Modern Sculpture', typescript (Read Archive, University of Victoria, British Columbia). Read used the terms British and English interchangeably.

10 The triumph of Post-Abstract Expressionist American Modernism was marked by Rauschenberg winning the Painting Prize at the *Biennale*; Read expressed his consternation publicly at the *Documenta* in a lecture entitled 'The Disintegration of Form in Modern Art', published in Read, Herbert (1965) *The Origins of Form in Art* (London, Thames & Hudson) Ch.IX.

11 Read, Herbert (1964) *A Concise History of Modern Sculpture* (London, Thames & Hudson) p.7.

12 Phillip King later said of the *Documenta* that in 1959 (mistaken for 1960): 'The sculpture there was terribly dominated by a post-war feeling which seemed very distorted and contorted … it was somehow terribly like scratching your own wounds – an international style with everyone showing the same neuroses'; in (1968) 'Phillip King talks about his sculpture', *Studio International*, June, p.300.

13 Greenberg, Clement (1962) 'How art writing earns its bad name', *Encounter*, Dec, and (1963) 'A critical exchange with Herbert Read', *Encounter*, Feb, both reprinted in O'Brian, John (Ed) (1993) *Clement Greenberg: The Collected Essays and Criticism*, vol.4 (Chicago, University Press) pp.135-44, 145-9. Greenberg's tirade was mainly provoked by what he regarded as the misinterpretation or, in Read's case, denigration of new American abstract painting.

14 See popular art history books such as Lucie-Smith, Edward (1984) *Movements in Art since 1945* (London, Thames & Hudson) pp.197-205.

15 Sprigge, Sylvia (1952) 'Britain strangely represented', *Manchester Guardian*, 24 June. Read denied this title, preferring to call himself the *commissario* for Britain at the 1952 Venice *Biennale*; see H. Read letter to *Manchester Guardian*, published 26 June.

16 Read was invariably a member of the sub-groups agreed to select their exhibitions of modern art, together with Sir Philip Hendy, Director of the National Gallery, Sir John Rothenstein, Director of the Tate Gallery, and Lilian Somerville, Head of the Fine Arts Department, all of whom were sympathetic towards modern sculpture. Only after 1960 was there a three-year time limit imposed on new members' service.

17 Venice *Biennales* included: 1948 Moore (International Sculpture Prize); 1950 Hepworth; 1952 Adams, Armitage, Butler, Chadwick, Clarke, Meadows, Paolozzi, Turnbull; 1954 Butler; 1956 Chadwick (International Sculpture Prize); 1958 Armitage (Bright Foundation Award); 1960 Clarke, Paolozzi; 1962 Adams, Dalwood; 1964 Meadows. São Paulo *Bienales* included: 1953 Moore (Best Foreign Sculptor); 1957 Adams, Armitage, Butler, Chadwick, McWilliam, Paolozzi, Turnbull, Wright (Acquisition Prize); 1959 Hepworth (Prefecture Prize); 1961 Chadwick.

18 For example, *Young British Sculptors* organised in collaboration with the Arts Club of Chicago toured four American cities and Toronto between March 1955 and February 1956; *Junge Englische Bildhauer* toured six German cities and Rotterdam between November 1955 and August 1956; *Yngre Brittiska Skuptörer* toured ten Swedish cities between 1956 and 1957; *Recent British Sculpture* toured Canada, New Zealand and Australia between 1961 and 1963.

19 Read wrote essays for Venice *Biennales*: 1948 Moore; 1952 eight sculptors as listed (n.17); 1958 Armitage; and São Paulo *Bienales*; 1953 Moore; 1957 *Young British Sculptors*; 1961 Chadwick.

20 H. Read letter to John Berger, 31 July 1955 (Read Archive, University of Victoria, British Columbia).

21 The collection was begun in 1946 and until 1977 selected by the Fine Arts Committee; by 1964 all of the sculptures it owned were by Hepworth, Moore, Dalwood and six of the eight sculptors shown at Venice in 1952; see British Council (1984) *The British Council Collection 1938-1984* (London, British Council).

22 By 1964 it owned sculptures by Hepworth, Moore, the eight shown at Venice in 1952 and six of the further eight consistently supported by Read; see Arts Council (1965) *Sculpture from the Arts Council Collection* (London, Arts Council) and Arts Council (1979) *The Arts Council Collection* (London, Arts Council).

23 See Calvocoressi, Richard (1981) 'Public sculpture in the 1950s', in Nairne, S. and Serota, N. (Eds) (1981) *British Sculpture in the 20th Century* (London, Whitechapel Art Gallery) pp.134-53; and Garlake, Margaret (1987) 'The Relationship Between Institutional Patronage and Abstract Art in Britain, c.1945-1956', unpublished PhD thesis, Courtauld Institute, London.

24 Three works on the South Bank by Epstein, Hepworth and Moore; one work in the Battersea Park *International Sculpture Exhibition* by Dobson; and eight works in the *60 Paintings for '51* exhibition at the RBA Galleries, London.

25 Thistlewood, David (1984) *Herbert Read: Formlessness and Form: An Introduction to his Aesthetics* (London, Routledge & Kegan Paul) p.17.

26 For the early history of the ICA see Thistlewood, David (1989) 'The MOMA and the ICA: a common philosophy of modern art', *British Journal of Aesthetics*, vol.29, no.4, Autumn; pp.316-27. Read received Rockefeller's unsolicited donation in March 1948; see King, James (1990) *The Last Modern: A Life of Herbert Read* (London, Weidenfeld & Nicolson) p.241.

27 ICA, London (1951) *Young Sculptors* (London, Lund Humphries), Dec-Jan 1951-2; included work by 16 British sculptors. *40,000 Years of Modern Art*, Dec-Jan 1948-9, held in the Academy Cinema Hall, Oxford Street.

28 Thistlewood, 1984 (n.25) p.199, note 50. These lectures formed the basis of his Andrew W. Mellon Lectures in Fine Art, National Gallery of Art, Washington, 1954.

29 Tate Gallery, London (1953) *International Sculpture Competition: The Unknown Political Prisoner* (London, Lund Humphries) 14 March – 30 April, sponsored by the ICA, Foreword by Herbert Read, Introduction by A.J.T. Kloman.

30 See Burstow, Robert (1987) 'The "Unknown Political Prisoner" International Sculpture Competition: ideological uses of modernist art in the Cold War', unpublished MA thesis, Birmingham Polytechnic (copy Tate Gallery Library). Read actually wished his old friend Naum Gabo to win the Grand Prize, admiring his project's symbolism: H. Read letter to N. Gabo, 19 March, 1953. Gabo had implored his support: N. Gabo letter to H. Read, 4 Jan, 1953 (Read Archive, University of Victoria, British Columbia).

31 H. Read letter to Will Grohmann, 20 Feb 1959 (Read Archive, University of Victoria, British Columbia).

32 Read, Herbert (1934) *Henry Moore, Sculptor, an Appreciation* (London, A. Zwemmer).

33 Published intermittently on Moore from 1944 and on Hepworth from 1952.

34 Butler 1950-3; Armitage 1953-5; Dalwood 1955-9; and Wright 1960-3. See Arts Council (1964) *The Gregory Fellows: University of Leeds* (London, Shenval Press), Introduction by Herbert Read.

35 Read's lectures included Washington (1954), Stockholm (1960), Berlin (1963) and Kassel (1964).

36 Read, Herbert (1951) *Contemporary British Art* (Harmondsworth, Penguin); Read, 1956 (n.7); Read, Herbert (1964) 'British art since 1945' in Brion, Marcel et al (1956) *Art Since 1945* (London, Thames & Hudson); Read, 1964 (n.11).

37 Heron, 1955 (n.5), p.269; this is a review of Read, Herbert (1952) *The Philosophy of Modern Art* (London, Faber & Faber).

38 H. Read letter to Ivon Hitchens, 16 Oct 1956 (Read Archive, University of Victoria, British Columbia).

39 Read, 1934 (n.32); Read, Herbert (1944) 'Introduction', *Henry Moore: Sculpture and Drawings* (London, Lund Humphries and A. Zwemmer) pp.xvii-xxxvi; Read, Herbert (1965) *Henry Moore: A Study of his Life and Work* (London, Thames & Hudson). The other biographee was Hans Arp: see Read, Herbert (1968) *Hans Arp* (London, Thames & Hudson).

40 Moore's reputation was securely established by retrospective exhibitions at MOMA, New York in 1946 and Tate Gallery, London in 1951, and his selection for the 1948 Venice *Biennale* with the award of the International Sculpture Prize.

41 For a sustained analysis of Read's aesthetic theories see Thistlewood, 1984 (n.25). 'Superrealism' was Read's preferred term for Surrealism.

42 See Read, 1944 (n.39) and Read, Herbert (1948) 'Sculpture and Drawings by Henry Moore', in British Council (1948) *The XXIV Biennale, Venice : The British Pavilion* (London, Westminster Press).

43 See Read, 1964 (n.11), p.163 where he quotes from Moore's statement in Read, Herbert (Ed) (1934) *Unit One* (London, Cassell).

44 Read, Herbert (1932) 'Introduction', *Barbara Hepworth and Ben Nicholson*, (London, Arthur Tooth & Sons Gallery) ; Read, Herbert (1952) *Barbara Hepworth, Carvings and Drawings* (London, Lund Humphries).

45 Venice *Biennale* in 1950; retrospective at the Tate Gallery in 1968.

46 Read, Herbert (1948) 'Barbara Hepworth : A New Phase', *The Listener*, 8 April, p.592

47 Read, 1952 (n.44) pp.ix-xii.

48 Read followed a Jungian notion of both man and woman containing a 'sexual ambiguity or dialectic' within their psyche; see Read, 1952 (n.44) p.ix and Read, Herbert (1957) 'C.G.Jung' in Read, Herbert (1957) *The Tenth Muse, Essays in Criticism* (London, Routledge & Kegan Paul) p.208.

49 Read, 1952 (n.44) p.xi-xii. Hepworth was puzzled by Read's remarks and told him that she did not think that 'either your integrity or my work should be penalised on account of my sex', admitting that previously he had 'always been both fair and free'; B. Hepworth letter to H. Read, 19 July 1952 (Read Archive, University of Victoria, British Columbia).

50 H. Read letter to B. Hepworth, 6 Dec 1951 (Tate Gallery Archive) ; see King (n.26) p.263.

51 H. Read letter to Wyndham Lewis, 10 Nov 1950 (Cornell University Library) ; cited in King (n.26) p.225. Read had mentioned Butler and Paolozzi in a lecture given in Germany and the United States, published as (1948) 'The situation of art in Europe at the end of the Second World War', *Hudson Review*, vol.1, no.1, Spring; reprinted in Read (n.37).

52 Read, 1951 (n.36) p.33. His 1964 thorough-going revision of this book attempts to explain the omission of Armitage and mentions or illustrates work by 23 sculptors.

53 Meadows, 1936-9; Butler, c.1947-8.

54 Read, 1951(n.36) p.39; see 1964 edition for his discussion of Surrealism.

55 Worringer, Wilhelm (1912) *Formprobleme der Gotik*; trans. H. Read, 1927, *Form in Gothic* (London, Tiranti). This was the first product of Read's efforts to learn German in the early 1920s. Worringer contrasts gothic art of the North with classical art of the South; for a fuller discussion see Thistlewood, 1984 (n.25).

56 See, for example, Ironside, Robin (1948) 'Painting since 1939' in (1948) *Since 1939* (London, Readers Union by arrangement with the British Council) pp.147-84.

57 Read, 1952 (n.1).

58 For example: Glaves-Smith, John (1979) 'Kenneth Armitage', *Artscribe*, No.16, Feb, p.30 (who relates the phrase to Worringer) ; Norbert Lynton, 'Introduction' in Arts Council (1979) *Hubert Dalwood, Sculptures and Reliefs*, p.9; Farr and Chadwick (n.2) p.8; Cork, Richard (1987) 'Aspects of Sculpture in the Fifties' in Compton, Susan (Ed) (1987) *British Art in the 20th Century* (London, Royal Academy & Munich, Prestel Verlag), p.300.

59 Worringer, Wilhelm (1908) *Abstraktion und Einfühlung*; trans, M. Bullock, 1953, *Abstraction and Empathy : A Contribution to the Psychology of Style* (London, Routledge & Kegan Paul) ; originally written in 1906. Read was a director of the British publishers.

60 Read, Herbert (1960) 'The Social Significance of Abstract Art', *Quadrum*, 9; pp.5-14; an address delivered at the Europa-Gespräch, Vienna, 21-25 June 1960.

61 *Ibid.* p.8.

62 See Read, Herbert (1948) *Ben Nicholson* (London, Lund Humphries) ; reprinted in Read, 1952 (n.37) pp.216-25.

63 Read, Herbert (1951-2) 'Jung at Mid-Century', *Hudson Review*, vol.IV, pp.259-68; reprinted as Read, 1957 (n.48), p.211. Read was then co-editing Jung's writings; see Read, H., Fordham, M. and Adler, G. (Eds) (1953-81) *The Collected Works of C.G.Jung* (London, Routledge & Kegan Paul).

64 See Read, 1952 (n.37) p.13; for a fuller explanation see Read, Herbert (1957) *Icon and Idea : The Function of Art in the Development of Human Consciousness* (London, Faber & Faber).

65 Read, 1952 (n.1).

66 Thistlewood, 1984 (n.25) p.42.

67 Read, Herbert (1958) *Lynn Chadwick*, Artists of Our Time No.4 (Amriswil, Bodensee-Verlag) pp.9-10.

68 Read, 1964 (n.11), p.218.

69 (1963) *Zeugnisse der Angst in Moderner Kunst*. The exhibition included Armitage, Butler, Chadwick and Moore.

70 Read, 'Henry Moore' lecture (n.9) (Read Archive, University of Victoria, British Columbia).

71 Read, Herbert (1959) 'Introduction', British Council (1959) *Kenneth Armitage, S. W. Hayter, William Scott*, Palais des Beaux-Arts, Bruxelles, 7-29 March. This was a repeat of the 1958 Venice *Biennale* showing.

72 Read, 1948 (n.62) ; reprinted in Read, 1952 (n.37) p.219.

73 Read, 1964 (n.11) p.212.

74 Read, Herbert (1960) 'Introduction', *Hubert Dalwood* (London, Gimpel Fils).

75 Read, 1958 (n.67) pp.9-10.

76 Read, 1952 (n.44) p.xii.

148

148 Bryan Kneale *Portrait of Sir Herbert Read* 1958. York City Art Gallery, Presented by the Friends of York City Art Gallery (cat.no.120)

77 Read, 1952 (n.1) and Read, 1964 (n.11) p.212. The revised (1964) edition of Read, 1951 (n.36) singles out Butler from the other sculptors for extended treatment, pp.42-3.

78 Read, 1964 (n.11) p.225.

79 H.Moore letter to H.Read, 26 April 1952; cited in Berthoud, Roger (1987) *The Life of Henry Moore* (London, Faber & Faber) p.244.

80 An address given at an international conference of artists organised by UNESCO and held in Venice, 22-28 Sept 1952; published in James, Philip (1966) *Henry Moore on Sculpture* (London, Macdonald) pp.84-90.

81 Read, 1944 (n.39); reprinted in Read, 1952 (n.37) p.215.

82 Read, 1952 (n.44) p.xi.

83 Read, Herbert (1955) *The Grass Roots of Art* (London, Faber & Faber) pp.81-2.

84 Read, 1953 (n.29).

85 Burstow, Robert (1989) 'Butler's competition project for a monument to "The Unknown Political Prisoner": abstraction and Cold War politics', *Art History*, vol.12, no.4, Dec, pp.472-96.

86 Read wrote that at the Berlin Congress the Americans shouted 'for bigger and better bombs to defend-what? Nothing that I could recognize as culture'; H.Read letter to Edward Dahlberg, 15 July 1950; cited in King (n.26) p.255.

87 Interview with Ewan Phillips, ICA Managing Director (c.1948-52) 4 Nov 1992.

88 The only ICA officials in contact with the American backer were Anthony Kloman, ex-American cultural attaché and ICA Organising Director (1951-3) and the Surrealist painter, Roland Penrose, ICA Vice-Chairman.

89 Reviews for *New Statesman & Nation* reprinted in Berger, John (1960) *Permanent Red, Essays in Seeing* (London, Methuen) pp.48, 75-9, 83-5, 96-8.

90 Berger, John (1952) 'The Biennale', *New Statesman & Nation*, 5 July. Berger and Read were 'friendly enemies', occasionally united by political issues, such as nuclear disarmament; see King (n.26) pp.299-301.

91 Greenberg, Clement (1947) 'Ideal climate for art: review of The Grass Roots of Art by Herbert Read', *New York Times Book Review*, 4 May, reprinted in O'Brian, John (Ed) (1986) *Clement Greenberg; The Collected Essays and Criticism*, vol.2 (Chicago, University Press) pp.146-7.

92 Greenberg, Clement (1947) Review of Gaston Lachaise and Henry Moore, *The Nation*, 8 Feb, reprinted in O'Brian (n.91), pp.125-8. Greenberg has recently expressed more favourable views on British sculpture: interviewed by author, 19 Nov 1992.

93 Greenberg, Clement (1949) 'The New Sculpture', *Partisan Review*, June, reprinted in O'Brian (n.91) pp.313-19.

94 Sylvester was employed as a personal secretary to Moore in 1944; he published on Moore's sculpture in the *Burlington Magazine* in 1948; he was invited to write a catalogue essay for Moore's retrospective in Wakefield in 1949 and was then invited, aged only twenty-six, by the Arts Council to select Moore's retrospective exhibition at the Tate Gallery in 1951.

95 Sylvester, David (1993) 'In Giacometti's Studio', *The Independent*, 10 July, p.29.

96 Kahnweiler, Daniel-Henry (1948) *Les Sculptures de Picasso*, with photos by Brassai (Paris, Editions du Chêne) translated as (1949) *The Sculptures of Picasso* (London, Rodney Phillips); the sculptor, Geoffrey Clarke, recalls the importance of this book: interviewed by the author, 4 Nov 1992. The journal *Cahiers d'Arts* was also important in this respect.

97 Hanover Gallery, London (1949) *Justin O'Brien, Reg Butler, Massimo Campigli*, Jul-Aug, with introduction Sylvester, David (1949) 'Microcosmos of a Sculptor' (where he described Butler's works as 'Beings affirming the tragic absurdity of existence'); Hanover Gallery, London (1950) *Eduardo Paolozzi, William Turnbull and Kenneth King*, Feb-March, with essay by Sylvester, David (1950); broadcast on 'Contemporary Sculpture' for the BBC Third Programme; published in *The Listener*, vol.XLVI, no.1173, 23 Aug 1951, pp.295-7. It was complete by the end of January 1952 (British Council Fine Arts Committee report on progress, 29 Jan 1952).

98 Selection for the *Biennale* was made at this time in Dec 1951; see King (n.26), p.203. *Young Sculptors* included Sarah Jackson and Rosemary Young.

99 Kramer, Hilton (1968) 'The Contradictions of Herbert Read', *New York Times*, 30 June; reprinted in Kramer, Hilton (1974) *The Age of Anxiety: an Art Chronicle of 1956-1972* (New York, Secker & Warburg) pp.506-9.

149 Bernard Meadows. Sculpture and drawings on exhibition, Venice *Biennale* 1952

149

The Gregory Fellowships

Hilary Diaper

150

151

An experiment with great potentialities
Eric Craven Gregory, 30 April 1943[1]

In 1943, Eric Gregory offered to finance a scheme for the institution of fellowships in the creative arts in the University of Leeds. A certain number of artists would be attached to the University and regarded as members of its staff; and while continuing to work independently, they would make themselves and their work accessible to the whole University community. The appointments were to range across all the arts, including possibly architecture, but Gregory intended that the main emphasis was to be upon poetry, painting and sculpture.

Herbert Read once described Gregory as 'a printer by calling but a patron of the arts by instinct'.[2] A Yorkshire businessman, deeply attached to Modernism in art and literature, Gregory was in close association with many of its leading figures. His publishing firm of Percy Lund Humphries and Company Limited had its presses in Bradford and its offices in Bloomsbury, and in the mid-1940s launched a series of monographs on English artists, including Henry Moore, Ben Nicholson and Barbara

Hepworth. As a collector and patron, Gregory's means were not extravagant, but his astute eye, irrepressible energy, and confirmed belief in the cause of English Modernism worked to the particular advantage of young artists. He was an early promoter and lifelong friend of Henry Moore, and was closely associated in a number of projects with Herbert Read, including the foundation of the Institute of Contemporary Arts, of which he was Honorary Treasurer and a member of the Managing Committee. He was undoubtedly much influenced by Read's ideas.

Read and Moore, together with two other friends, T. S. Eliot and Bonamy Dobrée, were his chosen advisers on the Committee which directed the Fellowships project. Gregory's scheme was not, as is often assumed in the artistic community and by the general public, merely to provide a setting in which artists might work free from commercial pressures. Gregory's vision was more complex than that, and in its complex terms lay its truly innovative character. The objects of the scheme, as suggested by Gregory, were twofold:

(i) to bring our younger artists into close touch with the youth of the country so that they may influence it; and (ii) at the same time to keep artists in close touch with the needs of the community. At present there is too great a gap between art and society, and it is hoped that this scheme would constitute a small step towards closing it.[3]

By 'younger artists' Gregory did not mean 'unproven', but rather members of the newest vanguards in art. In Gregory's mind the relay of the ideas of a creative élite would pass from artist to student, and then from student to the wider community. The students were to be the agents through whom the Modern Movement in art would permeate society. The University accepted the scheme in 1943, and it got underway in 1949, when Gregory was able to make the money available.[4] The full Gregory Fellowships Committee consisted of Gregory, Read, Eliot, Moore and Dobrée (as Professor of English Literature in the University), together with the Pro-Chancellor, Sir Hubert Houldsworth, and the Vice-Chancellor, Sir Charles Morris. The Committee's main function was to nominate candidates for the Fellowships. It is clear that Gregory and the other non-University members had a free hand in their selections, and that the University's acceptance of their recommendations was understood to be a formality. In fact, very few meetings of the full Committee ever took place during Gregory's lifetime. What generally happened was that Gregory and his friends consulted informally in the course of their normal round of activities and, having agreed on suitable names, would meet with the University representatives over lunch or dinner in Gregory's London flat (or sometimes in Leeds), where the nominations would be formalised. Prospective Fellows were given a formal interview, sometimes in London and sometimes in Leeds, but Gregory was in the habit of inviting them to dinner where a less formal and perhaps more searching interview could be conducted.

Gregory and his friends shared a view of what they hoped to accomplish through the Fellowships, and did not wish to be put in a position where their view of the purposes of the scheme and its standards might be compromised. When the University Senate proposed to add additional academic members to the Committee, the Vice-Chancellor had to report that 'while the Committee would wish to have consultations with a wide variety of persons interested in the scheme, it is of opinion that at present the Committee is not likely to be helped in its work by increasing its size'.[5]

The Committee operated with no precise division of labour. Read interested himself as much in the choice of poets as in the selection of painters, and Dobrée conducted an early campaign about the need to recruit a non-representational artist. They did not see themselves as judges of applications – for many years none were

sought. Rather, they were promoters of a cohort of artists, largely 'unknown' to the wider community, who were doing new things in art and were already co-opted into the circle of the creative élite. The prestige of the Committee, and the active efforts of its members – individually and collectively – usually enabled the University to induce people of high accomplishment and promise to spend a period in Leeds. A few of the invitees, however, such as C. Day Lewis and Victor Pasmore, got away.

At an early stage, we find Read expressing what was undoubtedly a common resolve never to relax standards. The Fellowships were not to become 'a sanctuary for the second-rate', Read wrote to Dobrée:

... I don't think you are going to enhance the prestige of the University ... by having some 'ingeniously obscure' minor poet hanging round the place – or a Bloomsbury beard or a Welsh inebriate or a Scottish potwalloper (no direct and libellous reference to any of the names under consideration) ... the main idea was to correct the academic atmosphere by the introduction of the creative artist. That is a perfect ideal, but it must be an artist of some presence and substance, or the whole purpose of the scheme is frustrated.[6]

Read remained on the Advisory Committee until his death in 1968, and in the eighteen years of his membership, eight Fellows in Poetry were appointed; six in Painting, five in Sculpture, and one in Music (see Table). His particular influence in the Committee's choice of painters is evident. They wished to set up an interplay between the various Fellows in Leeds which would have creative consequences for the Modern Movement in art – or at least a section of it – and it is interesting to reflect how closely the styles of the painters and sculptors appointed fit into the history that Read had been constructing in his *Contemporary British Art* (1951), and promoting as Founder-President of the ICA, as well as on the Fine Art Committee of the British Council.

GREGORY FELLOWS APPOINTED
DURING READ'S TIME ON THE COMMITTEE

Poetry		Painting	
James Kirkup	1950-52	Martin Froy	1951-54
John Heath-Stubbs	1952-55	Terry Frost	1954-56
Thomas Blackburn	1956-57	Alan Davie	1957-59
Jon Silkin	1958-60	Trevor Bell	1960-63
William Price Turner	1960-62	Dennis Creffield	1964-67
Peter Redgrove	1962-65	John Walker	1967-70
David Wright	1965-67		
Martin Bell	1967-69		
Sculpture		Music	
Reg Butler	1950-53	Kenneth Leighton	1953-56
Kenneth Armitage	1953-55		
Hubert Dalwood	1955-59		
Austin Wright	1961-64		
Neville Boden	1965-68		

The scheme envisaged that Gregory Fellows were to 'make themselves as much as possible part of the life of the University'.[7] The University, in turn, was to facilitate this process in practical terms. Easier said than done. The University was not used to having free-floating artists in its midst and was at first uncertain how to treat them: 'they were regarded as rather strange fish' Dobrée remarked, 'as of course they are in the University; they are meant to be'.[8]

Many academics were at first uneasy that the Fellows were not appointed in the usual way and were not formally attached to, and responsible to, departments. Neither were they clear about exactly how departments were to fulfil the intention that they were to take advantage of the artists' presence in the University. The artists, for their part, had no clear idea what precisely was expected of them, and what they could ask of the University. Both sides were feeling their way.

Over time, most of these problems were resolved in informal ways. With the help of Dobrée, poets soon settled into the Department of English Literature, where there were kindred souls and rooms in which to work. Within four months of his appointment James Kirkup, the first Fellow in Poetry, had, according to a letter from Dobrée to Charles Morris, 'made many contacts within the University and ... encouraged the young writers'.[9] The needs of the Fellows in Painting and Sculpture, however, were not so easily amenable to the normal arrangements for University housekeeping. The sculptor Reg Butler, appointed five months earlier than Kirkup, spent the first two years of his Fellowship in London, waiting for the University to arrange suitable accommodation for him. Try as they might (the written record of the University's efforts is voluminous), they could not earlier find a way to meet the needs of someone who did not work in 'normal materials', and whose activities consequently were likely to be a nuisance to his neighbours, and to reconcile this problem with the requirement of Gregory's scheme that Fellows be placed in the midst of student life.[10] Butler's insistence that he live next to his work sent the University Planning Engineer on endless searches around garages, stables and cycle sheds close enough to possible living quarters, and at one stage reduced him to banging a dustbin lid with an axe outside a women's hall of residence while inside the Warden moved from room to room to test the noise level. Rescue finally came when, due to a slipped disc, Butler was forced to suspend working with anvil and welding rod. His Fellowship was then extended for a further year, during which he produced his prize-winning entry for the International Competition for the *Monument to The Unknown Political Prisoner*.

Maurice de Sausmarez, the first Lecturer in Fine Art in the University, was appointed soon after the Gregory Fellowships were instituted, and, as the Fine Art Department grew and developed under Quentin Bell in the 1960s, it provided a natural link between the Fellows and the rest of the University. John Jones has written a lively

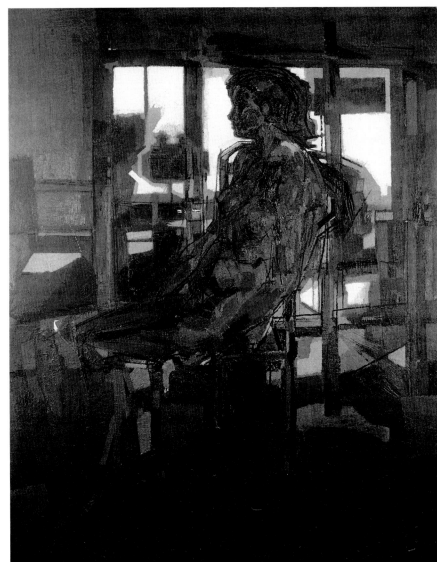

152

153

154

154 Terry Frost *High Yellow* c.1955. Leeds City Art Galleries (cat.no.80)

account of the impact of the Fellows upon the Fine Art Department and its students at that time.[11] Other activities of the Gregory Fellows brought them into contact with wider audiences: they gave talks to a variety of student societies, met students informally in halls of residence and received students from several departments in their studios, exhibited their own work in the central court of the Parkinson Building (the University Gallery had not yet been established), and helped with arrangements for other exhibitions. In some cases they contributed to academic seminars, and occasionally to more formal teaching periods. Hubert Dalwood had a group of

155

eight students practising sculpture in their 'free' time, and all the Fellows encouraged 'amateur' artists in the University. Martin Froy worked with the Theatre Group on decor and design, and both Froy and Dalwood produced articles and illustrative material for the student magazine, *The Gryphon*. Beyond all this, the Fellows were drawn, as Gregory had intended, into many of the University's social networks which were also circles of intellectual interchange, where philosophers and linguists, historians and lawyers, scientists and engineers – men

and women of all the disciplines – prompted and influenced one another.

It is a measure of the success of the scheme that it was thought necessary to call a special meeting of Senate in 1956 to consider its future. Gregory's original arrangement was to finance the scheme for a fixed period of nine years, putting £1,700 at the disposal of the University each year. Recognising the rewarding effects of the Fellowships scheme, not only on the University but on the artistic life of the region, and keen to maintain the inter-

155 Dennis Creffield
Leeds 1965. Leeds City
Art Galleries
(cat.no.51)

156

156 Alan Davie *In the Face of the Witch* 1955. Leeds City Art Galleries (cat.no.60)

national prestige which the University gained as a result of its participation in an imaginative act of patronage, it was resolved that the scheme ought not to be allowed to lapse when the existing funds came to an end in 1958.

It was first proposed to find the funds for the continuation of just one Fellowship after 1958. The Advisory Committee, however, as Gregory reported to the Vice-Chancellor, felt strongly that: 'one Fellow would cut very little ice ... it is the corporate body of three which is such a strong factor'.[12] Gregory was without doubt encouraged by the favourable comments which were issuing from the London art world (Bryan Robertson at the Whitechapel Art Gallery had written of the 'big work' the Fellows were doing in Leeds, and plans were underway for an exhibition of the Gregory Fellows at the ICA), and there was no doubt in his mind – or that of the Committee – that the multiplicity of the Fellowships had to be maintained if the scheme was to continue to exert national as well as local influence. As a result, he offered to fund one of the Fellowships for a further seven years if the University would finance the other two, and the University had already agreed to this when Gregory died on 9 February 1959. In the end, the University continued to fund all three Fellowships from 1959 until the early 1980s.

Gregory's death caused a short hiatus when no Fellows were in post, and when appointments were renewed late in 1960 the pattern of appointing had changed. The Vice-Chancellor was anxious to keep the Committee, and they agreed to continue as an advisory body, but there was a general feeling that the time had come to put the work on a different basis. Until then Gregory, as the presiding

figure, had provided most of the impetus and co-ordination. From that point on, the day-to-day organising fell into the hands of the University, which also played a greater part in selecting candidates. It was inevitable that with this change, the selection of Fellows came to rely more upon applications received, or recommendations made by members of the University. The Professors of Fine Art – Quentin Bell and afterwards Lawrence Gowing – took the lead in selecting Fellows in Painting and Sculpture. By 1967 we find Gowing writing to Read to suggest a Fellow in Painting, and Read, by then near the end of his life, acquiescing almost without comment.

When the basis for government funding of the universities began to change in the 1980s, the Gregory Fellowship Scheme could no longer be supported. It has been resumed in part by the decision of the Henry Moore Foundation in the late 1980s to fund a Gregory Fellow in Sculpture as part of its continuing support for sculpture studies within the University.

How, in retrospect, are we to assess the Gregory Fellowships, and how much of Gregory's original purpose did they achieve? Herbert Read, who in many ways was the co-inspirer of Gregory's experiment and who steered a firm course in its pursuit, was certain of its benefits for the artists involved.

I think they would all admit that they have benefited in a spiritual sense [he wrote], whether as a result of living and working in a community of young people; whether from the stimulus received from a vital and unsophisticated industrial community; or simply from a new and inspiring physical environment – for whatever reason the work of most of the poets, painters, sculptors and musicians who have held the posts has greatly improved, and in two or three cases has been transformed, by the experience.[13]

Nearly all those who were Gregory Fellows during Read's time, the period which concerns us here, are now known not merely in Leeds and London, but in the arts centres of the world. Their achievements are too many and too well known for repetition here.

So much for the Fellows. But what did the University, and particularly its students, gain? A more difficult question. Read rightly asked: 'Can the effect of the presence of a single poet or painter among the milling crowds of medical, engineering, textile, science and arts students be made evident?' His answer, the only one possible, was that he had 'met from time to time men and women whose interest in the arts was first aroused by contact with a Gregory Fellow in Leeds' (as his own interest had been aroused when, as an undergraduate, he had come into contact with Michael Sadler's art collection). He discerned, when visiting the University, 'a new spirit, a new liveliness ... about'. 'The final benefits', he concluded, 'will only be felt in the years to come, when the students of today become in their turn teachers and patrons of the arts'.[14]

The presence and example of the Gregory Fellows in the University was undoubtedly an influence in its decision to include the practical elements of art studies in the permanent staffing and curriculum of the Fine Art Department. Read had long campaigned against the 'entrenched heresy' in modern education which assumed that the arts could not be 'classified and analysed and thus made a fit subject for teaching until they are dead',[15] and Gregory had specifically expressed the hope that de Sausmarez's successor was not to be 'a mere scholar'.[16]

Through the Gregory Fellowships, the movement to bring the practice and critical appreciation of art – Read's 'a little aesthetic leaven'[17] – directly into the universities, begun by Felix Slade at the older universities in the 1860s and encouraged by Michael Sadler and Charles Morris at Leeds, gained substantial strength. Gregory's Fellowships had immediately attracted attention, nationally and internationally. As early as 1949, the Registrar at Oxford requested an account of the scheme from the Registrar at Leeds. It was not long before enquiries and applications were being received from other countries and, in due course, fellowships of a similar sort were set up in other universities.

Some other effects of the Gregory Fellowships were perhaps more diffuse but nonetheless real and discernible. The activities of the Fellows produced in the city and the region, as well as the campus, a buzz of interest in and excitement about modern art. They stimulated local enlightened patronage, and contributed a legacy of outstanding public and private collections. 'Taken altogether', Herbert Read judged, it was 'a manifestation of the creative spirit as encouraging as any that could be made in this country at the present time'.[18]

An experiment – with most of its potentialities realised.

158

Notes

1 Eric Gregory, known to his friends as 'Peter', was born in Scotland, but lived most of his life in Yorkshire. The choice of Leeds as the locus of the Fellowships was but one of many expressions of his attachment to the region. Unless otherwise indicated, information and quotations on the Gregory Fellowships are from letters and papers in the University of Leeds archives.

2 Read, Herbert (1964) introduction to the exhibition catalogue *The Gregory Fellows* (London, Arts Council).

3 Senate Minutes, 30 June 1943, 2909 (iii) 1.

4 The Fellows were not extravagantly paid. In the 1950s, they each received an emolument of between £400 and £600 a year from the Gregory fund (rising to around £1,050 by the mid-1960s). In some instances the Fellows were assisted with the payment of rates, or a proportion of rents, as well as removal to Leeds and other incidental expenses. Some of the Fellows in Painting and Sculpture were able to supplement their income by teaching at the Leeds College of Art for one or two half-days per week, and the University from time to time provided additional money for part-time lecturing.

5 Gregory Fellowships Committee Minutes, 9 Nov 1949, 4(i).

6 Read to Dobrée, 17 Dec 1949.

7 Senate Minutes, 30 June 1943, 2909 (iii) 7.

8 Dobrée, paper on the Gregory Fellowships, for a special meeting of the Senate, 29 Feb 1956.

9 Dobrée to Morris, 2 March 1951.

10 Morris to Gregory, 22 May 1952.

11 Jones, John (1986) 'The Gregory Fellowships in Painting and Sculpture', *The New Spirit – Patrons, Artists and the University of Leeds in the twentieth century*, exhibition catalogue (Leeds, University Gallery) pp.5-6.

12 Gregory to Morris, 20 Sep 1957.

13 Read, Herbert (1960) introduction to the catalogue of the *Gregory Memorial Exhibition* (Leeds City Art Gallery) (pp.5-7) p.6.

14 Read (n.2).

15 Read (n.13) p.6.

16 Morris, memorandum, 22 Dec 1958.

17 Read (n.13) p.6.

18 *Ibid.* p.7.

157

159

159 Patrick Heron
Portrait of Herbert Read
1950. National Portrait
Gallery, London
(cat.no.112)

BR : *Could we start by talking about the nature of the art criticism? It seems to me my father had obviously an amazing power with the use of words, which ties up with the poetry and his writing, but the accusation sometimes made against him is that with art he always, so to speak, philosophises rather than gives a detailed response, and therefore he never really looked at things and responded.*

PH : I actually reviewed *The Philosophy of Modern Art* in the *New Statesman*, and I said I did rather subscribe to the notion that Herbert had consciously swerved away from making, as it were, verbal evocation of visual realities his thing, because Roger Fry who preceded him had done that very, very well, and that Herbert therefore extended his activity into very great philosophical, not to say psychological domains, and in fact I called him the Philosopher of Modern Art, 'gave Modern Art its scientific credentials' was the phrase I used.

But when I picked up that first edition I read as a schoolboy in 1933, of *Art Now*, when I gave that little talk at Canterbury, I wanted to see if I was right about this, why somebody whose tastes were so extraordinarily sensitive, I wanted to confound that line of argument myself, so I thought, let's see what he says about Matisse, and it was absolutely fabulous actually. What is very extraordinary about Herbert is that he saw what so much was about, after all his contemporaries were furious, the Constructivists were furious because he saw the point of Surrealism and vice versa. Nobody was more didactic and merciless towards the enemy than Gabo. When I used to go and see Gabo in Carbis Bay during the war, Picasso really was the devil incarnate and Dali ditto, he loathed them both.

But to go back to Herbert's language, I actually think that he's got one of the purest prose styles on record anywhere. I think it's not surprising when you read one of the books that I immensely admire, *English Prose Style*, there is a very great purity in Herbert's use of the English language, it is absolutely spare, accurate, critical, poetic; it's both poetic and scientific, absolutely equal in terms of chemistry on both sides, don't you think so?

BR : *There is obviously something inherent ; before he went to the Victoria and Albert Museum he was employed in the Treasury and was chosen to write the minutes of very complicated meetings, because he had this clarity and precision of language, and I don't think he learnt it from reading, he must have just had it, somehow naturally.*

PH : Well, I think Yorkshire is a great centre of the English language, look at the Brontës, and my own parents, their feel for the language was very remarkable, and all their friends.

BR : *What do you think was so significant about his writing and his philosophy of Art?*

PH : Well it is partly the fact that he was the first person to write about so many of these people in English. If you asked Braque or Picasso, 'who was their supporter in England?', there would only be one person they would tell you of, apart from personal friendships like Roland [Penrose] with Picasso. The whole of the School of Paris would have said the same.

I still think that the point that I was making all those years ago, that he gave modern art its scientific credentials, is quite a valid one in a way, because he discussed things in ways in which someone like myself was totally

160

incompetent. He was profoundly acquainted with all kinds of areas of thought, from psychoanalysis to the history of art, in many many phases. Look what he has written about ceramics.

I'm sure that Herbert thought too the art of children, you know it's not just an educationalist's fad or fantasy that it is very beautiful, it is very beautiful, it's as beautiful as a natural object, they can't make a mistake, children cannot make a mistake, it works, pictorially, in every way, it works, it's fabulous. Matisse said he spent all his life trying to paint like a child, that is simply a statement of the truth. So there again, Herbert's interest in children's art. There is a genuine openness of his sensibility.

BR : *And it is almost a poetic response going on, rather than a hard line, linguistic philosophy.*
PH : At no point did Herbert pursue a policy, and therefore at no point did he in fact advance himself or his position, in fact the opposite, because as soon as there was one group going 'Ah, Hail Herbert Read', they would suddenly find he had written an eloquent piece about something completely different. His range was so very considerable, I think he had this difficulty in the literary world too, don't you, because at one moment he is writing the best things about Wordsworth ...
BR : *And he wrote the very early article on psychoanalysis, which didn't go down very well.*

160 Patrick Heron *Still Life* 1947. Private collection* (cat.no.110)

PH: Oh no, at every turn he was asking for trouble, from the established gang so to speak, but what none of them could deny or stomach was that he floated high above them all in international esteem and fame, purely and simply, to put it crudely, amazing!

I'll tell you a story about his international renown – at the old Unesco House in the Avenue Wagram, there was this international conference, the second ever get-together of the recently founded International Association of Art Critics. This was 1949, and I was in Paris with Delia, and had been for ten days, and we were both coming home, and Lilian Somerville heard about this and sent me a telegram or something, to say if I would stay an extra week and represent us, I suppose the country or something, at this conference, she would pay for my expenses for staying another week. She said go and look up our new representative, Frank McEwan whom I have established in a little office in the Champs Elysées, because he is doing a great job, and he of course knew all the great artists on Christian name terms, he just picked up his phone and got through to Braque, and made a date for me to see him. So Lilian, once again, was doing brilliantly.

So anyway, I went to this conference, and I think there can't have been more than three or four English people there. One was Benedict Nicholson who seemed to be playing noughts and crosses all the time, and there was me, and there was Eric Newton, unfortunately, who was the National Chairman and therefore one of the Co-Chairmen, and there was Fierens from Belgium who was the president of the whole caboosh that year, and there must have been about five hundred French critics, quite a lot from other countries, but we were a minute particle. Fierens suddenly said: 'And now I would like to ask you all to think of any names of critics who are not yet members, or who are not here, that you would recommend that we should invite to become members of the International Association', and names were handed in, and they were very strong, and results were put up on a huge blackboard at the head of the room, behind the President's head, which in my memory was a blackboard about ten feet high, and when the results came out the names were up or down, according to the number of votes they had got, and right at the very top was Herbert Read, and there was nothing, completely ten feet of blank blackboard until you got to the bottom eighteen inches where there were about 250-300 names. It's an astonishing image. That was his eminence internationally then.

BR: *You were mentioning earlier how you thought that the Kenneth Clark people somehow had it in for Herbert.*
PH: Oh yes, well all I can tell you is that Coldstream on some occasion, standing next to me on some public occasion, suddenly said to me 'Oh Herbert Read, of course the trouble with Herbert is he hasn't got a trained mind you know, didn't go to Oxford' and I realised I was in the presence of the received opinion inside the Clark pyramid. I mean if you consider that there were two pyramids internally in the English art world, and Clark was at the apex of one and Herbert was at the apex of the other, and certain canny souls like Sutherland and Henry managed to get on equally well with both of them.

BR: *Why do you think that somebody like Ben liked him so much, because he obviously did?*
PH: Of course you have got to realise, Ben was profoundly egotistical, wildly so, and quite unkind, though never to me. Ben was very nice to me. I met Ben in the Leach pottery when I was a hired hand for Bernard, and nobody thought I was going to be a potter, least of all me [though] I can throw very expertly. I was helping out because the place was being run by three conscientious objectors, and Bernard was helping me out, because I had been in a chain-gang digging drainage ditches, and had to find because of medical reasons some other acceptable thing for Ministry of Wartime service. So I went to Bernard's, so I had this fascinating thing, that I met Ben, Barbara and Gabo, and Adrian Stokes as a matter of fact. One very funny thing happened many years later, I happened in one week to bump into both Herbert and Adrian in London in the open, and the subject turned to the other in each case, and each said exactly the same thing in effect about the other. Herbert looked at the sky – I was standing on the curb outside Broadcasting House – and said, 'I have very great admiration for Adrian, he is extremely intelligent, but I can't help feeling there is something fundamentally confused and obscure at the heart of it', or something like that. And lo and behold, Adrian I met at a gallery and somehow the subject went round to Herbert, and he said, 'Of course Herbert is a wonderful man, and has done an immense amount for us all, and I am terribly attached to him, but I think his ideas are slightly confused'. Wasn't that amazing! exactly the same thing.

BR: *I suppose when they were all living cheek by jowl in Hampstead, there was a very close feeling of comradeship?*
PH: They were a movement in the making, and Herbert was the mild man, an amazingly indispensable ambassador of them all to the outside world. I've often thought that. When did that first Henry Moore book by Herbert come out? Three Yorkshiremen, the publisher, the artist and the critic, an amazing production really, I mean infinitely superior in every conceivable way to anything that had ever emerged from France by that time, let alone America. I don't think that there was such a thing as a hardback on Braque, Matisse or Picasso, no, there was this little Matisse one of 1939, but they weren't in the habit of producing volumes of that sort, so I have always thought Herbert in that book alone created Henry Moore. It wasn't Sir Kenneth Clark who created Henry Moore by sending him around the country with Piper and Sutherland in a little CEMA exhibition, that's all very well, but reputations are created outside, in the great outside world, and that book by Lund Humphries, by your father, on first Henry and then Ben went into the museum libraries of the world just as the war ended, you know, so when later they saw the sculpture, they knew what it

161

was all about. That's why Greenberg has hated your father so much, because your father was an infinitely more successful promoter.

BR: *We've coined in Leeds, over the last few years, the term 'The Yorkshire Mafia', which I think encompasses my father, Eric (or Peter to his friends) Gregory, Barbara and Henry, and of course you.*

PH: Well, I'm rather later on, but I can tell you a very funny thing, Victor Pasmore, who is quite a lot older than me, was responsible for keeping myself, Roger Hilton, Peter Lanyon and one or two others out of the London Group, which we all decided to send something into, so Victor chucked them all out, and when I subsequently became friends with him because I'd written a whole page in defence of his first venture into abstraction in the *New Statesman* (may I say that Coldstream who I was never on unfriendly terms with, nevertheless wrote me a little letter saying 'I must just thank you, for coming to the aid of my friend in his hour of need' – wasn't that amazing?) anyway, so when I became friendly with Victor, much later, somehow or other I remember him using this, saying 'Of course, we had a hell of a job getting going, the Yorkshire Brigade wherever you looked …'. 'The Yorkshire Brigade', he said, 'It's always them blocking it off'. I said 'It's bloody funny you should say that, because our lot always refer to the Coldstream Guards blocking us off, if you really want to know'.

BR: *Did you go to the ICA a lot?*

PH: I did quite a bit, but more to join in discussion, I never exhibited there, I thought that was rather in the hands of some kind of clique, which certainly included Paolozzi who never ceased to exhibit there (I don't know who was responsible for that).

BR: *They have started writing up the so called Independent Group at the ICA, whom Dorothy Morland encouraged.*

PH: When they appointed Lawrence, I remember Peter Gregory asking me what I thought of Lawrence Alloway, because he is the arch enemy of me and of all our generation, but in spite of that I said that I thought he would be rather good, not that Lawrence Alloway would ever know that.

BR: *But he was obviously a sort of key figure, then seems to have disappeared.*

PH: Yes, he did in fact do fantastic and lasting damage to my generation. We were really pushed right under the carpet for twenty years, and we are really only emerging now. The British Council did do things for us, we were sent to biennales and so on, but the Arts Council, my god, and then the Tate actually, have never done anything for any of us, perhaps they are going to change.

BR: *They have got a lot of ground to make up. We are getting an enormous Sam Francis from Stuttgart – we used to have a lovely small one at Stonegrave.*

PH: Well, it was Herbert who introduced me to the painting of Sam Francis, it must have been in 1952, because Herbert had just come back from Paris, and he said there is a chap whose painting I think you ought to see, extremely interesting, he's called Sam Francis, and I've just been visiting him in Paris. And when in January 1953 the ICA put on an exhibition called *Opposing Forces* it consisted of the first Jackson Pollock ever to be seen on this side of the Atlantic, and it was a big one, plus three little bits of paper about Pollock, with black oily paint blobbed onto them so that the oil made a yellow ring around them, which Alan Davie liked very much. That big painting was at the head of the old room at the ICA, and these were just around the corner, on your way to the bar, but the rest of the show was all from Paris, so it was painters like Serpan, Michaux and Sam Francis. The point is, Sam began his professional life in Paris you see, and for this reason he was ostracised by official America. For years he never appeared in official American shows abroad, of course he's San Francisco.

Mrs Thatcher was with me and Tony Caro at the Tate, looking at the big Sam Francis through the plate glass while we were all having drinks, Tony said 'That's by Sam Francis', and I said 'Yes, born in San Francisco, which they'll ultimately rename Sam Francisco, in his honour'. She was furious, she said 'All this will have to go', pointing to the entire contents in the sculpture hall. 'All this, you have got this entirely wrong!', she gave a Hitler salute when she said 'Now you have got this great space here, this fantastic voluminous great height, you want to get something that goes from top to bottom, and if you haven't got it you should commission it!', she gave the Hitler salute nine times in four seconds. I recorded all this in the *Guardian* (but omitting the raised arm detail!) which I expect she didn't like either. I said I presume she had something like the Victor Emmanuel monument in mind, she condemned the entire lot.

It was Herbert who saw the point of Sam Francis, so that when I saw them I was very impressed with them, in fact I have often said that the only influence really that I admit to from the other side of the Atlantic was the Sam Francis, both Sam Francises did have an effect on me, and I've always recorded that, even in writing.

BR: *We have been very keen to include in the exhibition a number of the less widely known artists he wrote about, because it seems to me that he was prepared to champion art of all sorts and at all levels.*

PH: Are you including the Jacob Kramer etchings, from the passage?

BR: *No, but we are trying to get a wonderful Kramer which I've never seen, it's called* Improvisation to Music, *I think it is about 1920.*

PH: That would have been after Kandinsky's visit.

BR: *He actually went to Leeds?*

PH: My father [Tom Heron, member of the Leeds Arts Club] always said he did, and explained his colour organ.

He went because, with Michael Sadler, Leeds was the headquarters you know in those days.

BR: *That's what we are trying to show, we've got an article commissioned from somebody to write about it.*

Coming back to my father, when he bought those two paintings, the two still lives of yours, did he come into the gallery, see them, and say 'I must have them'?

PH: Well, funnily enough, one of them I gave to him. (Piers obviously thought that he'd bought them both, and I never mentioned it). But the one over the fireplace, he bought at the Redfern at my 1950 show which is also the show which had the portraits of himself and of Eliot.

BR: *So did he choose the one that you gave him?*

PH: Oh yes. You see, at Addison Avenue, one evening I suddenly surprised him very much by saying 'Let's get down to business'. Herbert said 'What business?' I said 'I want to give you a picture – for coming all the way to Wakefield.' So he chose it, there and then, we went up into the studio/bedroom and he very nearly chose another one which I've still got, but I'm glad he chose that one: it's much bigger and much better too. I gave it to him some months after he had been to Wakefield to open an exhibition of mine; it was a long speech, a most astonishing speech, I don't know where the text of it is. It was marvellous, and a lot of my 1951 paintings were purely linear, out of the tube, and his opening remark was a pun, he said 'Patrick Heron may be said in the last eighteen months to have developed a line of his own', looking sideways over the top of his glasses.

As for the portrait of your father, the moment he saw it (I painted it in thirty minutes you know in his absence) and he came to look at it, and he walked right across the room, and he was immediately very excited. He said 'I'll try to get the British Council to buy this, they ought to have it', he said with a smile. And so they did, they bought it at the show.

But now, when he died and they enquired about it, where was it, I said it's at the British Council. Now, the British Council had a rule that they couldn't sell art in their collection, but Lilian managed to get that waived on this occasion, to everybody's agreement, and Henry and Barbara subscribed and bought it from the Council, I don't know what for, and they presented it to the National Portrait Gallery.

Well, I've described as it were the blackboard voting position in 1949, which revealed that, statistically, he was about 5000% more celebrated in the international world of art, than anybody writing about art in the English language. Art of any kind actually, not just modern art, he had a tremendous reputation, how many languages have his books been translated into, scores? What's wrong with the bloody English? Why can't they understand, that's what has really got me, somehow this centenary has got to start to ram this home hasn't it?

Transcript of an interview conducted in August 1993.

162

With what purpose does this artist paint? It will satisfy no-one to say that he is trying to touch the intangible, see the invisible, grasp the Encompassing. But that ... is his highly original aim ... He is highly conscious of the incompleteness of man's vision and consciousness, and he seems to be striving to grasp just this – another dimension of awareness.

A Letter to a Young Painter, p.118

Herbert Read 1893-1968
The Turbulent Years of 'The Pope of Modern Art'

A Chronology and Select Bibliography compiled by Terry Friedman and David Thistlewood

163

163 Muscoates Grange c.1900

Historical material has been drawn from: Clapp, J. (1972) *Art Censorship A Chronology of Proscribed and Prescribed Art*; Lucie-Smith, E. (1979) *Cultural Calendar of the 20th Century*; Mercer, D. (Ed) (1988) *Chronicle of the 20th Century*; and Remy, M. (1986) 'British Surrealism: A Chronology' in: *Angels of Anarchy and Machines for Making Clouds: Surrealism in Britain in the Thirties* (Leeds City Art Galleries) pp.189-99. Material devoted to Read himself has been gathered chiefly from (1975) *A Tribute to Herbert Read 1893-1968* (The Manor House, Ilkley) – including Read, B. 'Herbert Read: His Life and Work', pp.7-15; 'Catalogue' pp.16-30; and Parrington-Jackson, R. 'Herbert Read The Yorkshire Background', pp.74-5; King, J. (1990) *The Last Modern: A Life of Herbert Read*; and Thistlewood, D. (1984) *Herbert Read: Formlessness and Form: An Introduction to his Aesthetics*. Additional material has been taken from Mitchinson, D. (1968) *70 Years of Henry Moore* (Rijksmuseum Kröller-Müller, Otterlo); Hepworth, B. (1970) *Barbara Hepworth: A Pictorial Autobiography*; and Lewison, J. (1983) *Ben Nicholson: the Years of Experiment 1919-39* (Cambridge, Kettle's Yard Gallery).

The selected bibliographic listings have been compiled from: Skelton, Robin (Ed) (1970) *Herbert Read: a memorial symposium* (London, Methuen); Annual volumes of *The Art Index* (Wilson Publishing Co); Ghanem, Salma Mohammed (1963) *The literary criticism of Sir Herbert Read* (unpublished PhD, University of Liverpool); and private bibliographic records compiled by Clive Philpott, Director of the Library of the Museum of Modern Art, New York, and David Thistlewood.

1893

■ Herbert Read (henceforth HR) is born on 4 December at Muscoates Grange, a farm near Kirkby Moorside in the Vale of Pickering, North Riding of Yorkshire, the eldest of four children of Herbert Edward Read and Eliza Strickland Read. The Read family had been linked to the area as farmers at least since 1725.

1901

Death of Queen Victoria (22 January). Whitechapel Art Gallery, London opens (12 March).

■ HR and his brother William (born 1895) are admitted to Nunnington School, North Yorkshire (26 April): 'These boys … have never been to school before and just know their letters'.

1902

Boer War (begun 1899) ends (31 May). Edward VII crowned (9 August).

■ Death of HR's sister Mariana (born 1900).

1903

Death of Paul Gauguin (8 May). Leeds School of Art (by Bedford and Kitson), city's first 'modernist' building.

■ HR's father dies (3 February) from a fall from a horse. Eliza Read, now penniless, moves from Muscoates Grange to Kirkby Moorside. HR and William are sent to the Crossley and Porter Orphan Home and School at Halifax, West Riding of Yorkshire; here HR reads avidly (Sir Walter Scott and Rider Haggard) and begins writing stories (1903-8).

1908

Rise of Cubism in Paris (Braque, Gris, Léger, Picasso). Roger Fry defends Paul Cézanne in *Burlington Magazine*. Die Brücke founded 1905 (Heckel, Kirchner, Nolde, Schmidt-Rottluff); exhibits in Dresden (September). Frank Rutter, editor of *Art News* and *Sunday Times* art critic, founds Allied Artists Association (AAA): artists' utopian 'trade union'.

164

■ HR wins second class honours in the Cambridge Junior Certificate and is awarded a Second Class Certificate from Crossley's School (December). He joins his mother, now living in Leeds, where she works as a laundry manageress at Weetwood Grange, then as a matron at St Anne's Hill Hostel in Headingley. HR attends evening school, studying English Literature, French, German, History, Latin, Maths and Science. He soon joins the local branch of the Conservative Party and the local Territorial Unit of the Royal Army Medical Corps.

1909

F.T. Marinetti, 'The Foundation and Manifesto of Futurism', in *Le Figaro*, Paris (20 February): 'a speeding automobile is more beautiful than the Victory of Samothrace'. Victoria and Albert Museum, London, opens (26 June) (formerly the South Kensington Museum).

■ HR obtains a job as clerk with the Leeds, Skyrack & Morley Trustee Savings Bank in Leeds (22 January) at an annual salary of £20.

1910

Der Sturm (The Assault) magazine and art gallery founded in Berlin (until 1924) to publicise Expressionism. Rutter *Revolution in Modern Art*. Fry's *Manet and the Post-Impressionists* exhibition, Grafton Galleries, London. Henri Matisse *The Dance* (second version).

■ Eliza Read rents a house for HR, William and Charles (born 1897) at 24 Delph Lane, near Leeds University.

1911

Kaiser Wilhelm II proclaims Impressionists and Van Gogh 'too depraved for the Prussians'. Der Blaue Reiter (The Blue Rider) founded in Munich (until 1914) and hold first exhibition (Kandinsky, Marc, Macke, Klee). Camden Town Group formed in London (Gilman, Gore, Augustus John, Lamb, Lewis, Lucien Pissarro, Rutter, Sickert). Edward Carpenter *Non-Governmental Society* a decisive influence on HR's political thought.

■ Through his brother William, HR meets William Prior Read (no relation), a Leeds tailor, who unofficially 'adopts' him: 'It is his kindness that has balanced the sadness of our early life, and, I believe, saved me from a bitter heart, and so earthly damnation'. Read introduces HR to the works of Browning, Chekhov, Dostoevsky, Ibsen, Tennyson, Turgenev, Yeats and, above all, William Blake. HR matriculates with a second division pass, assuring entrance to a university.

1912

Titanic sinks in North Atlantic (15 April). Fry's second *Post-Impressionist* exhibition in London. Italian Futurist Painters exhibition in Paris and London (Balla, Boccioni, Carra, Severini). Marcel Duchamp *Nude Descending a Staircase No.2*. Rutter appointed Curator of Leeds City Art Gallery.

■ HR enrols at Leeds University (September), studying English and French Literature, Law, Political Economy, Social Economics, European History and Geology; in Arthur Greenwood's class he is introduced to the writings of Marx and the anarchist philosophers Bakunin and Kropotkin. He joins the Leeds Arts Club (or 'Platonic Lodge'), founded in 1903 by A.R.Orage and which in 1912 is run by Rutter as a platform

165

for advanced ideas in art and literature: for instance, in 1914 Wyndham Lewis lectured on 'Cubism and Futurism'. HR is writing poetry, completes two plays in Yorkshire dialect and publishes a letter referring to a controversy over spelling in *The New Age*, a weekly periodical edited by Orage and published in London, to which Arnold Bennett, G.K. Chesterton, Thomas Ernest Hulme, Ezra Pound and Bernard Shaw are contributors.

The Read family move to 7 Buckingham Mount, near the home of Michael Sadler (Buckingham House, Headingley Lane). Sadler, a pioneer collector of Cézanne, Gauguin (including *The Vision after the Sermon*, 1888), Paul Klee and Van Gogh, as well as Augustus John, William Nicholson and Puvis de Chavannes, was appointed Vice-Chancellor of Leeds University in October 1911 (until 1923). Michael Sadler Jr has purchased woodcuts by Wassily Kandinsky at the AAA exhibition in London in 1911; in the following year father and son visit the painter in Bavaria and in 1913 Sadler Sr acquires *Composition VII*. HR gains access to the collection through the housekeeper, a close friend of his mother. He also meets Jacob Kramer (who had emigrated from the Ukraine to Leeds in 1900), the first artist he ever knew personally. Though confirmed at the wealthy suburban church of St Michael, Headingley, HR loses his religious faith: 'the first year at the university, and the open access to the very fount of heresy [leads him to a] state of unbelief'.

1913

International Exhibition of Modern Art (Armory Show), New York (opens 17 February). Igor Stravinsky, *The Rite of Spring* ballet premiered in Paris causes riot (29 May). Richard Aldington becomes editor of *The Egoist*. Camden Town Group merges with Lewis to form London Group (Epstein, Fry, Gill, Paul Nash, Nevinson, Wadsworth). Omega Workshop founded by Fry in London (Vanessa Bell, Grant). Henri Alain-Fournier, *Le Grand Meaulnes* (author killed in action in 1914). Umberto Boccioni *Unique Forms of Continuity in Space*. David Bomberg, *The Mud Bath*.

    Stanley Cursiter *Princes Street, Edinburgh*.

■ HR publishes an essay on Francis Thompson, praising the poet's 'genius-endowing Poverty' as 'veritably god-like and life-giving', in the Leeds University students' magazine *The Gryphon*.

1914

Suffragette slashes Velasquez's *Rokeby Venus* in National Gallery, London (10 March). 140,000 Yorkshire miners strike for minimum wage (from 30 March). First issue of *BLAST*, edited by Lewis (20 June), launches Vorticist movement. Archduke Franz Ferdinand and Duchess assassinated at Sarajevo (28 June). Britain declares war on Germany (4 August): The Great War. August Macke, German Expressionist, killed in action (26 September). *Twentieth Century Art: A Review of Modern Movements* exhibition, Whitechapel Art Gallery, London. Kandinsky's *Über das Geistige in der Kunst* (1912) published in English, translation by Michael Sadler Jr as *Concerning the Spiritual in Art*.

■ HR passes the LL.B (Law) Intermediate examination (Summer) and due to the call-up is granted a degree without taking his finals. He meets Evelyn Roff, a native of Bradford and fellow university student. Applies for a commission in the Territorial Force (11 August). Eliza Read dies in Leeds (9 December).

    Jacob Kramer *Portrait of Herbert Read*.

'The apotheosis of poverty', *The Gryphon*, no.XVII, p.89. 'August Strindberg', no.XVIII, p.5

1915

Ypres offensives (April). Death of Rupert Brooke (23 April). Henri Gaudier-Brzeska killed in action (5 June). *BLAST War Number* (July). Nurse Edith Cavell, shot by Germans on spy charge (12 October) 'Patriotism is not enough. I must have no hatred or bitterness towards anyone'. Gallipoli Evacuation (19 December), Michael Sadler lecture 'Premonitions of the War in Modern Art' delivered in Leeds (26 October). Ford Madox Ford *The Good Soldier*. Epstein dismantles *Rock Drill* (begun 1913) and decapitates torso. Duchamp begins *The Bride Stripped Bare by Her Bachelors, Even*.

■ HR, supported by Sadler Sr, is commissioned as a Second Lieutenant in the Green Howards (6 January) and posted to Wareham in Dorset. Passing through London he arranges for the publication of his first book *Songs of Chaos* (Elkin Mathews, London), a volume of poems with an epigraph from Friedrich Nietzsche, dedicated to W. P. Read: 250 copies are published at HR's own expense, of which only 22 are sold. 'Essays in Imagism' prefixed with extracts from the *Affirmations of Ezra Pound*, is published in *The Gryphon* (November). HR confronts the 'primitive filth, lice, boredom and death' of the Ypres Salient (recounted in *War Diaries*, 1962).

Songs of Chaos (London, Elkin Mathews)
'Essays in Imagism', *The Gryphon*, no.XIX, p.5

1916

Battle of Verdun (21 February–16 December). Death of Henry James (28 February), which HR learns about in the trenches. Easter Uprising, Dublin (25 April–11 May). Battle of the Somme (1 July–8 November). Pound *Gaudier-Brzeska A Memoir*. Dada group, in violent revolt against smugness, formed in Zurich (Arp, Tzara, Duchamp, Picabia, Ray from 1918).

    Harold Gilman *Factories and Barges*.

■ HR is wounded on the battlefield and invalided to England (February). The poem 'Ypres' appears in *The Gryphon*. Rutter introduces him to Robert P. Bevan, Gilman and Charles Ginner. He has taken to drawing and painting by this time and contemplates studying art in London and Paris rather than returning to university after the war. During the next few years he reads the Brontës, Ford, Hardy, Hudson, James, D. H. Lawrence, Lewis, Marx, Morris, Pound, Plato, Wells.

'Sorel, Marx and the war', *The New Age*, vol.XIX, pp.128-9

1917

Czar Nicholas II of Russia abdicates (16 March). United States declares war on Germany (6 April). October Revolution in Russia. T. E. Hulme killed in action. Death of Rodin (17 November). Thomas Stearns Eliot *Prufrock and Other Observations* (which HR reads). Carl G. Jung *The Psychology of the Unconscious*. *De Stijl (The Style)* periodical launched in Holland, with concurrent Modernist movement in painting and architecture (Mondrian, Oud, Rietveld, van der Leck, van Doesburg, Vantongerloo). Tony Garnier *Cité Industrielle*, utopian Modernist architecture, Charles Ginner 'Modern Painting and Teaching', *Art and Letters*, no.1.

■ HR is transferred to the 7th Yorkshire Regiment at Brocton Camp, Staffordshire (January), where he defends socialism against imperialism at a public debate. Returning to France he subsequently joins the 10th Yorkshire Regiment (April), reads Bertrand Russell's *Principles of Social Reconstruction* and in the trenches draws *The Road to Polygonveld*. Some 'weird drawings' are sent to the AAA exhibition at the Grafton Gallery, London, where some are sold (June). With Rutter (who had recently been dismissed as Curator of Leeds City Art Gallery over a disagreement with the city fathers and is now working at the Admiralty) HR founds the journal *Art and Letters* (Autumn until 1920). On returning from Buckingham Palace to receive the Military Cross (for conducting a raid and capturing a German officer), HR is introduced at Monico's Restaurant, Piccadilly Circus, to Eliot, leading to the poet agreeing to contribute to *Art and Letters*.

'The world and the guild idea (I): The natural basis', *The Guildsman*, no.5, Apr, p.6. '(II): The future peace', no.6, May, p.4 Review of Joyce, J. *A Portrait of the Artist as a Young Man, Art and Letters*, vol.I, pp.26, 28, 30

1918

Russian Ex-Czar and family executed (16 July). Wilfred Owen killed in action (4 November). Armistice (11 November): Great War ends, 10 million dead.

    Kasimir Malevich *Suprematist White Square on a White Background*. Oswald Spengler *The Decline of the West*. Paul Nash *We Are Making a New World* (1917) shown in *The Void of War* exhibition, Leicester Galleries, London.

    Wyndham Lewis *Great War Drawing No.2*.

THE ROAD TO POLYGONVELD

166

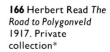
ber). Bauhaus established at Weimar, Germany to teach Modernist design and industrial techniques (Bayer, Breuer, Feininger, Gropius, Kandinsky, Klee). Robert Wiene's Expressionist film *The Cabinet of Doctor Caligari*. Seven and Five Society (7 painters, 5 sculptors) formed in London as foil to 'Bloomsbury'.

Edward Wadsworth *Roofs*.

■ HR leaves the army and enters the Civil Service (January) on the advice of Arthur Greenwood (former economics lecturer at Leeds University who is now Secretary to the Minister of Reconstruction). He gets a job in the Ministry of Labour, Trade Board division (February) and, showing an aptitude for drafting succinct minutes, takes part in the negotiations for the establishment of the Whitley Council, then transfers to the Treasury (August). Arnold Bennett notes HR as 'a very young poet' at a dinner party at Osbert Sitwell's in London, also attended by Aldous Huxley, Siegfried Sassoon, Lytton Strachey and Virginia Woolf (June). HR sells catalogues, answers enquiries and attempts to quiet protests at the Sitwell brothers' exhibition of work by Archipenko, Derain, Dufy, Matisse, Modigliani, Soutine, Utrillo, Vlaminck and Zadkine at Heal's Mansart Gallery, Tottenham Court Road, London. HR marries Evelyn Roff at the Register Office, North Brierley, Yorkshire (7 August); they set up house at 35 Beaumont Road, Purley, Croydon. *Eclogues: A book of Poems* dedicated to her, is illustrated by Ethelbert White.

About this time HR purchases his first original work of art, a Vorticist print by Edward Wadsworth.

Eclogues. A book of poems (London, C. W. Beaumont)
Naked Warriors (London, Art & Letters)
'Bomberg', *Arts Gazette*, 13 Sep, pp.391-2
'La jeune littérature Anglaise: I – Observations Préliminaires', *L'Art Libre*, no.14, p.154. 'II – Nos journaux', no.16, pp.180-1. 'III – Les Imagistes', no.18, pp.203-4

1920

'La jeune littérature Anglaise: IV – Les Vorticistes', *L'Art Libre*, no.1, pp.4-5. 'V – T. S. Eliot', no.3, pp.31-2. 'VI – James Joyce', no.5, pp.54-6. 'VII – Conclusions', no.7, pp.78-9
'Lay criticism', *Athenaeum*, 13 Aug, pp.199-201

1921

Lewis *Mr Wyndham Lewis as a Tyro*.

■ HR becomes private secretary to the Controller of Establishments (January); dissatisfied with the Civil Service, he contemplates returning to Yorkshire to write but is dissuaded by Ford. Orage is persuaded to allow him to edit Hulme's papers (May) and he also takes over the former's 'Readers and Writers' column in *The New Age* (July–December). Pound describes HR as 'too bloody dull' in the *Little Review*.

'Readers and Writers': weekly column in *The New Age*, vol.XXIX, Jun–Dec, commencing no.11, 14 July, esp. review of Croce, B. *Ariosto, Shakespeare and Corneille*, vol.XXIX, no.15, 11 Aug, pp.176-7; review of Russell, B. *The Analysis of Mind*, vol.XXIX, no.18, 1 Sep, pp.211-12. Series ends vol.XXX, no.9, 29 Dec, p.103

1922

British Broadcasting Company [Corporation] (BBC) established in London (18 October). Fascist march on Rome (30 October). Carter discovers Tutenkhamen's tomb in Valley of Kings (5 November). Russian manifesto *Artists of the Revolution*

■ HR (carrying the 1916 Everyman edition of Thoreau's *Walden* in his pocket) survives the retreat from St Quentin at the Second Battle of the Somme (21-28 March); for leading the retreat he is awarded the Distinguished Service Order. Sent back to England, he is rejected by the medical board for transfer to the Flying Corps (June–July). HR's younger brother Charles is killed at Beaurevoir (5 October) and is mourned in the poem *Auguries of Life and Death* (1918). HR arrives in London (24 October), living briefly in rooms in Half Moon Street near Piccadilly, then at 24-9 Nottingham Terrace, Marylebone. Rutter introduces him to Osbert and Sacheverall Sitwell at the Café Royal (26 October) and on the same day he meets Pound and Lewis (writing to Evelyn Roff on 30 October that 'Lewis and Eliot are by far the most important figures. They have strength'). Lewis makes drawings to illustrate HR's collection of war poems *Naked Warriors* but only that for the cover is used because the publisher refuses to pay the artist the minimum fee of £10. In October he also becomes 'very pally' with the poet Richard Aldington, is taken up by Ginner and at Redcar, North Yorkshire is introduced to Ford Madox Ford.

'Definitions towards a modern theory of poetry', *Art and Letters*, vol.I, no.3, Jan, pp.73-8
'An approach to Jules Romains', *Art and Letters*, vol.II, pp.44-52. 'A neglected aspect of Edgar Allan Poe', pp.137-41

1919

Ernest Rutherford splits the atom in Manchester (3 January). League of Nations established to prevent war (14 February). Mussolini founds Fascia di Combattimento (Fascists) in Italy (23 March). Hitler founds National Socialist German Workers (Nazi) Party. Treaty of Versailles (28 June). Matisse, Derain and other modern French painters exhibit in London (6 Decem-

perpetuates 'the greatest event in history' through pictorial representations of workers and peasants; reported 33 million Russians near starvation. James Joyce *Ulysses*. Eliot *The Waste Land*.

■ HR is transferred by the Civil Service from the Treasury to a curatorial post in the Department of Ceramics at the Victoria and Albert Museum, where he specialises in the study of domestic glass, stained glass and pottery, and publishes articles in *The Burlington Magazine* (from 1923), *Country Life* and *The Connoisseur* (from 1924) and *Apollo* (from 1925). He dines with E. M. Forster at Leonard and Virginia Woolf's in Richmond, Surrey (October).

'The nature of metaphysical poetry', *The Criterion*, vol.I, pp.246-66
'The notebooks of T. E. Hulme', *The New Age*, vol.XXX, no.12, 19 Jan, pp.148-9; no.13, 26 Jan, pp.167-8; no.15, 9 Feb, pp.193-4; no.16, 16 Feb, pp.207-8; no.22, 30 March, pp.287-8; no.23, 6 April, pp.301-2; no.24, 13 April, pp.310-12
'Critics in Arabia', *The Tyro*, no.1, p.12. 'A note on the imagination', no.2, pp.44-5

1923

Eliot launches *The Criterion*, review of literature, politics and religion (until 1939). George Grosz's lithographs *Ecce Homo*, depicting contemporary Berlin life, charged with 'defaming public morals' in Germany. Eric Gill's relief *Our Lord Driving the Money Changers Out of the Temple*, commissioned by Sadler for Leeds University (1921), unveiled to great controversy (May). Le Corbusier, *Vers une Architecture*: 'The house … a machine for living'.

■ HR and Evelyn's son, John, is born (7 June). *Mutations of the Phoenix*, The Hogarth Press, London (Leonard and Virginia Woolf), a collection of poems. HR becomes a regular contributor of articles and book reviews to *The Criterion*.

Mutations of the Phoenix (Richmond, Leonard & Virginia Woolf)
'The labours of the months: a series of stained glass roundels', *Burlington Magazine*, vol.XLIII, pp.167-8. 'The Blés collection of English and Irish glass', vol. XLIII, pp.247-8

1924

Death of Lenin (21 January). First Labour government in Britain (22 January-31 October). Stalin emerges as Russian leader (May). Deaths of Franz Kafka (3 June) and Joseph Conrad (3 August). Leon Trotsky *Literature and Revolution*. André Breton *Manifeste du Surréalisme*. *La Révolution Surréaliste* magazine founded in Paris.

■ HR edits *Speculations by T. E. Hulme*, propagandising a rigorous virile Modernism, with a foreword by Jacob Epstein. HR and Bernard Rackham collaborate on the first modern classification of all branches within the field of English pottery.

Speculations, Essays on humanism and the philosophy of art by T. E. Hulme (London, Kegan Paul, Trench, Trubner & Co) [1936]; (1924; New York, Harcourt, Brace & Co); (1965; London, Routledge and Kegan Paul); (1965; New York, Humanities Press)
(and Rackham, Bernard) *English pottery: its development from early times to the end of the eighteenth century* (London, Ernest Benn)
'English and Irish glass: the Blés collection; I – Historical glass', *Country Life*, no.LV, pp.945-6. 'II – Decorated glasses', no.LVI, pp.471-2. 'III – Cut glass', no.LVI, pp.615-16
'The definition of comedy', *Dial*, vol.LXXVI, pp.257-64
'Swiss stained glass', *Architectural Review*, vol.LV, pp.147-9

'Charlotte and Emily Brontë', *Yale Review*, vol.XIV, pp.720-38
'Psychoanalysis and the critic', *The Criterion*, vol.III, pp.214-30. Review of Fry, R. *The artist and psychoanalysis*, pp.471-2

1925

Exposition des Arts Décoratifs et Industriels Modernes, Paris (April–October). Epstein's *W. H. Hudson Memorial* (Rima) unveiled in Hyde Park, London to bitter controversy (19 May). *Neue Sachlichkeit* ('New Realism') exhibition, Munich: Beckmann, Dix, Grosz (opens 14 June). Hitler *Mein Kampf* (published 18 July).

■ Evelyn Read has a miscarriage and shortly afterwards becomes ill with a thyroid condition.

In retreat (London, Leonard & Virginia Woolf); (1930; London, Faber & Faber)
'The future of poetry', *Times Literary Supplement*, pp.573-4
'A set of Italian painted enamels in the Victoria and Albert Museum', *Apollo*, vol.II, pp.208-12. 'English pottery: an aesthetic survey', pp.318-23

1926

Eliot launches *The New Criterion* (January), moving away from HR's beliefs in politics and theology. Fritz Lang *Metropolis* (premiered 10 January). General Strike in Britain (3-12 May). Fascist Party assumes total control in Italy (7 October). Death of Rainer Maria Rilke (29 December). Bauhaus reopens at Dessau, Germany (designed by Walter Gropius).
   Paul Klee *Rauferei*.

■ HR travels widely in Spain under the auspices of the Victoria and Albert Museum (24 April–27 May) recording his observations on works of art of all ages in journals and notebooks. His versifying is parodied in *Punch* (June issue): 'More Jackdaw in Georgia', 'The Poets at the Round Pond'.
   Jean Cocteau's *Night of the Night*, a drawing inscribed 'amical souvenir au professeur Read' (later used as the frontispiece of *Art Now*, 1933).

Collected poems, 1913-25 (London, Faber & Gwyer)
Reason and romanticism (London, Faber & Gwyer)
Review of Whitehead, A. N. *Science and the Modern World*, *The Criterion*, vol.IV, pp.581-6
'Walter Bagehot', *Times Literary Supplement*, pp.49-50. 'English prose', pp.149-50. 'The dethronement of Descartes', pp.585-6
'Walt Whitman', *Nation and Athenaeum*, vol.XXXIX, p.447. 'Blake', vol.XL, p.272

1927

BBC broadcasts first programmes (1 January): 3 million homes have wireless sets. Charles Lindberg's first non-stop trans-Atlantic solo flight, New York to Paris (21 May). Anarchists Sacco and Vanzetti executed (23 August) USA. Anarchist International Federation founded. Ernst Barlach's *Hovering Angel* in Gustrow church destroyed by Nazis as 'un-German'.

■ HR and family move from Purley to Broom House, Seer Green near Beaconsfield, Buckinghamshire (15 June), which he has a hand in designing: semi-Tudor outside, resolutely contemporary inside. By this time Herbert and Evelyn are more and more drawing apart.

(Ed and trans.) Worringer, Wilhelm *Form in Gothic*, (London, G. P. Putnam's); (1957; London, A. Tiranti); (1964; New York, Schocken)
Review of Whitehead, A. N. *Religion in the Making*, *The Criterion*, vol.V, pp.259-63. 'The raid', vol.VI, pp.40-9. Review of Vivante, L. *Notes on the Originality of Thought*, vol.VI, pp.363-9

'Potted Ruskin', review of Ruskin, J. *Modern Painters*, *Nation and Athenaeum*, vol.XLII, no.4, 29 Oct, pp.158-9. 'Time and Mr Wyndham Lewis', review of Lewis, P.W. *Time and Western Man*, no.7, 19 Nov, pp.282-4

1928

Twenty-three countries, including Germany, sign Kellogg-Briand pact outlawing war (26 September). US Customs rule Constantin Brancusi's *Bird in Flight* duty-free 'work of art' (26 November). Luis Buñuel and Salvador Dali's Surrealist film *Un Chien Andalou* causes scandal when premiered in Paris. Paul Schulze-Naumberg *Art and Race*: birth of Nazi concept of 'degenerate art'. Grosz convicted of blasphemy and sacrilege in Berlin for drawing crucified Christ wearing gas mask. Barbara Hepworth (born 1903, West Riding of Yorkshire) moves to 7 The Mall, Parkhill Road, Hampstead, London. D.H.Lawrence *Lady Chatterley's Lover*.

■ HR travels in Southern France exploring its art. *English Prose Style* an essential handbook on rhetoric. 'Herbert Read is the best mind in England' (proclaims the American poet and critic Allen Tate).

English Prose Style (London, G.Bell) [1928; 1931; 1952] (1928 New York, H.Holt) [1952 New York, Pantheon; 1955 Boston, Beacon Press]
Phases of English poetry (London, Leonard & Virginia Woolf) [1950]; (1929, New York, Harcourt, Brace)
'The implications of Behaviourism', *The Criterion*, vol.VII, pp.64-75. Review of Aldington, R. (trans.) Benda, J. *The Great Betrayal* [La Trahison des Clercs], vol.VIII, pp.270-6
'The making of meaning', review of Barfield, O. *Poetic Diction: a Study in Meaning*, *Nation and Athenaeum*, vol.XLIII, no.13, 30 June, pp.429-30

1929

Ernst Ludwig Kirchner prevented by Nazis from executing murals at Folkwang Museum, Essen. German artists speak out for artistic freedom at anti-censorship meeting in Berlin. Museum of Modern Art founded in New York. Wall Street Crash (24 October): The Great Depression. Richard Aldington *Death of a Hero*. Robert Graves *Goodbye to All That*. Ernest Hemingway *A Farewell to Arms*. Erich Maria Remarque *All Quiet on the Western Front: evocations of The Great War*.

Henry Moore marries Irina Radetsky and moves from Hammersmith to 11A Parkhill Road, Hampstead, where he carves brown Hornton stone *Reclining Figure*.
Naum Gabo *Construction in Space: Soaring*.
Paul Nash *Northern Adventure*.

■ HR delivers the Clark Lectures at Trinity College, Cambridge (Eliot had put forward his name in 1927) on the subject of William Wordsworth (1929-30). He becomes personal assistant to Sir Eric Maclagan, Director of the Victoria and Albert Museum. Maclagan introduces him to Henry Moore (born 1898, Castleford, West Riding of Yorkshire). 'The Meaning of Art' is published as a supplement to *The Listener* (29 September), the first of many articles on the visual arts to appear in the BBC's weekly literary magazine. This association allows HR to recommend Eric Gill to carve the figurative sculpture on the new BBC headquarters in Portland Place, London, resulting in *Prospero and Ariel*, *The Sower* and three reliefs (by 1931).

The sense of glory; essays in criticism (Cambridge, Cambridge University Press) (1967; Freeport, New York, Books for Libraries Press)

Staffordshire pottery figures (London, Duckworth)
(Ed) *A sentimental journey by Laurence Sterne* (London, Scholartis Press)
'Aesthetics and the science of art', *Times Literary Supplement*, 18 April, p.xxi
'The meaning of art', *The Listener*, vol.II, Supplement no.1, 25 Sep, pp.i-viii

1930

All-India National Congress demands 'complete independence' from Britain (2 January); Gandhi begins civil disobedience campaign: 'Victory gained by violence is tantamount to a defeat' (14 February). Death of D.H.Lawrence (2 March). International Bureau of Revolutionary Artists in Russia define role of art in Communist state: 'Art must be a class weapon'. Alfred Rosenberg *Myth of the Twentieth Century*. Bible of Nazi ideology Hitler's *Mein Kampf* illustrated by 200 full-page plates, 'The Most Widely Discussed Book of the Modern World ... The original Edition entirely Unexpurgated ', price 6d. Nazis eliminate Expressionist art from Weimar museum as work of 'a mankind subnormal from the racial point of view'.
László Moholy-Nagy *Collage*.

Ambush (London, Faber & Faber)
Julien Benda and the new humanism (Seattle, University of Washington Book Store)
Wordsworth (London, Jonathan Cape) [1949; 1958]; (1931; New York, J.Cape and H.Smith)
'A recipe for the Italian Exhibition', *The Listener*, vol.III, p.17. 'What is a good portrait?', p.55. 'Ancient art and modern sensibility', p.108. 'Modern Italian painting', p.148. 'Art and manufacture', p.192. 'Venetian glass', p.238. 'Art and culture', p.281. 'An outline of art', p.292. 'The drawings of the Italian masters', p.316. 'Method in art criticism', p.371. 'Picasso', pp.412-13. 'Children's drawings', p.460. 'Art and scholasticism', p.508. 'Nudity in art', pp.546-7. 'Tolstoy's theory of art', pp.592-3. 'Masterpieces', p.627. 'Beyond Realism', p.679. 'Psychoanalysis and art', p.737. 'Art and photography', p.766. 'Art and decoration', p.805. 'English Gothic', p.853. 'English illuminated manuscripts', p.898. 'Pieter de Hooch', p.939. 'Cézanne', pp.987-8. 'Two kinds of truth', pp.1025-6. 'The evolution of a modern artist', p.1083. 'Egyptian sculpture', p.1112. Vol.IV: 'The history of art', p.24. 'Renoir', p.64. 'Landscape painting', pp.101-2. 'Art, beauty and ugliness', p.142. 'Architecture and sculpture', p.169. 'Eugène Delacroix – I', p.225. 'Eugène Delacroix – II', p.250. 'The high priest of modern literature', p.296. 'Bushman art', p.329. 'Annotations', p.362. 'Peasant art', p.411. 'Rousseau le Douanier', p.450. 'Impressionism', p.490. 'Realism', p.525. 'The Antwerp Exhibition of Flemish Art', pp.578-9. 'Rubens', p.616. 'Art in two countries', p.660. 'Modern German painting', p.708. 'Post-war art in Germany', p.738. 'El Greco', pp.786-7. 'Greek Sculpture', p.832. 'Distortion', pp.882-3. 'Architect or engineer?', pp.926-7. 'Van Gogh', p.973. 'Form and expressionism', p.1026. 'Persian art', p.1060. 'Art and religion', pp.1094-5
'The form of modern poetry', *Symposium*, vol.I, pp.293-309
'Josiah Wedgwood: prince of potters', *International Studio*, vol.XCVI, pp.31-4

1931

Spanish Republic declared (14 April). Epstein proclaims Moore 'vitally important for the future of sculpture in England' (catalogue to one-man show at Leicester Galleries, London, April). Ben Nicholson (born 1894) joins Hepworth in Hampstead.

■ HR's inaugural lecture, Edinburgh University: 'The Place of Art in a University' (published under the same title in 1931) envisages the city reasserting the position it held in the Late Georgian intellectual world. Subsequent lectures deal with aspects of European art (controversially, El Greco is defended at the expense of Velasquez) and up-to-the-minute developments in Continental painting, sculpture and architecture. Attempts are made in the Department to reduce the impact of such modernity by putting the slides in the projector upside down. HR is living at 9 Tipperlinn Road, for which he designs a 10 foot long Modernist desk. He discusses with Canon John Gray and André Raffalovich the creation of a modern art centre in Edinburgh, modelled on the German Bauhaus, but the project comes to nothing. However, at a lunch given by Gray and Raffalovich HR meets Margaret Ludwig (nicknamed Ludo), a lecturer in the University's music department, of Scottish-German stock, and they mutually fall in love immediately (Autumn). 'Bildhauerkunst in England: Henry Moore', *Kunstblatt* (31 June issue). The magazine *Kreis von Halle* (September–October issues) feature some of HR's *Listener* articles on contemporary German art, translated by Max Sauerlandt, Director of the Hamburg Museum für Kunst und Gewerbe, whom HR had met at least as early as 1926 and who, in 1931, purchases Moore's brown Hornton stone *Head*, his first work to enter a European public collection.

(1931) *The meaning of art* (London, Faber & Faber) [1936; 1942; 1951] (1947; Harmondsworth, Penguin Books) [1949; 1959]; (1951; New York, Pitman); (1959; Baltimore, Penguin Books); American editions (1932; New York, Dodd, Mead & Co) [1932; 1936] have title: *The anatomy of art; an introduction to the problems of art and aesthetics*
The place of art in a university. An inaugural lecture given at the University of Edinburgh (Edinburgh, London, Oliver & Boyd)
(and Bonamy Dobrée) (Eds) *The anthology of English prose* (New York, Viking)
(and Bonamy Dobrée) (Eds) *The London book of English prose* (London, Eyre & Spottiswoode) [1949; 1951; 1963] (1949; New York, Macmillan)
'Art and nature', *The Listener*, vol.V, pp.19-20. 'Wilson Steer and the English tradition', p.56. 'Matisse', p.116. 'The Golden Section', pp.142-3. 'On looking at a picture', pp.193-4. 'A new theory of art', pp.232-3. 'The city of tomorrow', pp.272-3. 'The house of tomorrow', p.324. 'Mosaics', p.366. 'Homage to Gainsborough', p.407. 'The Morris Movement', pp.463-4. 'Paul Klee', p.509. 'Design and industry', pp.552-3. 'War memorials', p.587. 'Henry Moore', pp.688-9. 'The art of Egypt', p.762. 'Marc Chagall', p.860. 'Byzantine art', p.986. 'Paul Gauguin', p.1021. Vol.VI: 'Painting and poetry', p.22. 'Pyramid vs. mosque', pp.106-7. 'Baroque art, pp.171-2. 'What London might be', pp.214-15. 'Chinese art', pp.254-5. 'Turner revived', pp.338-9. 'Domestic interiors', pp.493-4. 'Modern photography', p.582. 'From the first stroke', pp.693-4. 'Jehan Foucquet', p.818. 'Edvard Munch', p.962. 'Old Crome', p.1148.

1932

Nazis win plurality in Dessau City Council and dissolve Bauhaus: 'one of the most prominent centres on the Jewish-Marxist art programme'. Sir Oswald Mosely forms British Union of Fascists. Alberto Giacometti *Woman with Her Throat Cut*. Aldous Huxley *Brave New World*. R.H.Wilenski *The Meaning of Modern Sculpture*.

Hepworth and Nicholson visit Picasso at Gisors and the studios of Arp and Brancusi, Paris (Spring); meet Calder, Giacometti and Miró (Summer).
Moore *Half-Figure*.
Hepworth *Kneeling Figure*.
Nash *Harbour and Room*.

■ HR gives a lunch attended by Hugh MacDiarmid, poet and pioneer of the Scottish literary renaissance (New Year's Day). He attends a Seven and Five Society exhibition at the Leicester Galleries in London (February), where he is particularly struck by Hepworth's sculpture. He is awarded a D.Litt (honoris causa) by Leeds University (July). In one of the forewords to the catalogue *Carvings by Barbara Hepworth; Paintings by Ben Nicholson*, Arthur Tooth & Sons Gallery, London (9 November–3 December) he writes of Hepworth's 'leading position … in redeeming art from its present triviality and insignificance'.

Form in modern poetry (London, Sheed & Ward) (1948; London, Vision Press) [1964]
'Foreword', *Carvings by Barbara Hepworth; Paintings by Ben Nicholson*, (London, Arthur Tooth & Sons)
'Towards a film aesthetic', *Cinema Quarterly*, vol.I, pp.7-11
'Cézanne and Classicism', *The Listener*, vol.VII, pp.18-19. 'The crystalline art', p.168. 'Rainer Maria Rilke', p.247. 'Drawings at the French Exhibition', p.276. 'English painting in perspective', pp.450-1. 'The anatomy of style', p.500. 'Modern stained glass', pp.686-7. 'Frans Hals', p.792. 'The modern museum (I)', p.943. Vol.VIII: 'The modern museum (II)', p.24. 'Leonardo and the decline of painting', pp.160-1. 'The problem of the provincial picture gallery (I): painted mill-wheels', p.301. 'The problem of the provincial picture gallery (II): the remedy', p.339. 'André Derain', p.492. 'Celtic art', p.690. 'The teaching of art', p.789. 'The painter-critic', p.820

1933

Hitler becomes German Chancellor (30 January). Nazis open Dachau, first concentration camp (20 March) and order nationwide burning of banned books (10 May). Goebbels' Ministry of Propaganda for Popular Enlightenment assumes total control of arts in Germany. Gestapo closes Bauhaus School in Berlin: 'breeding place of cultural Bolshevism': Bayer, Breuer, Feininger, Gropius, Klee, Mendelsohn, Mies van der Rohe, Moholy-Nagy flee mainly to England and United States. Spanish Fascist Party (Falange Espanola) founded. Nash announces in *The Times* (2 June) formation of Unit One, standing for 'the expression of a truly contemporary spirit' in art. H.G.Wells *The Shape of Things to Come* (published 1 September). *Unit One* exhibition opens, Mayor Gallery (October). *Minotaure*, influential Surrealist journal, launched in Paris. Misha Black and Cliff Rowe found Artists' International Association (AIA) in London to champion proletarian art (HR is sympathetic). Everyman Cinema opens in Hampstead to show European avant-garde films: its Foyer Gallery exhibits Bomberg, Hepworth, Klee, Nicholson. Geoffrey Grigson edits *New Verse*.
Max Ernst *La Ville Pétrifiée*.
Francis Bacon *Crucifixion*.

■ HR and wife have a 'showdown' while holidaying on the Isle of Islay (Spring). He resigns his post of Watson Gordon Professor (28 June) 'to save the University a public scandal', and with Ludo visits her former music teacher in Cologne, Walter Braunfels, who is related by marriage to the sculptor Adolf von Hildebrandt. HR and Ludo elope to London (July); HR lives temporarily in Moore's Parkhill Road house, then both permanently settle at the nearby No.3 The Mall, which is furnished with paintings by Nicholson and Alfred Wallis, sculpture by Hepworth, and furniture by Aalto and Mies.
During this decade Hampstead becomes the 'modernist fortress' in London: residents in Parkhill Road and the neighbourhood include Grigson, F.E.McWilliam, E.L.T.Mesens,

Roland Penrose, John Cecil Stephenson, Adrian Stokes, John Summerson, Hepworth, Moore, Nash and Nicholson, and the foreign exiles Sigmund Freud (1933-9), Marcel Breuer (1934-7), Gropius (1934-8), Moholy-Nagy (1935-7), Gabo (1936-9) and Piet Mondrian (1938-40). Thus Hampstead becomes HR's base as he develops into the foremost defender of modern art in Britian. With Roger Fry's support, he becomes editor of *The Burlington Magazine*, the leading art history journal in Britain, at an annual salary of £500 (in the years up to 1939 he is responsible for publishing works by many young scholars including Friederich Antal, Erwin Panovsky, John Pope-Hennessy and Ellis Waterhouse). HR 'is a nice man & has a v. wide knowledge of ancient & modern art and an appreciation of the latter possessed by few' (Eric Gill, 17 November letter).

Art now; an introduction to the theory of modern painting and sculpture (London, Faber & Faber) [1936; 1948; 1960; 1968]; (1937; New York, Harcourt, Brace) (1948; New York, Pitman) [1960]
The innocent eye (London, Faber & Faber); (1947; New York, Holt)
(Ed) *The English vision; an anthology* (London, Eyre and Spottiswoode); (1939; G. Routledge)
'Rudolph Arnheim's Film', *Cinema Quarterly*, vol.I, pp.172-5. 'The poet and the film', pp.197-202. 'Herbert Read replies', vol.II, pp.35-6
'Unit One', *Architectural Review*, vol.LXXIV, pp.125-8
'Obscurity in poetry', *The Bookman*, vol.LXXXV, pp.12-15
'The innocent eye', *Atlantic Monthly*, vol.CLI, pp.267-77, 447-57
'Carlton House Terrace', *Burlington Magazine*, vol.LXII, p.103. 'Laurence Binyon', p.153. 'The galleries and the public', p.203. 'Breaking up the Hermitage', vol.LXIII, p.53. 'The National Gallery', p.145. 'English art', pp.243-76
'Line', *The Listener*, vol.IX, p.218. 'Tone values in painting', pp.318-19. 'Colour in painting', p.534. 'Form in painting', pp.588-90. 'Mr. Wilenski's Ruskin', pp.817-18. 'Max Ernst', p.899. Vol.X: 'The function of decor', pp.47-8. 'Seeing is believing', p.172. 'The Hindu view of art', p.318. 'The poetry and the prose of painting', pp.354-5. 'Vulgarity: the antithesis of art', pp.497-8. 'The origins of geometric art – I: past and present', pp.628-9. 'The origins of geometric art – II: the psychological necessity', pp.831-2. 'An essay in aesthetics', p.1002

1934

Paul Hindemith's opera *Mathis der Maler* premiere banned by Nazis. Leni Riefenstahl's film *Triumph of the Will*. Huntington Hartford *Art or Anarchy* condemns Abstract Expressionism as 'gigantic Communist plot against America'. 'Getting Ready at Burlington House An attempted gate-crash by the Moderns is frustrated' – *Punch* cartoon using works illustrated in *Art Now*. Wells Coates, 'Isokon' Flats, Lawn Road, first International Style building in Hampstead (occupants include Breuer, Gropius, Moholy-Nagy). Moholy-Nagy introduces Hepworth and Nicholson to Mondrian in Paris (Summer). Death of Roger Fry (September).

■ HR and Sauerlandt had been planning an exhibition of German post-war art for London but the project is abandoned with Sauerlandt's death (January).

Joan Miró *Composition*, a drawing, inscribed 'à Monsieur Herbert Read, très affectueusement, Miró, 934'.

Art and industry, the principles of industrial design (London, Faber & Faber) [1944; 1953; 1956; 1966]; (1954; New York, Horizon Press) (1961; Bloomington, Indiana University Press)
Henry Moore, sculptor, an appreciation (London, Zwemmer)
(Ed) *Unit One: the modern movement in English architecture, painting, and sculpture* (London, Toronto, Melbourne, Sydney, Cassell & Co)
'The Walpole Society', *Burlington Magazine*, vol.LXIV, p.153. 'Roger Fry', vol.LXV, p.145
'Experiments in counterpoint', *Cinema Quarterly*, vol.III, pp.17-18, 21
'Paul Klee', *The Listener*, vol.XI, pp.108-9. 'British art for sevenpence', p.140. 'Romanticism in poetry and painting', pp.360-2. 'The modern aesthete', pp.527-8. 'The aesthetics of tombstones', pp.738-40. 'Eclecticism and tradition', pp.916-17. Vol.XII: 'The expatriates', pp.296-7. 'The intellectual and liberty', pp.497-80. 'Seurat's *La Baignade*', pp.608-9. 'Bosch and Dali', pp.824-6. 'Max Liebermann', pp.980-2
'Vincent van Gogh', *The Spectator*, vol.CLII, p.468. 'The intellectual crisis in Paris', pp.734-5. 'Art and work', vol.CLIII, p.197. 'Art: Roger Fry', p.359. 'Christianity and Communism', pp.1002-3
'Picasso and the Marxists', *London Mercury*, vol.XXXI, pp.95-6. 'Richard Sickert', pp.207-8. 'Modern drama: the architectural hold-up', vol.XXXII, pp.427-32

167

167 Herbert Read at Edinburgh 1931-3

1935

'Non-Aryans' expelled from German Chamber of Writers and banned from literary work (12 April). Italy invades Abyssinia (3 October) Hitler stigmatises German modern artists as 'corrupters of art' and 'insane'. Seven and Five Society, under Nicholson's *aegis*, holds first all-abstract exhibition in England: Hepworth, Hitchens, Moore, Piper (2-22 October). *Axis*, edited by Myfanwy Evans, magazine devoted to abstract art. AIA exhibition *Artists Against War and Fascism* in London shows work by some 500 artists (November–December). Henry Miller *Tropic of Cancer* (admired by HR). Maxwell Fry *Sun House*, Hampstead.

Piet Mondrian *Composition with Red and Blue*.
John Piper *Forms on a White Ground*.

■ HR expresses his hostility towards Eliot's *Murder in the Cathedral* (premiered 1935) to Stephen Spender. He and Ludo rent Charleston, Vanessa Bell's Sussex house; Ludo plays the viola in the Glyndebourne orchestra (Summer). HR meets Roland Penrose and attacks Kenneth Clark (Director of the National Gallery) on his view, published in *The Listener*, that 'advanced' (modern) art is out of touch with reality and can only lead to a dead end. David Gascoyne, Grigson and HR contribute to the 'Engish art to-day' issue of *Konkretion* (November), published in Copenhagen, Oslo and Stockholm. HR delivers the Sydney Jones Lectures in Art at the University of Liverpool (1935-6), and discusses with Nicolete Gray, J. L. Martin and Nicholson plans for founding a Museum of Living Art in London devoted to abstractionism.

Essential Communism (London, Stanley Nott Ltd)
The Green Child; a romance (London, Heinemann); (1945; London, Grey Walls Press); (1947; London, Eyre & Spottiswoode); (1948; New York, New Directions)
Poems, 1914-1934 (London, Faber & Faber); (1935; New York, Harcourt, Brace & Co)
(and Denis Saurat) *Orage, Alfred Richard. Selected essays and critical writings* (London, Stanley Nott)
'What is Revolutionary Art?', in: Rea, Betty (Ed) (1935) *5 on Revolutionary Art* (London, Wishart), pp.11-22
'Novelism at the Royal Academy', *Architectural Review*, vol.LXXVII, pp.45-50. 'A museum to the rescue', vol.LXXVIII, pp.37-8. 'A new Humanism', review of Moholy-Nagy, L. *The New Vision*, pp.150-1
'Our terminology', *Axis*, no.1, pp.6-8. 'Ben Nicholson's recent work', no.2, pp.15-16. 'Jean Hélion', no.4, pp.3-4
'A general impression of the exhibition', *The Listener*, vol.XIII, pp.51-2. 'African art', p.276. 'Modern Chinese painting', pp.398-9. 'Twenty five years of British painting', pp.705-6. 'The International Style', pp.866-8. 'Writing into pattern – a new way of teaching art to children', pp.1034-6. 'Multiple reviewing', p.1065. Vol.XIV: 'Universality in art', pp.190-1. 'Toulouse-Lautrec', pp.326-7. 'Soviet Realism', p.579. 'Ben Nicholson and the future of painting', pp.604-5. 'Expressionism in art', pp.1108-10
'Why the English have no taste', *Minotaure*, no.7, pp.67-8
'Art and the revolutionary attitude'; *Southern Review*, vol.I, pp.239-52
'Semantic criticism', *The Spectator*, vol.CLIV, pp.490-2. 'A theory of art', pp.985-6. 'Kierkegaard', vol.CLV, p.471

1936

Abstract and Concrete An Exhibition of Abstract Painting & Sculpture 1934 & 1935, organised by Nicolete Gray at Oxford, subsequently shown at Liverpool, Cambridge and London: Calder, Hélion, Hepworth, Moholy-Nagy, Mondrian, Nicholson. German army reoccupies Rhineland (7 March). Gascoyne translates Breton's *What Is Surrealism?* (Spring). Spanish Civil war erupts (July). Federico Garcia Lorca assassinated by Franco agents (19 August). Jarrow hunger marches (begin 5 October). Goebbels abolishes all art criticism in Germany; 16,500 'undesirable' modern art works purged from German museums. 'Leftist' art in Russia attacked as 'petty bourgeois Westernistic formalism'. Gabo 'Constructive Art', *Listener* (4 November issue). *Fantastic Art, Dada, Surrealism* exhibition, Museum of Modern Art, New York (December).

■ HR and Evelyn Read's divorce is granted (20 January). HR marries Ludo at the Hampstead Registry Office (12 February); they honeymoon in northern Spain. *International Surrealist Exhibition* masterminded by Penrose assisted by a committee which includes Hugh Sykes Davies, Gascoyne, Moore, Nash and HR, is held at the New Burlington Galleries, London. 392 paintings and sculptures (by Agar, Arp, Brancusi, Burra, Calder, de Chirico, Dali, Duchamp, Ernst, Giacometti, Klee, Magritte, Miró, Moore, Nash, Picasso, Ray, Tanguy etc) as well as ethnographical, Surrealist and found objects (including a *Found Object* contributed by HR) attract 25,000 visitors.

HR writes an introduction to the catalogue: 'Do not judge this movement kindly. It is not just another amusing stunt. It is defiant – the desperate act of men too profoundly convinced of the rottenness of our civilization to want to save a shred of its respectability'. He delivers a lecture 'Art and the Unconscious' standing on a spring sofa (19 June) and speaks on behalf of the movement at the AIA Open Meeting for Discussion on 'The Social Aspects of Surrealism' (23 June). HR, Ludo and John Read vacation at Dieppe, where they visit Braque (Summer). Agar, Gascoyne, Moore, Nash, Penrose, HR and others sign a Surrealist Group manifesto condemning the London Non-Intervention Committee's policy voiced at the international convention for non-intervention in the Spanish Civil War held in London (9-17 September). HR writes an introduction 'The Significance of Edvard Munch' (extracted from *Art Now*) to the catalogue of the exhibition *Works by Edvard Munch* at the London Gallery (October).

Paul Nash *Study for Encounter on the Downs* inscribed 'souvenir for Herbert Read from Paul Nash'.

In defence of Shelley & other essays (London, Heinemann)
(Ed) Arnheim, Rudolph, *Radio*. Trans. Margaret Ludwig and Herbert Read (London, Faber & Faber)
(Ed) *Surrealism* (London, Faber & Faber) [1971]
'The designer in industry', *Architectural Review*, vol.LXXIX, pp.143-6
'Abstract art: a note for the uninitiated', *Axis*, no.5, p.3
'Surrealism: the dialectic of art', *Left Review*, vol.2, no.10, July, Supplement fac. p.508, pp,ii-iii
'Dealers in art', *The Listener*, vol.XV, pp.434-6. 'The triumph of Picasso', pp.1023-25. Vol.XVI: 'Art and religion', pp.256-8. 'The Modern Movement', Early Autumn Supplement, p.xviii. 'The spontaneous self', p.1017
'The artist as individual', *Virginia Quarterly Review*, vol.XII, pp.376-91

1937

George Orwell *The Road to Wigan Pier* (published 9 March). AIA *Unity of the Artists for Peace, Democracy and Cultural Development* exhibition, London (March–April). Picasso paints anti-war masterpiece *Guernica* following bombing of Basque capital (26 April). Guggenheim fund for art set up in New York

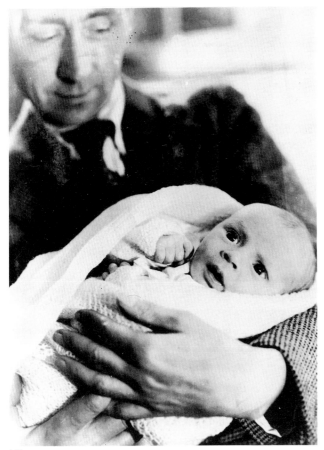

168

(28 June). *Degenerate Art* exhibition, Munich (opens 19 July) demonstrating 'Jewish Democratic' and 'Kultur-Bolshevistic' influences: Cubism, Expressionism, Futurism, Impressionism, work by Archipenko, Barlach, Beckmann, Braque, Chagall, Dix, Gauguin, Grosz, Heckel, Kandinsky, Kirchner, Kokoschka, Marc, Munch, Nolde, Picasso, Van Gogh. Hitler dedicates alternative Munich exhibition of 'true German art' with 90-minute speech to 30,000 visitors, castigating 'degenerate half-wits who ... see blue fields, green sky, and sulphurous clouds'. Goering orders German museums cleansed of all modern art. Euston Road School founded in London (Graham Bell, Coldstream, Pasmore, Rogers). Adrian Stokes *Colour and Form* (challenging HR's aesthetic theories). Myfanwy Evans *The Painter's Object*.

André Masson *Mass at Pamplona*.
Moore *Carving*.

■ HR, Epstein, Gill and Nash sign a letter of co-operation with the International Peace Campaign against Fascist aggression in Spain. HR begins acting as a literary adviser to both Heinemann and Routledge. 'Life without a Shoehorn', comic essay, published under the pseudonym James Murgatroyd in *Night and Day* (at the suggestion of Graham Greene). He and Ludo move from Hampstead to Broom House near Beaconsfield. HR is Eileen Agar's *Angel of Anarchy*. In *Surrealist Objects and Poems* he defines the Surrealist object, as 'the chance meeting of the umbrella and the sewing machine on the dissecting table'.

Ludo gives birth to Thomas Bonamy Read (21 December) her first child and HR's second son, named after Bonamy Dobrée and T. S. Eliot; Gill is the godfather.

Acquires Hepworth's *Single Form*.

Art and society (London, Heinemann) (1945; London, Faber & Faber) [1956; 1967]; (1937; New York, Macmillan) (1950; New York, Pantheon Books) (1966; New York, Schocken Books)
'The faculty of abstraction', in: Martin, L.; Nicholson, B. and Gabo, N. (Eds) *Circle: International Survey of Constructive Art* (London, Faber & Faber), pp.61-6
'Introduction', *Paul Nash* (London, Soho Gallery)
'Introduction', *Surrealist objects and poems* (London Gallery)
'The necessity of Anarchism', *Adelphi*, vol.XIII, pp.458-63; vol.XIV, pp.12-18. 44-8
'Why I am a Surrealist', *New English Weekly*, vol.X, 4 March, pp.413-14. 'Surrealism and Communism', pp.479-80
'False Romanticism', *The Listener*, vol.XVII, pp.182-3. 'The present state of watercolour', pp.598-9. 'The first British Artists Congress', pp.816-8. Vol.XVIII: 'An enquiry into public taste', pp.31-2. 'Hitler on art', pp.605-7

1938

Anschluss: German army occupies Austria (11 March): 'Brute force and the immediate fear of torture and death have been set up as the keystone of national organization' (Moore, 'Collective security: the People's answer to dictators', *Yorkshire Post*, 31 March). Peggy Guggenheim opens Guggenheim Jeune, London, showing Cocteau (January), Kandinsky (February), Arp, Brancusi, Calder, Moore (April). First English exhibition of Magritte and Delvaux, London Gallery (April–June). British Surrealists demonstrate against Chamberlain's non-intervention policy regarding German aggression (1 May). Hitler orders confiscation of 'degenerate art' owned by German citizens (3 June). Breton and Trotsky *Manifesto Towards a Free Revolutionary Art*, calling on revolution for complete liberation of art (English text published in *Partisan Review*, Autumn). Chamberlain returns from Berchtesgaden: 'Peace for our time' (30 September). German army occupies Sudetenland (1 October). Orwell *Homage to Catalonia*: 'by far the best book I have read on this Spanish war' (HR). Penrose *The Road is Wider Than Long* (London, Gallery Editions).

Oscar Kokoschka *Prague Nostalgia*.
Paul Delvaux *L'Appel de la Nuit*.
John Cecil Stevenson *Bright Triangles*.

■ HR quarrels with *The Listener* over its refusal to publish an article by him on Guggenheim's Kandinsky exhibition (February). He attacks the precepts of the Euston Road School in the *London Bulletin* (April issue). The AIA sponsors a discussion between the supporters of Realism (Anthony Blunt, Coldstream, Bell) and Surrealism (Penrose, HR and others). HR serves as the 'mouthpiece' for the exhibition of modern 'degenerate' German art (highlighting Expressionism) at the New Burlington Galleries, London (opens 7 July), which is savagely attacked by Hitler: 'lamentable unfortunates who plainly suffer from defective sight. They can live and work where they choose but not in Germany' (11 July).

Guernica, with 67 preparatory studies, is exhibited at the New Burlington Galleries (4-29 October) and the Whitechapel Art Gallery (December), attracting 15,000 visitors. Organised by the National Joint Committee for Spanish Relief, of which HR is Vice-Chairman. He describes 'Picasso's great fresco [as] a monument to destruction ... the modern Calvary' (*London Bulletin*, October issue).

Epstein, Moore, Nash, HR and others publish a letter – 'Homeless German Artists' – in *The Manchester Guardian* (9 November) drawing attention to 'artists who found asylum in Czech-Slovakia [who] are in immediate danger of being sent

168 Herbert Read with his son, Thomas (photographed by Barbara Hepworth) 1938

back to Germany, where concentration camps await them'. HR eulogises Herschel Grynszpan, who shot Ernest van Rath, Third Secretary at the German Embassy in Paris, in protest against the Nazi expulsion of Jews from Germany (7 November); the assassination ignites Kristallnacht (9-10 November). HR recommends Samuel Beckett's *Murphy* and Jack B. Yeat's *The charmed life* to Routledge.

Collected essays in literary criticism (London, Faber & Faber) [1951]; American editions (1956; New York, Horizon Press); (1958; New York, Grove Press) have title: *The nature of literature*
Poetry and anarchism (London, Faber & Faber); (1947; London, Freedom Press)
'Introduction', Thoene, Peter (1938) *Modern German art* (Harmondsworth, Penguin Books) pp.7-11
'Introduction', catalogue of the exhibition *Realism and Surrealism* (Gloucester, Guildhall) May–June
'The death of a contemporary', *Burlington Magazine*, vol.LXXII, p.103. 'French art of the C19th', p.253
'Art contemporain en Angleterre', *Cahiers d'Art*, nos 1-2, pp.29-42
'The art of children', *The Listener*, vol.XIX, p.180. 'Kandinsky and others', p.458. 'What is art?', Late Spring Supplement, p.xiv. 'The effect of the war', p.1298. 'The significance of Paul Delvaux', pp.1336-7. Vol.XX: 'The problems of primitive art', pp.340-1. 'At the Tate Gallery', p.896. 'Art and the state', p.904. 'The duality of Leonardo', pp.1312-13
'Picasso's *Guernica*', *London Bulletin*, no.6. p.6
'The museums scandal', *London Mercury & Bookman*, vol.XXXIX, pp.386-92

1939

German troops occupy Czechoslovakia (14 January). Spanish Republican Government collapses. Civil War ends (1 April). 'The arts cannot thrive except where men are free to be themselves ... Crush individuality in the arts, and you crush art as well.' (Franklin D. Roosevelt at May opening of *Art in Our Time* exhibition, Museum of Modern Art, New York). Nazis burn 5,000 banned works of modern art pilfered from German museums (June).

Gabo, Hepworth and Nicholson move to St Ives, Cornwall (August).

Britain and France declare war on Germany (3 September) following invasion of Poland. Death of Sigmund Freud (23 September). Wilhelm Lehmbruck's *Kneeling Woman* condemned for deriding Nazi ideal of Woman (October). Christopher Isherwood *Goodbye to Berlin*. 'Low dishonest decade' (W. H. Auden *September, 1939*).

■ 'It is vitally necessary for those of us who intend to oppose the coming of war to start organising for illegal anti-war activities' (Orwell to HR, 4 January). HR pledges allegiance to Trotsky in *Clé*, the bulletin of the Fédération Internationale des Artistes Révolutionnaires Indépendants (February issue). He is involved in discussions (March) with Peggy Guggenheim about setting up a Museum of Modern Art in London, with himself as Director, modelled on the New York institution; the project is abandoned due to the war (but the list of artists and their works made by HR and revised by Duchamp becomes the cornerstone of the Guggenheim collection now in Venice).

HR and Ludo holiday in Italy (June). He becomes a director of the publishing firm George Routledge and Sons, London (1 July). This collaboration results in the 'English Master Painters' series, which HR edits (including E. K. Waterhouse *Reynolds*, 1939); later Routledge publishes the poets Sidney

Keyes, John Heath-Stubbs, Henry Treece and the New Apocalypse, as well as works sponsored by the Paul Mellon Foundation for British Art, of which HR becomes a director. HR and Ludo's first daughter, Sophia Teresa born (7 October). He gives up the editorship of *The Burlington Magazine*.

(Ed) *The knapsack; a Pocket-book of Prose and Verse* (London, G. Routledge) [1943]
'The art of the blind', *The Listener*, vol.XXI, pp.350-1. 'Cézanne 1839-1906', pp.936-8. 'The Brescian School', p.1364. Vol.XXII: 'A doomed profession?', p.148. 'Art in the universities: a new centre', p.187. 'Art in education (I): the problem stated', pp.214-15. 'Roger Fry as an art critic', pp.725-6. 'New methods in art criticism', p.922. 'Round the art exhibitions', pp.1001-2
'In what sense living?', *London Bulletin*, nos 8-9, pp.5-7. 'The development of Ben Nicholson', no.11, pp.9-10. 'An art of pure form', no.14, pp.6-9
'A museum of the future', *Museums Journal*, vol.XXXVIII, pp.566-8
'Three English Sculptors' [Moore, Hepworth, Nicholson], *XXe Siècle*, Année II, no.1, p.45 (a special issue with English text)

1940

Dunkirk (29 May–4 June). Britain, France and United States withdraw from Fascist-dominated Venice *Biennale* (May–June). 'We shall never surrender' (Churchill, 4 June speech). Italy declares war on Britain and France (11 June). German troops occupy Paris (14 June). 'FIGHT HITLER AND HIS IDEOLOGY WHEREVER IT APPEARS WE MUST' (*London Bulletin*, June issue). Death of Paul Klee (29 June). Stalin's agents assassinate Trotsky in Mexico (21 August). Battle of Britain (begins 4 September). London Blitz (begins 30 September). Moore begins shelter drawings; moves to Perry Green, Hertfordshire. Coventry devastated by German bombs (14 November). RAF drop 2,000 bombs on Hamburg (16 November). Death of Eric Gill (17 November). Kurt Schwitters fled Germany (1937) and now flees Nazi-occupied Norway to England. Arthur Koestler *Darkness at Noon*.

■ HR is awarded the Leon Fellowship at London University (July) for research on the place of art in the educational system (he has been writing intermittently on children's art since 1930 and now produces a lucid and practicable *vade mecum* on the subject and subsequently *The British Council Exhibition of British Children's Drawings* tours North and South America, 1941-2, and Paris, 1945).

Annals of innocence and experience (London, Faber & Faber)
The philosophy of anarchism (London, Freedom Press) [1941; 1947]
Thirty-five poems (London, Faber & Faber) [1941]
(Ed) *English master painters* (London, Kegan Paul)
'The United Artists Exhibition', *The Listener*, vol.XXIII, pp.67-70. 'The fate of Western art', pp.740-1. 'Adolescent art', p.842. Vol.XXIV: 'Pictures of the war', p.22. 'Public styles and private languages', p.207. 'The vitality of abstract art', pp.407-8. 'How shall we rebuild?', pp.586-7. 'Indian art', pp.729-30

1941

Death of Virginia Woolf (28 March). Leeds City Art Galleries stage Moore's first retrospective (July–September); purchases brown Hornton stone *Reclining Figure*, 1929. Germany invades Russia (22 June). United States enters War following Japanese attack on Pearl Harbor (7 December).

■ HR suggests to Moore that he draws Yorkshire coal-miners at work. He writes the introduction to the catalogue of the *Klee* exhibition at the Leicester Galleries, London. HR and Ludo's second son Piers Paul, is born (7 March).

169

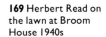

'Introduction', *Kropotkin: selections from his writings* (London, Freedom Press) pp.7-16
'Is British art fighting?', *Art and Industry*, vol.XXXIII, pp.2-4
'Art in relation to education', *Athene*, vol.I, pp.2-9. 'Design', vol.II, pp.6-8
'Vulgarity and impotence: speculations on the present state of the arts', *Horizon*, vol.V, no.28, pp.267-76
'Nicholson and Yeats at the National Gallery', *The Listener*, vol.XXVII, p.50. 'Round the art exhibitions', p.404. 'The new Romantic school', pp.533-4. 'Stone carving', p.809. Vol.XXVIII: 'The universal harmony', review of Thompson, D.W. *On Growth and Form*, p.187. 'The reputation of Raphael', p.335. 'Polish painting', p.655
'Modern art and French decadence', *Studio*, vol.CXXIV, pp.179-89

1943

German army surrenders at Stalingrad (31 January). Warsaw Ghetto uprising (begins 19 April). Italy surrenders to Allies (8 September). Reverend Walter Hussey begins commissioning contemporary art for St Matthew's, Northampton: Moore's *Madonna and Child* (1943-4), Sutherland's *Crucifixion* (unveiled November 1946).

■ HR acts as Director (until 1945) of the Design Research Unit (DRU), founded on 1 January with the aim of joining together the forces of art and industry; he helps promote the prototype for a post-war automobile designed by Gabo for Jowett Cars Ltd, Bradford, though the project subsequently falls through.

Education through art (London, Faber & Faber) [1958; 1945; 1956; 1961]; (1945; New York, Pantheon Books)
The politics of the unpolitical (London, Routledge & Kegan Paul)
'The future of industrial design', *Four lectures on design. The future of industrial design* (London, Hutchinson; Design and Industries Association) pp.26-32
'Creative ability in children', *The Listener*, vol.XXIX, p.111. 'The art of the portrait', p.299

1944

Siege of Leningrad ends (19 January). Deaths of Edvard Munch (23 January) and Piet Mondrian (1 February). Rome liberated (4 June). Allies land in Normandy: D-Day (6 June). Paris liberated (25 August). Deaths of Aristide Maillol (27 September) and Wassily Kandinsky (13 December).

■ HR introduces *Henry Moore Sculpture and Drawings* (Lund Humphries and A. Zwemmer), the first of a series of monographs on English artists promoted by Eric (called Peter) Gregory, one of the directors.
Exhibition of Sculpture and Drawings by Barbara Hepworth, Wakefield City Art Gallery (12 February–11 March) and Bankfield Museum, Halifax (18 March–15 April), with an introduction by HR.
Kurt Schwitters *Merzbild* and *Collage Incorporating Photograph of Herbert Read*.

The education of free men (London, Freedom Press)
Paul Nash (Harmondsworth, Penguin Books)
A world within a war, poems (London, Faber & Faber); (1945; New York, Harcourt, Brace)
(Ed) *Flicker. Three essays on the cinema* (Croydon, R.S.O. Poole)
'Threshold of a new age', 'Philosophy of change', Brumwell, J.M.R. (Ed) *This Changing World* (London) pp.7-14, 263-8
'Introduction', *Henry Moore Sculpture and Drawings* (London, Lund Humphries, Zwemmer); (1949; London, Lund Humphries); (1965; New York, Wittenborn) pp.xvii-xxxvi

To hell with culture; democratic values are new values (London, Kegan Paul, Trench, Trubner)
'The war as seen by British artists', Wheeler, M. (Ed) *Britain at War* (New York, MOMA) pp.11-12
'Culture and liberty', *Programme for Victory* (London, Fabian Society) pp.57-77
'The drawings of Henry Moore', *Art in Australia*, no.3, pp.10-16
'Art in an electric atmosphere', *Horizon*, vol.III, pp.308-13
'English watercolours and continental oils', *The Listener*, vol.XXVI, pp.121-2. 'What to look for in a picture', pp.529-30. 'Etruscan sculpture', p.602. 'The tragical history of Dr Faustus, pp.790-2. 'English art and the Mediterranean', p.819
'Eric Gill: Anarchist', *War Commentary*, vol.III, no.1, pp.3-4

1942

Singapore surrenders to the Japanese (15 February). *New Movements in Art* exhibition, London Museum: Agar, Gabo, Moore, Nash, Tunnard (18 March–9 May). Rommel defeated at El Alamein (4 November).

■ HR commends work by the Surrealists and abstract Constructivists, particularly Gabo's *Spiral Theme*, in his 'speculations on the present state of the arts' in *Horizon*. He broadcasts 'Aerial in Wartime; the question of abstract art' on the BBC Home Service (1 May).

'Education of the designer', *Architectural Review*, vol.XCVI, pp.183-4
'Art and crisis', *Horizon*, vol.IX, pp.336-50. 'Constructive art: an exchange of letters between Naum Gabo and Herbert Read', vol.X, no.55, pp.57-65
'Education through art', *Studio*, vol.CXXVII, pp.89-97

1945

RAF devastate Dresden (14 February). Tokyo destroyed by Allied bombing (10 March). United Nations born (25 April). Mussolini executed (28 April). Hitler commits suicide (30 April). Fall of Berlin (2 May). The Louvre reopens (10 July). Japan surrenders (14 August) following A-bomb drops on Hiroshima and Nagasaki. United Nations Educational, Scientific and Cultural Organisation (UNESCO) founded in Paris (16 November).

■ HR praises George Orwell *Animal Farm*: 'All animals are equal, but some are more equal than others'. *Freedom: Is It a Crime? Two Speeches by Herbert Read*, Freedom Press, London; a spirited defence of British anarchists put on trial, convicted and jailed for possessing literature of a 'seditious' character. This case leads to the setting up of the Freedom Press Defence Council, of which HR is Chairman. HR and Ludo's third son, Benedict William, is born (26 March).

Anarchy and order; essays in politics (London, Faber & Faber)
A Coat of Many Colours; occasional essays (London, Routledge & Kegan Paul) [1947; 1956]; (1956; New York, Horizon Press)
Freedom: is it a crime? (London, Freedom Press)
'The present state of design and its relation to the industrial system', *Architects Yearbook*, no.1, pp.86-91
'British children's art in Paris', *Athene*, vol.III, pp.112-13
'Primitive art', *The Listener*, vol.XXXIV, p.18. 'South Kensington revisited', p.74. 'Art in Paris now', p.188

1946

Inaugural session of United Nations General Assembly, London (30 January). 'An Iron Curtain has descended across the Continent' (Winston Churchill, 5 March). Death of H.G. Wells (13 August). Moore's first major retrospective in America, Museum of Modern Art, New York. Gabo emigrates to United States (December). Death of Paul Nash (10 July).

■ HR, Penrose and Mesens convene a meeting of the Museum of Modern Art Organising Committee (January) for the purpose of attracting 500 subscribers to finance the opening of a museum in London by 1950. Cooper's inflammatory policy ridiculing the Tate Gallery and the British Council rejected for a milder statement proposed by Grigson and HR (Spring). The enterprise soon became the Institute of Contemporary Arts (ICA). Peggy Guggenheim writes to HR from New York (2 February) to introduce her new 'discoveries': Robert Motherwell, Jackson Pollock and Clifford Still.

HR makes his first visit to the United States: he delivers the four Woodward and Trowbridge Memorial Lectures at Yale University (March), visits Moholy-Nagy near Chicago (Easter) and negotiates with the Bollingen Foundation to support the publication of an English edition of Jung's collected works (HR is on both the Editorial Committee and Executive Subcommittee representing Routledge). He departs from New York on the *Queen Mary* (12 May). During the Summer he meets with Jung while attending the annual Eranos conference (established in 1933 by Olga Froebe-Kapteyn) at Ascona on Lake Maggiore.

HR and Clive Bell are buying contemporary art in London for British Council institutions abroad (Nicholson, Pasmore, Matthew Smith): 'I suppose the urge to discover new things

170

instead of repeating oneself is merely an urge towards life instead of death … The excitement of discovering a new ptg "idea" is terrific … a kind of transformation – as much beyond oneself as being in love' (Nicholson to HR, 21 August).

Poem *1945* illustrated by Moore.

Collected poems (London, Faber & Faber) [1953; 1966]; (1951; Norfolk, Conn., New Directions) (1966; New York, Horizon Press)
'The problem of Picasso', *Journal of the Royal Society of Arts*, 18 Jan, pp.127-8
'Paul Klee', *The Listener*, vol.XXXV, pp.20-1. 'Art and healing', p.120. Vol.XXXVI: 'Britain can make it', pp.429-30. 'Neither Liberalism nor Communism', pp.844-5
'Century of English painting', *Magazine of Art*, vol.XXXIX, pp.220-5
'De Tocqueville on art in America', *Adelphi*, vol.XXIII, pp.191-5

1947

Indian Independence and creation of Pakistan (15 August). Director of Moscow's Tretjakov Gallery attacks modern art as 'decadent, anti-humanist, and pathological'.

Kurt Schwitters *Merzbild* '*Dundrennan*', a collage and watercolour inscribed 'For Herbert Read Kurt Schwitters 1947'.

■ HR, who believes great art avoids the depiction of the horrors of life, condemns Sutherland's Northampton *Crucifixion* (1946) as a 'wreck' (letter to Hepworth, 6 February). HR announces in *The Times* (26 June) the existence of the ICA; he is its first President. He lectures on art and literature in Belgium, Czechoslovakia, Denmark, France and Sweden: 'I have become a sort of Wandering Jew of British Culture'.

The Grass Roots of Art (London, Drummond) [1955]
'Introduction', *Policy statement: proposed Institute of Contemporary Arts* (London, Lund Humphries)
'The fate of modern painting', *Horizon*, vol.XVI, no.95, Nov, pp.242-54
'The artist's attitude to nature', *The Listener*, vol.XXXVII, pp.189-90. 'Why I was inspired by Nietzsche', pp.295-6. 'The ethics of power, pp.466-7. 'A scholar's essay', p.684. Vol.XXXVIII: 'Pre-Columbian art', pp.13-14. 'The Oxford Wordsworth', p.1027
'Chains of freedom', *Now*, vol.VIII, pp.4-10. Vol.IX, pp.17-22
'Education for peace (I)', *Adelphi*, vol.XXIV, pp.193-8

1948

Death of Schwitters (8 January). Gandhi assassinated (30 January). Communist coup in Czechoslovakia (27 February). State of Israel established (14 May). First *Sculpture in the Open Air* exhibition, Battersea Park, London (Summer). Eliot wins Nobel Prize for Literature (10 December).

■ HR, the 'dean of highbrow art critics' and 'our most distinguished lover of bad painting', is interviewed in *News Review* (22 January) about his anarchism (not of the bomb-throwing type) and the ICA: 'we want to strengthen the production of art. Today there is not a sufficient flow of vital ideas'. *Forty Years of Modern Art* at the Academy Hall, Oxford Street, London (15 February–6 March), an exhibition organised by the ICA comprising 127 works from British collections, including Braque, de Chirico, Dali and Matisse as well as Bacon, Colquhoun, Craxton, Freud, Hepworth, Lewis, MacBryde, Moore, Nash, Nicholson, Paolozzi and Sutherland. In his opening speech HR stresses that the ICA is 'not another museum ... but an adult play-centre, a workshop where work is joy, a source of vitality and daring experiment'. The critics of *The Sunday Times*, *Daily Worker* and *New York Times* give sympathetic reviews but the show attracts only 16,000 visitors and the organisers are prosecuted at Marlborough Street Magistrates Court for obstructing the pavement.

HR flies to New York (28 March) and delivers a paper on Coleridge at the Symposium on the Great Critics at Johns Hopkins University, Baltimore. He helps organise the first *National Exhibition of Children's Art* in London and speaks on art in education at a UNESCO conference in Paris (May).

HR is on the British Council's selection committee for the British Pavilion at the 24th Venice *Biennale* and writes the introduction to the catalogue. Moore is awarded the International Sculpture Prize, which launches his world-wide reputation. HR is also a member of the Council's selection committee for Moore's exhibition tour to Paris, Brussels and Amsterdam (which took place in 1949-50). HR stresses that the aim of the ICA's exhibition *40,000 Years of Modern Art*, which opens in the Academy Cinema Hall, London, on 21 December and includes Picasso's *Les Demoiselles d'Avignon* (lent by the Museum of Modern Art, New York) was to juxtapose primitive and modern art as a way of demonstrating 'some of the sources of inspiration in the most important trends in painting and sculpture since the beginning of this century'. He lectures in Germany (December and again in January 1949).

Barbara Hepworth *Poet reading to his Children* portrays HR with Thomas, Sophie and Piers.

Culture and education in a world order (New York, Museum of Modern Art)
Klee (1879-1940) (London, Faber & Faber) 2 vols; (1949; New York, Pitman)
'Introduction', *Ben Nicholson; paintings, reliefs, drawings* (London, Lund Humphries) pp.1-32
'The dialectic of art', Thiessing, F. C. (Ed) *Erni: elements of future painting* (Zurich) pp.12-14
'Introduction', *Forty years of modern art* (London, Institute of Contemporary Arts) 3pp. unpag.
'Preface', *Forty thousand years of modern art* (London, Institute of Contemporary Arts) pp.6-7
'Aristotle's mother' and 'Thieves of mercy', Heppenstall, Rayner (Ed) *Imaginary conversations* (London, Secker & Warburg) pp.35-47, 97-110
'Introduction', *Naum Gabo and Antoine Pevsner* (New York, Museum of Modern Art) pp.7-13
'Introduction', *Paul Klee on Modern Art* (London, Faber & Faber) pp.5-6
'Paul Nash as artist', Eates, Margot *Paul Nash, paintings, drawings and illustrations* (London, Lund Humphries) pp.7-13
'The plight of the visual arts', Hardman, D. (Ed) *Reflections on our age* (Paris, UNESCO) pp.177-90

'A great teacher', review of Moholy-Nagy, L. *Vision in Motion*, *Architectural Review*, vol.CIII, no.647, May, p.221
'Barbara Hepworth: a new phase', *The Listener*, vol.XXXIX, p.592
'The moral principle in education', *Question*, vol.I, pp.26-45
'Coleridge as critic', *Sewanee Review*, vol.LVI, pp.597-624
'Culture and education in a world order', *World Review*, Sep, pp.36-42

1949
Pound wins the first Bollingen Poetry Prize (19 February). Tate Gallery fully reopens for first time since 1939 (25 February). North Atlantic Treaty Organistion (NATO) established (18 March). G. A. Dondero, Republican Congressman from Michigan, attacks modern art and modern art museums, in series of Congressional speeches: 'Modern Art as Communist Heresy' (11 March), 'Communism in the Heart of American Art: What To Do About It' (17 May: 'Modern Art is communistic because it is distorted and ugly, because it does not glorify our beautiful country'), 'Modern Art Shackled to Communism' (16 August). Mao-tse-tung proclaims Communist People's Republic of China (1 October). Orwell *Nineteen Eighty-Four*.

■ HR becomes President of the Penwith Society (February), a group of Modernist painters and sculptors (including Hepworth, Lanyon and Nicholson) which breaks away from the traditionalist-dominated St Ives Society, whose recently elected President, Alfred Munnings attacks modern art, vilifying Matisse, Moore and Picasso, at the Royal Academy's annual dinner (30 April). HR acquires Stonegrave – 'Only 7 acres, but a nice old parsonage to live in, with stables and pigsties' – located some three miles from Muscoates, his birthplace (June). He and Basil Taylor select paintings (June) for the British section of the international exhibition at the Musée d'Art Moderne and the Salon des Realités Nouvelles, Paris. HR lectures at Kenyon College, Ohio (26 June–6 July). HR supports Richard Hamilton's plan (Autumn) for a *Growth and Form* show at the ICA, which is mounted in 1950, and proposes that the Arts Council commissions five paintings for £500 each, recommending Colquhoun, Craxton, MacBryde, Nicholson and Sutherland (9 November report to Philip James).

171

Coleridge as critic (London, Faber & Faber)
Education for peace (New York, Scribner); (1950; London, Routledge & Kegan Paul)
Existentialism, Marxism and anarchism (London, Freedom Press)
Atelier 17 (New York, Wittenborn, Schultz)
(Ed) *Gauguin (1848-1903)* (London, Faber & Faber); (1951; New York, Pitman)
(Ed) *Paul Nash: Outline, an autobiography, and other writings* (London, Faber & Faber)
(and Bonamy Dobrée) (Eds) *The London book of English verse* (London, Eyre & Spottiswoode) [1956; 1965]; (1952; New York, Macmillan)
'Coleridge as critic', The Johns Hopkins University Lectures in Criticism (New York, Johns Hopkins University) pp.73-116
'Education for peace (II)', *Adelphi*, vol.XXV, pp.12-16
'The present situation of art in Europe', *Hudson Review*, vol.I, pp.50-64
'The revival of Europe', *World Review*, Jan, pp.9-14. 'Conversation in the ruins', March, pp.25-8. 'A reply to Mr. Priestley', April, p.3. 'Primitive and modern art', June, pp.34-9. 'Poetry and love', July, pp.29-33

1950

Death of George Orwell (21 January). McCarthyism in America. Museum of Modern art, Whitney Museum of American Art, New York, and Institute of Contemporary Art, Boston issue *Manifesto on Modern Art* to counter attacks of radicalism and subversion (March). Korean War begins (25 June), Britain sends troops: 'The whole idea that we can fight communism with firearms is an illusion: it merely blows the smouldering embers to a flame' (HR to Gabo, 21 December). *American Symbolic Realism* at ICA (July–August). Burgess and MacLean 'infiltrate' Institute. Death of Bernard Shaw (2 November).

Bertrand Russell wins Nobel Prize for Literature (10 December). Death of Max Beckmann (27 December). The ICA's inaugural exhibition in its new premises, 1950, *Aspects of British Art* (realism, neo-romanticism and international art), is opened by Lord Harewood in the ICA's new London home at 17 Dover Street. Peter Gregory, an early Moore supporter, establishes the Gregory Fellowships in Painting, Sculpture, Poetry and Music at Leeds University. HR is closely associated with the venture. Reg Butler is appointed the first Sculpture Fellow (1950-3), Martin Froy the first Painting Fellow (1951-4).

■ HR visits Peggy Guggenheim in Venice (July); he also obtains an invitation for Hepworth to represent Britain at this year's *Biennale*. He 'tyrannically censored all further dissension' at an ICA poetry reading during which Emmanual Litvinoff grossly insults Eliot for his anti-semitism (Autumn). Wyndham Lewis attacks *Education Through Art* (1943) as being too formulaic and rigid (November).
Moore *Standing Figure*.
Lynn Chadwick *Maquette for Poseidon*.
Gabo *Opus 4*, a woodcut inscribed 'Gabo ... 50, for Herbert Op4'.
Patrick Heron *Portrait of Herbert Read*.

'Realism and abstraction in modern art', *Eidos*, no.1, pp.26-37
'The critic as a man of feeling', *Kenyon Review*, vol.XII, no.4, Autumn, pp.575-80
'Goethe and art', *The Listener*, vol.XLIII, pp.13-14. 'Marxist critic', pp.700-1. 'Wordsworth and *The Prelude*', pp.775-7. Vol.XLIV: 'Shelley the optimistic philosopher', pp.377-8
'Wordsworth's philosophical faith', *Sewanee Review*, vol.LVIII, pp.563-85
'Malraux and The Psychology of Art', *World Review*, Jan, pp.44-7. 'The mystery of landscape', Feb, pp.65-8. 'The plays of Henry

James', March, pp.45-50. 'The price of culture', April, pp.44-8. '1984', June, pp.58-9. 'An irregular genius: the significance of D.H. Lawrence', July, pp.50-6

1951

Festival of Britain (design director Hugh Casson) and Royal Festival Hall (designed by J. L. Martin) open (3 May); ICA organises *Ten Decades of British Taste*, ironic comment on persistence of philistinism. Anthony Kloman, ICA's American-born Director of Public Relations, introduces idea of *Unknown Political Prisoner* competition as way of contrasting 'open' society of West with Soviet totalitarian repression (ICA May meeting). United States tests first H-bomb (12 May). Burgess and MacLean defect to Russia (25 May). Hepworth and Nicholson separate.
Butler *Girl and Boy*.

■ HR lectures on *Art and the Evolution of Man* at the Conway Hall, London. He opens the Hepworth retrospective at Wakefield, West Yorkshire (May). *Moon's Farm*, a verse drama, is broadcast on the BBC (July). HR lectures at Princeton University, delivering the first part of *The True Voice of Feeling: Studies in English Romantic Poetry*, and is invited to Paul Mellon's home at Upperville, Virginia (Autumn). HR and Alex Comfort write a letter to *The New Statesman* (10 November) condemning the Conservative government's willingness to rearm Britain according to the United States' anti-Red dictates, and they call for immediate disarmament.

Art and the evolution of man (London, Freedom Press)
Byron (London, New York, British Council and Longmans Green) [1961; 1966]
Contemporary British art (Harmondsworth, Penguin Books); (1964; Baltimore, Penguin Books)
'Preface', Whyte, L. L. (1951) *Aspects of Form* (London, Lund Humphries) pp.v-vi
'Psychoanalysis and the problem of aesthetic value', *International Journal of Psychoanalysis*, vol.XXXII, part 2, pp.73-82
'The paradox of liberalism', *The Listener*, vol. XLV, p.671. 'The method that kills', pp.1013-14
'Jung at mid-century', *Hudson Review*, vol.IV, pp.259-68

1952

Britain explodes first Atomic bomb off Australian coast (3 October). United States explodes first Hydrogen bomb in Pacific atoll (30 November). Independent Group formed in London (Reyner Banham, Hamilton, Paolozzi, Turnbull and later Lawrence Alloway): avant-garde not committed to 'received' history of art reacting against precepts championed by HR (November).
Moore *Time/Life Screen* working model.

■ HR co-chairs the Central Committee for the ICA's *International Competition for a Monument to the Unknown Political Prisoner*, which is announced in January. He invites Benjamin Britten, E. M. Forster, Graham Greene and Moore to take part in a demonstration against political murders in Spain (March). He and Ludo meet Igor Stravinsky in Paris and attend a performance of Britten's opera *Billy Budd*.

HR travels on to Venice, where he is a jury member which awards a prize to Dufy. As a member of the selection panel for the British Pavilion at the Venice *Biennale*, he writes an essay 'New Aspects of British Sculpture' for the catalogue, featuring Robert Adams, Kenneth Armitage, Reg Butler, Lynn Chadwick, Geoffrey Clarke, Bernard Meadows, Moore, Eduardo Paolozzi and Turnbull. While staying with Peggy Guggenheim he meets the Paris-based Czech-Jewish painter Ruth Francken and a close friendship is formed (Summer).

Graham Sutherland, an exhibition organised by the British Council and the Museums of France, held at the Musée National d'Art Moderne, Paris, with an introduction to the catalogue by HR (November–December). HR receives a letter (3 December) from the Palace offering him a knighthood 'for services to literature' (awarded 1953). Writes introductory text to *Barbara Hepworth Carvings and Drawings* (London, Lund Humphries). His book *The Philosophy of Modern Art* is dedicated to Wilhelm Worringer, 'my esteemed master in the philosophy of art'.

The philosophy of modern art; collected essays (London, Faber & Faber) [1964]; (1953; New York, Horizon Press); (1955; New York, Meridian Books)
'Introduction', Wölfflin, H. *Classic Art* (London, Phaidon) pp.v-viii
'Farewell to Formalism', *Art News*, vol.LI, no.4, pp.36-9
'Art and the development of the personality', *British Journal of Medical Psychology*, vol.XXV, parts 2-3, pp.114-21
'The art of art criticism (I)', *The Listener*, vol.XLVII, pp.714-16. '(II)', pp.797-800
'Sign and symbol', *Question*, vol.V, pp.46-68

1953
Death of Stalin (5 March). Coronation of Elizabeth II (2 June). Korean War ends (27 July). First showing of Jackson Pollock in Britain, organised by the ICA. Kenneth Armitage appointed Gregory Fellow in Sculpture (1953-5)
 Moore *King and Queen*.
 Meadows *Black Crab*.

■ HR, as President of the ICA, represents Britain on the International Jury of the *Competition for a Monument to the Unknown Political Prisoner* and writes the foreword to the exhibition catalogue (14 March–30 April): Butler is awarded the Grand Prize – his original maquette is smashed by a member of the public while on view at the Tate Gallery. Gabo, Hepworth and Chadwick are also prize winners. HR, Ludo and Benedict leave (Autumn) for a seven month visit to the United States. In New York, HR meets Georges Simenon, one of his authors, and is both fascinated and terrified by the menacing spectacle of McCarthy's televised anti-Communist 'witch-hunt'. At Harvard University he lectures as the Charles Eliot Norton Professor of Poetry (1953-4). HR and Alfred Barr, Director of the Museum of Modern Art, New York, travel to Brazil as jury members of the 2nd São Paulo *Bienal*; Moore wins the International Sculpture Prize (December).

The true voice of feeling; studies in English romantic poetry (London, Faber & Faber) [1968]; (1953; New York, Pantheon Books)
(Ed; 1953f-)*The collected works of C.G.Jung* (London, Routledge & Kegan Paul); (1966; New York, Pantheon Books)
'Foreword', *International Sculpture Competition: the Unknown Political Prisoner* (London, Tate Gallery) 1p unpag.
'Introduction', *Sutherland* (London, Arts Council) 2pp unpag.
'Everyman as artist', *Athene*, vol.VI, pp.35-8
'The Zeitgeist', *Encounter*, vol.I, pp.64-6
'The dynamics of art', *Eranos Jahrbuch*, Band XXI: 1952, pp.255-85
'Presentation of the RIBA Gold Medal to Le Corbusier', *Journal of the Royal Institute of British Architects*, vol.LX, pp.215-16
'What does art create?', review of Langer, S. *Feeling and Form*, *New Republic*, vol.CXXVIII, 1 June, pp.17-18. 'Primitive art and modern man, vol.CXXIX, pp.16-17. 'Against the betrayal of architecture', pp.20-21
'The artist in the world', *New Statesman & Nation*, vol.XLV, p.316. 'Tragic art', p.366
'The longing for truth-knowledge', *Question*, vol.VI, pp.60-83
'Originality', *Sewanee Review*, vol.LXI, p.533-56

1954
'Convention for the Protection of Cultural Property in the Event of Armed Conflict' signed by 50 countries at The Hague (14 May). UK Atomic Energy Authority established (1 August). Moore's *King and Queen* removed from lobby of 380 Madison Avenue, New York after 75% of tenants express disapproval (October). Death of Henri Matisse (3 November).
 Chadwick *The Stranger*.
 Moore *Internal/External Form*.

■ HR delivers the six A.E. Mellon Lectures in the Fine Arts at the National Gallery of Art, Washington DC (beginning in March) on the theme of sculpture. He gives the opening address at the First General Assembly of the International Society for Education through Art. Nicholson visits Stonegrave (October) and makes a series of drawings of the house and village, including *The Invisible White Cat*, and of nearby Rievaulx Abbey.

HR becomes increasingly disillusioned by the ICA's (indiscriminate) commitment to 'contemporary art', which he regards as an imprecise adjective covering a multitude of sins (December meeting).

Terry Frost, Gregory Fellow in Painting (1954-6), paints *Red Black and White* after a visit to Stonegrave. Lewis published a vitriolic attack on HR in *The Daemon of Progress in the Arts*.

'Introduction', *Australia: aboriginal paintings, Arnhem Land* (Greenwich, Conn., New York Graphic Society; UNESCO) pp.5-9
'The museum and the artist', *College Art Journal*, vol.XIII, pp.289-93
'The true voice of John Keats', *Hudson Review*, vol.VI, pp.90-105
'Art and the evolution of consciousness', *Journal of Aesthetics and Art Criticism*, vol.XIII, pp.143-55
'W.B.Yeats', *The Listener*, vol.LII, pp.582, 585. 'Pascal-Napoleon', review of Grohmann, W. *Paul Klee*, pp.967, 969

1955
Russell's declaration urging nations to renounce war published (15 July). 250,000 visit Royal Academy, London to see Annigoni's portrait of *Queen Elizabeth* (14 August–13 October). Hubert Dalwood appointed Gregory Fellow in Sculpture (1955-9).

■ HR's review in *New Statesman* claiming that the Catholic Church has instigated a campaign to discredit Epstein leads to a public squabble with Graham Greene. HR writes the introduction to the catalogue of the Nicholson retrospective exhibition at the Tate Gallery.

The Grass Roots of Art; lectures on the social aspects of art in an industrial age (London, Faber & Faber); (1955; New York, G. Wittenborn); (1961; Cleveland, World Publishing Co)
Icon and idea; the function of art in the development of human consciousness (London, Faber & Faber); (1955; Cambridge, Harvard University Press)
Moon's Farm, and poems mostly elegiac (London, Faber & Faber); (1956; New York, Horizon Press)
The psychopathology of reaction in the arts (London, Institute of Contemporary Arts) [reply to Lewis]
'Introduction', *Ben Nicholson: paintings, reliefs, drawings*, Vol.2 (London, Lund Humphries) pp.1-24
'The drift of modern poetry', *Encounter*, vol.IV, Jan, pp.3-10. 'A blot on the scutcheon', vol.V, July, pp.54-7
'Baudelaire as art critic', *The Listener*, vol.LIV, p.665. 'Michelangelo and Bernini', pp.886-8
'The Romantic revolution', *London Magazine*, vol.II, pp.68-74
'The lost leader, or the psychopathology of reaction in the arts', *Sewanee Review*, vol.LXIII, pp.551-66 [reply to Lewis]

1956

Death of Emil Nolde (15 April). John Osborne's tirade against English Establishment *Look Back in Anger* (premiered 10 May). US Information Agency cancels *100 American Artists of the Twentieth Century* tour: 10 artists are 'politically unacceptable ... pro-Communist' and 'social hazards' (June). Suez Crisis (begins July). Deaths of Jackson Pollock (11 August) and Bertolt Brecht (14 August). Hungarian National Rising (begins October). Harwell nuclear reactor opens (21 November). Richard Hamilton *Just what is it that makes today's homes so different, so appealing?* Alan Davie appointed Gregory Fellow in Painting (1956-9).

■ HR, grappling with American Abstract Expressionism, finds Willem de Kooning's 'titanic struggle with the Shadow, the dark aspects of the mind' appealing. He lectures on children's art at the University of British Columbia, Vancouver (Summer). He refuses the call from Koestler and Spender to join them in a protest against the Soviet's brutal suppression of Hungary because he disagrees with the revolutionaries' use of force: 'the only way to end war is to refuse to fight, under any provocation'. His book *The Art of Sculpture* (the 1954 Mellon Lectures), dedicated to Gabo, Hepworth and Moore 'Sculptors and Friends in Gratitude'.

The Art of Sculpture (London, Faber & Faber) (1956; New York, Pantheon Books) (1961; New York, Pantheon Books)
(Ed) *This way, delight; a book of poetry for the young* (New York, Pantheon, 1956); (1957; London, Faber); (1961; New York, Pantheon)
'The architect as universal man', *Architects Yearbook*, vol.VII, pp.7-10
'Gauguin: the return to symbolism', *Art News Annual*, vol.XXV, pp.122-58
'The psychology of art', *The Listener*, vol.LV, p.423
'An art of internal necessity', *Quadrum*, no.1, pp.7-22

1957

Death of Constantin Brancusi (16 March). European Common Market established: Treaty of Rome (25 March). Britain drops first H-bomb on Christmas Island (15 May). J.B. Priestley's letter to the *New Statesman* criticising development of British H-bomb causes uproar and sparks Campaign for Nuclear Disarmament (CND). Russia launches Sputnik (4 October). NATO agreement to accept United States nuclear missile bases in Europe (19 December).

■ HR travels to Switzerland (August), Italy (September) and on Routledge business to Canada and the United States (November–December).

The significance of children's art: Art as symbolic language (Vancouver, University of British Columbia)
The tenth muse; essays in criticism (London, Routledge & Kegan Paul); (1958; New York, Horizon Press)
'Introduction', *Henry Moore* (London, Lund Humphries), pp.xvii-xxxvi
'New realms of art', *New frontiers of knowledge: a symposium* (Washington) pp.77-9
'The problem of aesthetic consciousness', *Proceedings of the Third International Congress on Aesthetics*, 1956, University of Torino, pp.257-60
'Poetic consciousness and aesthetic experience', *Eranos Jahrbuch*, Band XXV: 1956, pp.357-89
'Art, industry and national decay', *The Listener*, vol.LVII, pp.175-7.
'Constantin Brancusi: 1876-1957', pp.642-3

1958

CND launched in Britain (17 February); Aldermaston March (7 April). Alberto Burri's sewn-burlap collage refused duty-free entry by United States Customs because not 'art' (November). John Betjeman wins Duff Cooper Prize for poetry (18 December).

Jean Arp *Brass Figure*.
Bryan Kneale *Portrait of Herbert Read*.
Moore *UNESCO Reclining Figure*, Paris.

■ HR receives the Bollingen Foundation's agreement to give him an annual stipend of £4,000 to reduce the ever-increasing burden of administrative work. Visits to London and lecture tours (April). He defends Jung in *New Statesman* (31 May issue) against allegations of having been pro-Nazi and anti-Semitic. Member of International Committee of Experts for exhibition *50 Years of Modern Art*, Brussels. Though unsure of some others of the younger generation of artists, HR contributes an essay on Armitage, Bacon, Butler and Chadwick as well as on Hepworth, Moore, Nicholson, Pasmore and Sutherland, to *Art Since 1945*, edited by Marcel Brion.

Lynn Chadwick (Amriswill, Bodensee-Verlag)
'Recent tendencies in abstract painting', *Canadian Art*, vol.XV, pp.192-203
'Limitations of a scientific philosophy', *Educational Review*, vol.X, pp.92-107
'The creative nature of Humanism', *Eranos Jahrbuch*, Band XXVI: 1957, pp.315-50
'Sam Francis', *Quadrum*, no.5, p.92

1959

Deaths of George Grosz (6 July) and Sir Jacob Epstein (19 August). Opening of F.L. Wright's Solomon R. Guggenheim Museum, New York. In a letter to *The Times* (January) HR, Spender and others oppose the government's claim that Vladimir Nabokov's novel *Lolita* (1955, published in Britain in 1959) is obscene.

■ HR, responding to C.P. Snow's advocacy of technology, expresses his belief that the technological revolution would lead to the extermination of humanity (*London Magazine*, August issue). During a three-week visit to China on a Cultural Exchange (September) – via Moscow, where he sees work by Gauguin, Matisse and Renoir in the Pushkin Museum – HR is overwhelmed by Peking's physical beauty and describes the commune system as 'a dream come true', though he finds China yet 'another country committed to technological doom [which] fills me with horror' (letters, reprinted in *A Tribute to Herbert Read 1893-1968*, 1975, pp.43-9). HR writes 'A Letter of Introduction' to the Hepworth exhibition catalogue at the Galerie Chalette, New York (November). He receives a Maillol bronze *Bather* from the late Peter Gregory's estate.

A concise history of modern painting (London, Thames & Hudson) [1961]; (1959; New York, Praeger) [1965]
'Introduction', *Kandinsky (1866-1944)* (London, Faber & Faber); (1959; New York, Wittenborn) pp.1-24
'The flower of peace', *Eranos Jahrbuch*, Band XXVII: 1958, pp.299-332
'Aspirations in perspective', *The Listener*, vol.LXI, pp.793-4.
'David Jones: Epoch and Artist', p.853
'Art and life', *Saturday Evening Post*, vol.CCXXXII, pp.34-5, 103-4, 106
'A literary correspondence [with Edward Dahlberg]', *Sewanee Review*, vol.LXVII, pp.177-203, 422-45

172

1960

Third Congress of Artistic and Literary Workers decree art and literature 'the nerve centre of the class struggle' and 'the victory of Marxist-Leninist principles' in China (July). Russell resigns as CND leader (24 October). 200,000 copies of Penguin edition of *Lady Chatterley's Lover* sell out first day of publication (10 November). *Gregory Memorial Exhibition*, Leeds City Art Gallery. Trevor Bell appointed Gregory Fellow in Painting (1960-3).

■ HR has a frenzy of lectures at American universities (Spring). He speaks at the Europa-Gespräch conference in Vienna (June), launches the British Society of Aesthetics (July), attends the 4th International Congress of Aesthetics in Athens and visits Olympia and Bassae (September). He gives a speech in honour of Kramer at Leeds City Art Gallery (September). He disputes Jung's diagnosis of Picasso's enormous success as a symptom of the failure of contemporary art (19 October letter).

Nicholson *Tenement*, an etching incorporating HR's poem of the same title.

The forms of things unknown: essays towards an aesthetic philosophy (London, Faber & Faber) (1960; New York, Horizon) (1963; Cleveland, World Publishing Co, Meridian Books M168)
The parliament of women; a drama in three acts (Huntingdon, Vine Press)
'Introduction', *Peter Gregory Memorial Exhibition* (Leeds City Art Gallery), pp.5-7
'The aesthetics of architecture', *Architectural Association Journal*, vol.LXXV, pp.202-9
'Dialogue on modern U.S. painting', *Art News*, vol.LIX, pp.32-6
'Nihilism and renewal in the art of our time', *Eranos Jahrbuch*, Band XXVIII: 1959, pp.345-76
'Rock paintings in South Africa', *The Listener*, vol.LXIII, pp.263-4. 'The problem of style', p.671
'Avantgardism and modernism', review of Shattuck, R, (1959) *The Banquet Years*, *London Magazine*, vol.7, no.3, March, pp.57-60
'In defence of abstract art', *New York Times Magazine*, April, pp.32-3, 40, 42, 45, 48
'The social significance of abstract art', *Quadrum*, no.9, pp.5-14
'Esthetics: enemy of violence', *Saturday Review*, Dec, pp.9-11

1961

United States fires first intercontinental ballistic missile (1 February). Soviet Union launches first man in space (12 April). Death of Carl Gustav Jung (6 June). Berlin Wall built (13-20 August). Austin Wright appointed Gregory Fellow in Sculpture (1961-4).

■ HR (a member of the recently formed CND Committee of 100, prominent citizens opposed to nuclear war) participates in sit-downs at the Ministry of Defence in London (February), and in Trafalgar Square (17 September); but now disillusioned by the Campaign's 'fascist' tactics, he resigns. HR in Venice, where he writes *Daphne*, one of his finest long poems. The honeymoon with Routledge comes to an end: 'my services were no longer considered essential'. HR's son, John, makes the film *Barbara Hepworth* for BBC TV.

Aristotle's mother; an imaginary conversation (North Harrow, Middlesex, P. Ward)
(and Dahlberg, Edward) *Truth is more sacred; a critical exchange on modern literature: James Joyce, D.H. Lawrence, Henry James, Robert Graves, T.S. Eliot and Ezra Pound* (London, Routledge & Kegan Paul); (1961; New York, Horizon Press)
'The origins of form in art', *Eranos Jahrbuch*, Band XXIX: 1960, pp.183-206

1962

Coventry Cathedral, with art by Epstein, Piper, Sutherland and others, consecrated (25 May). Cuban Missile Crisis (October). Benjamin Britten *A War Requiem*.

■ HR visits South America (Summer) and the United States (Autumn) on a lecture tour. 'A Nest of Gentle Artists' describes his reminiscences about avant-garde art in Hampstead in the 1930s.

Karel Appel *Portrait of Herbert Read*.

Ben Nicholson (London, Methuen) (Paris, Hazan) (Gütersloh, Mohn)
Design and tradition (Hemingford Grey, Vine Press)
A letter to a young painter and other essays (London, Thames & Hudson); (1962; New York, Horizon Press)
Vocal avowals: Worte sagen aus (St Gallen, Tschudy Verlag)
'A nest of gentle artists', *Apollo*, vol.LXXVI, no.7, Sep, pp.536-8
'What is there left to say?', *Encounter*, vol.XIX, no.4, Oct, pp.27-31
'Ape art', *Studio*, vol.CLXIII, pp.172-3

1963

President John F. Kennedy assassinated (22 November).

■ HR is instrumental in publishing Worringer's *Abstraktion und Einfühlung* (1908) in an English trans., *Abstraction and Empathy* (London, Routledge & Kegan Paul). He lectures in New Zealand and Australia (Spring) and Canada (Summer). His 70th birthday is celebrated with dinners at the Arts Club, London, and in Leeds (December).

The contrary experience; autobiographies (London, Faber & Faber) (1963; New York, Horizon Press)
Reason and romanticism, essays in literary criticism (New York, Russell & Russell)
Selected writings; poetry and criticism (London, Faber & Faber)
To hell with culture, and other essays on art and society (London, Routledge & Kegan Paul); (1963; New York, Schocken Books)
'The beginnings of art', *Apollo*, vol.LXXVIII, pp.319-20

173

1964

United States at war in Vietnam. Pop Art shown for first time under official United States government patronage at Venice *Biennale*; artists condemned as 'impudent crooks' by European critics (September).

■ HR is the best-known promoter of Modernism in the English-speaking world: 'Do you think Sir Herbert Read takes something to keep him so avant-garde?' (*Punch* cartoon, 26 February issue). He is appointed a Fellow of the Center for Advanced Studies at Wesleyan University, Conn., and goes on an American lecture tour. 'The Disintegration of Form in Modern Art', a lecture in which HR airs his misgivings about some recent artistic tendencies, is delivered at *Documenta III*, in Kassel, Germany. During a trip to Switzerland, HR visits Nicholson in Ticino (August). Writes introduction to *The Gregory Fellows University of Leeds*, an Arts Council exhibition. A malignant tumour (an epithelium) is removed from HR's tongue, followed by radiotherapy and hospitalisation (November–December).

A concise history of modern sculpture (London, Thames & Hudson) (1964; New York, Praeger) [1965]
High noon and darkest night (Middletown, Conn., Center for Advanced Studies, Wesleyan University Press)
'High noon and darkest night: Ortega y Gasset's philosophy of art', *Journal of Aesthetics*, vol.XXIII, no.1, pp.43-50

174

'Jan le Witt: conflicting concepts of reality in abstract art', *Quadrum*, no.17, pp.119-24
'Limits to painting', *Studio*, vol.CLXVII, pp.2-11

1965

Death of T.S. Eliot (4 January). Russell tears up Labour Party card in protest at British support for United States in Vietnam (14 October).

■ HR finds Pop Art 'tedious' (letter to Penrose, 28 February). He and Ludo travel to Wesleyan University (en route reading *Paradise Lost* and Saul Bellow's *Herzog* – 'a shapeless mass of unleavened dough'); lectures at Yale, Berkeley and in Virginia (Spring) and receives an honorary doctorate from Boston University (6 June). To Switzerland (August). He warns Misha Black that design in England has become infected with 'adolescent pruriency' and 'beatnikery' (15 October letter).

HR and his son Piers Paul visit Japan: 'a vast unplanned mechanised chaos' (October). Concerned about the American presence in Vietnam, he tells the poet Allen Tate: 'I don't want to come to the States again so long as this bloody aggression goes on' (28 December letter). HR is awarded the Erasmus Prize, which he shares with René Huyghe, and an Honorary Doctorate at York University; he is made an honorary member of the American Academy of Arts and Letters and is invited to become a Trustee of the Tate Gallery.

Henry Moore; a study of his life and work (London, Thames & Hudson); (1966; New York, Praeger)
The origins of form in art (London, Thames & Hudson)
(Ed) *The styles of European art* (London, Thames & Hudson)
'British art 1930-1940'; 'A nest of gentle artists', *Art in Britain, 1930-40, centred around Axis, Circle and Unit One* (London, Marlborough Fine Art, Ltd) pp.5-8
'Wilhelm Worringer', *Encounter*, vol.XXV, no.5, Nov, pp.58-60
'Disintegration of form in modern art', *Studio*, vol.CLXIX, pp.144-55

1966

HR writes an introduction to the Hepworth exhibition catalogue at The Marlborough-Gerson Gallery, New York (April–May). He undergoes a second operation for cancer of the tongue (October): 'I have no energy left for creative tasks: all is consumed in the will to live'. He and Hepworth are among the Tate Trustees who object to the purchase of Roy Lichtenstein's painting *Whaam!* (1963): 'This sort of thing is just nonsense' (November).

The redemption of the robot; my encounter with education through art (New York, Trident Press); (1970; London, Faber & Faber)
T.S.E., a memoir (Middletown, Conn., Center for Advanced Studies, Wesleyan University)
(Ed) *The Thames and Hudson encyclopaedia of the arts* (London, Thames & Hudson); American edition (1966; New York, Meredith) has title: *Encyclopaedia of the arts*
'Man and his world', *Canadian Art*, vol.XXIII, pp.25-40
'T.S. Eliot: a memoir', *Sewanee Review*, Winter
'Mondrian in London: reminiscences', *Studio*, vol.CLXXII, p.289.
'What kind of art education?', pp.136-8, 166-7, 226-7, 284

1967

200,000 demonstrate against Vietnam War in New York and San Francisco (15 April). Deaths of Siegfried Sassoon (1 August) and René Magritte (15 August).

■ HR is hospitalised to undergo further surgery and doses of radium (January). *The Naked Ape* by Desmond Morris, Director of the ICA, an overnight success: 'It shows that it pays to write on Apes rather than Art' (HR to Penrose).

Art and alienation: the role of the artist in society (London, Thames & Hudson); (1967; New York, Horizon Press)
Poetry and experience (London, Vision Press); (1967; New York, Horizon Press)
'Whatever happened to the great simplicities?', *Saturday Review*, 18 Feb, pp.21-3, 48-9

175

1968

Martin Luther King assassinated (4 April). Venice *Biennale* closed down by students attempting to overthrow 'bourgeois capitalistic international art establishment'.

■ HR speaks on 'The Problems of Internationalism in Art' at the International Cultural Congress in Havana (4-11 January); he is stirred by Cuba's socialism, and through Graham Greene meets the painters Jacob Milian and Portocarrero. He also visits Puerto Rico and Haiti. After another major operation (March), HR tells Hepworth that he looks 'like one of Francis Bacon's worst nightmares'.

Sir Herbert Read dies in his sleep at Stonegrave (12 June). He is buried in Kirkdale churchyard, near his parents: 'Here lies HERBERT READ Knight Poet Anarchist'. 'Herbert was my first sponsor and friend ... His great courage and understanding helped me so much ... Without him there is an awful blank' (Barbara Hepworth).

176

176 Herbert Read in his study at Stonegrave 1960s

Arp (London, Thames & Hudson)
'Will Grohmann', *Burlington Magazine*, vol.CX, p.413
'Pragmatic Anarchism', *Encounter*, vol.XXX, no.1, Jan, pp.54-61

Obituaries

Apollo, vol. LXXXVIII, pp.160-3
Martin, J.L. *Architectural Review*, vol.CXLIV, p.306
Michelis, P.A. *British Journal of Aesthetics*, vol.IX, p.3
Taylor, B. *Burlington Magazine*, vol.CX, pp.433, 462
Connaissance des Arts, vol.CXCIX, p.27
Gray, N. *Design*, vol.CCXXXV, p.71
Gazette des Beaux-Arts, vol.LXXII, suppl.24
Studio, vol.CLXXVII, pp.2-4

Writings on Herbert Read by other authors

BOOKS

Berry, Francis (1953, 1961) *Herbert Read* (Writers and their work no.45) (London, Longmans Green/British Council)

Hortmann, Wilhelm (1976) *Wenn die Kunst Stirbt : zum Prinzip des Organischen in der Kunst und Gesellschaftstheorie von Herbert Read* (Duisburg, Walter Braun Verlag)

King, James (1990) *The last modern : a life of Herbert Read* (London, Weidenfeld & Nicolson)

Skelton, Robin (Ed) (1970) *Herbert Read : a memorial symposium* (London, Methuen)

Thistlewood, David (1984) *Herbert Read : Formlessness and Form : an introduction to his aesthetics* (London, Routledge & Kegan Paul)

Treece, Henry (1944) *Herbert Read : an Introduction to his work by various hands* (London, Faber & Faber)

Woodcock, George (1972) *Herbert Read : the stream and the source* (London, Faber & Faber)

(1975) *A Tribute to Herbert Read 1893-1968* (Bradford Art Galleries and Museums)

(1984) *Homage to Herbert Read* (Canterbury College of Art)

CHAPTERS OF BOOKS

Fishman, Solomon (1963) 'Herbert Read', *The Interpretation of art* (Berkeley, University of California Press) pp.143-86, 190-1

Ray, Paul C. (1971) *The Surrealist movement in England* (Ithaca and London, Cornell University Press) ; esp. pp.108-32

Thistlewood, David (in press) 'Herbert Read' in: Tedesco, J.C. and Morsy, Z. (Eds) *Thinkers of Education* [*Penseurs de l'Education*] [*Pensadores de la Educación*] (Paris, UNESCO, 1994).

ARTICLES

Hodin, J.P. (1965) 'Herbert Read : the man and his work : a tribute on his 70th birthday', *Journal of Aesthetics*, vol.XXIII, no.2, pp.169-72

Ray, P.C. (1966) 'Sir Herbert Read and English Surrealism', *Journal of Aesthetics*, vol.XXIV, no.3, pp.401-13

De Gennaro, A.A. (1968) 'Benedetto Croce and Herbert Read', *Journal of Aesthetics*, vol.XXVI, no.3, pp.307-10

Frankston, L. (1968) 'A talk with Herbert Read', *Art Journal*, vol.XXVII, no.4, p.371-4

Thistlewood, David (1979) 'Herbert Read's aesthetic theorising 1914-1952', *Art History*, vol.II, no.3, pp.339-54

Thistlewood, David (1980) 'A dialectical model of modern art', *Malahat Review*, no.55, University of Victoria BC Press, pp.73-103

Thistlewood, David 'A study of Herbert Read's criticism', *Malahat Review*, no.61, University of Victoria BC Press, pp.49-95

Thistlewood, David (1982) 'Organic art and the popularisation of a scientific philosophy', *British Journal of Aesthetics*, vol.XXII, no.4, pp.311-21

Thistlewood, David (1986) 'Creativity and political identification in the work of Herbert Read', *British Journal of Aesthetics*, vol.XXVI, no.4, pp.345-56

Thistlewood, David (1993) 'Herbert Read : a critical appreciation at the centenary of his birth', *Journal of Art and Design Education*, vol.XII, no.2, pp.143-60

Critic's Choice – but am I a critic in the accepted meaning of the word? In the past twenty-five years I have written much about contemporary art, but generally with a philosophical or perhaps sometimes a psychological intention. I have tried to be as objective as possible, and have deliberately refrained for confusing a would-be scientific activity with any expression of my likes and dislikes. For this reason I have occasionally been accused of having no direct relation to the work of art as such – of being, that is to say, an intellectualist without any sensuous response to aesthetic values.

I suppose there are theorists of art who work with their nerves carefully insulated – I have known historians of art, who always use photographs for their researches and feel uncomfortable when confronted with an original painting. But that has not been my method of work. I have lived among artists and have had the privilege of close friendship with some of the leading painters and sculptors of my time. I have visited hundreds of studios and exhibitions in many parts of the world, and have always realised that a theory of art must be based, not only on a knowledge of the history of art, but also on a close contact with the contemporary practice of it. Only in this way can a critic appreciate the miracle of transformation that takes place in the actual *process* of creation.

On this occasion, however, I am to abdicate my role of objectivity and freely declare my personal tastes! I accept the challenge with some trepidation – because my freedom is so carefully circumscribed. I am limited to less than 30 paintings, and to about half a dozen artists. More seriously, I am limited to living British artists, and even with that category, to artists of certain age limits. How comparatively easy my task would have been if I could have expressed my personal choice from the works of Renoir and Vuillard, Braque and Klee, or any of a dozen artists to whom I am passionately devoted, but who are beyond my imposed pale! How 'safe' my revealed taste would then have seemed, how sensuous and serene! But I have no such liberty, and must turn my eyes to the contemporary scene in England.

One further limitation I have imposed on myself. This is the second exhibition of its kind – last year Mr Eric Newton made his choice, and at least two of the painters he chose might have competed for a place in my exhibition. I have deliberately excluded these painters because it seemed to me that the field was wide enough for two critics to avoid each other's tracks. In other words, my choice has been to that extent restricted by what is perhaps an irrelevant sense of fairness.

Now for some explanation of my final selection of paintings! It will at once be seen that they all tend towards that extreme in contemporary art which is known as 'abstraction', and this will immediately reinforce the already prevalent suspicion of an intellectual approach to art. I must insist, therefore, that I *like* this kind of art – it gives me a directly sensuous and profound enjoyment. Let me be as emphatic as possible at this point: I do not intend this exhibition to be another demonstration in the bitter conflict between realism and abstraction in modern art. I follow the dictates of my own sensibility alone, and this exhibition is the result.

I have in the past written so much about abstraction in general, and this is not the place for philosophical discourse. What must be reaffirmed, however, is that the kind of art misrepresented by the word 'abstraction' is neither 'formalist' nor 'pure' nor 'academic' in the perjorative sense of these words. It differs from so-called realist art (again an ambiguous term – used generally to indicate expressionist art with a class conscious scope) in that it accepts as realistic the constituent elements of the medium of expression. That is to say the realistic elements of the art of painting are: *paint* as a plastic substance of infinite variations of substance and tone; *formal relations* as a reflection of the essential nature of the real world; and *intuitive vision* as the artist's power to create a symbolic discourse of universal validity. The vision is, of course, the first necessity, for without it the artist cannot exploit his medium as formal and plastic language. Granted this vision, this creative power of expression, he can communicate to us a consciousness of the nature of reality far more profound than any that is present in the representation of the superficial appearance of objects. *To live in the realm of forms* (Cassirer has said) *does not signify an evasion of the issues of life; it represents, on the contrary, the realisation of one of the highest energies of life itself.*

I know that in identifying realism with the 'superficial appearance of objects' I am begging the question. I shall be told that the effort of evey realist since Cézanne (if not since Masaccio) has been to get beneath the superficial appearance of objects, to reveal the inner structure of things, to realize, as Cézanne said, the structure of what we actually see. But Cézanne's aim, rigorously followed, has led step by step with inexorable logic to the kind of painting I have chosen for this exhibition.

Catalogue

The catalogue entries may include the following:

Number
Artist; Dates of birth and death
Title and date of work
Signature, date, description
Medium
Dimensions (in centimetres: height, width, diameter and, in the case of some furniture and sculptures, depth)
Illustration (in a Read publication)
Exhibited (in an exhibition with Read associations)
Comments
Lender

* denotes a work formerly in the collection of Herbert Read

The present exhibition also includes a selection of Herbert Read's publications

1
ALVAR AALTO; 1898-1976
Chair 1934
Moulded birch plywood
82.5 × 42.5 × 57
The Board of Trustees of the Victoria and Albert Museum, London

2
JANKEL ADLER; 1895-1949
*Woman with Cat**
Signed: Adler
Etching
46 × 35.5
Read wrote the Introduction to Adler's exhibition at the Redfern Gallery, London, June-July 1943
Private collection

3
Africa, Kinshasa Baluba, Zaire
Figure, probably 19th century
Wood
68.6
Ill: H. Read, *The Art of Sculpture*, 1956, pl.166
The British Museum, Department of Ethnography

4
Africa, Songye, Zaire
Dance mask, probably 19th century
Wood
38.1
Ill: H. Read, *The Art of Sculpture*, 1956, pl.168
The British Museum, Department of Ethnography

5
Anonymous
*c.*1940-1
Poster paint on paper
Chosen by Read for inclusion in an exhibition of *Drawings and Paintings by British Schoolchildren*, which toured North and South America, 1941-2.
National Arts Education Archive, Bretton Hall, University of Leeds

6
Anonymous
Dining chair, produced by Practical Equipment Ltd for Broadcasting House, Portland Place, London 1931-3
Tubular steel and leather
77 × 52 × 53
The Museum of London

7 (cover & fig.102)
KAREL APPEL; born 1921
Portrait of Sir Herbert Read 1962
Oil on canvas
115.9 × 89.2
The Montreal Museum of Fine Arts Collection. Purchase, Horsley and Annie Townsend Fund

8
KENNETH ARMITAGE; born 1916
Study for sculpture 1951
Signed and dated: KA 51
Watercolour on paper
40.6 × 50.8
The Ronnie Duncan Collection

9
KENNETH ARMITAGE; born 1916
Standing Group No.2, 1952
Bronze
102
Related to the work shown in the British Pavilion, Venice *Biennale*, 1952 (104)
Gimpel Fils and New Art Centre, London

10 (fig.153)
KENNETH ARMITAGE; born 1916
Figure lying on its Side (version V) 1957
Bronze
82
Ill: H. Read, *A Concise History of Modern Sculpture*, 1964, fig.255
The British Council

11
KENNETH ARMITAGE; born 1916
Pandarus (version 8) 1963
Brass
178
Armitage was Gregory Fellow in Sculpture, 1953-5
Collection of the artist

12
JOHN ARMSTRONG; 1893-1973
*Untitled c.*1930
Signed: JA
Oil on canvas
73.7 × 62.2
Armstrong was a member of Unit One.
Private collection

13
JEAN/HANS ARP; 1887-1966
Figure 1958*
Brass
Approx. 10 × 11 × 8
Private collection

14
Australia, Aborigine
*Painting**
Pigment on bark
26 × 43
Private collection

15 (fig.76)
FRANCIS BACON; 1909-92
Study for a Crucifixion 1933
Oil on canvas
61 × 48.3
Ill: H. Read, *Art Now*, 1933, pl.61 as 'Crucifixion 1933'. Exh: 'Art Now', Mayor Gallery, London, Oct 1933 as 'Composition 1933'
Private collection

16 (fig.145)
VOJIN BAKIC; born 1915
*Torso c.*1960*
Signed: V. Bakic pour Sir Herbert
Bronze on wood base
29 × 10 × 8
Private collection

17 (fig.44)
ERNST BARLACH; 1870-1938
*Mors Imperator** *(Death the Emperor)* 1919
Woodcut
27 × 36
Private collection

18 (fig.54)
WILLI BAUMEISTER; 1889-1955
Apollo 1933
Signed on verso: Baumeister 1.33
Oil and sand on canvas
81.5 × 65.2
Baumeister features in H. Read, *Art Now*, 1933. Read wrote the introduction to the artist's exhibition at the Institute of Contemporary Art, London, 1956
Staatsgalerie Stuttgart

19
TREVOR BELL; born 1930
Image of Red 1958
Inscribed on verso: Image of Red by Trevor
Bell 1958
Oil on canvas
71.1 × 63.5
The Ronnie Duncan Collection

20
TREVOR BELL; born 1930
Italian 1959
Signed and dated: Bell 59
Oil on canvas
121.9 × 91.4
University of Leeds Art Collections

21
TREVOR BELL; born 1930
To Tuscany 1959
Signed and dated: Bell 59
Oil on canvas
167.6 × 76.2
University of Leeds Art Collections

22
TREVOR BELL; born 1930
Widdale 1962
Inscribed on verso: Trevor Bell 1962
Widdale
Oil on canvas
60.8 × 121.8
Bell was Gregory Fellow in Painting,
1960-3
University of Leeds Art Collections

23
WILLIAM BLAKE; 1757-1827
Songs of Innocence 1789 (facsimile published
by Benn, London, 1926, from a copy in The
British Museum)
'The poetry of William Blake descended on
me like an apocalypse. Though I have
submitted to many influences and have
been fired to more than one enthusiasm in
the intervening years, there is no poet with
whom today I would more readily identify
the poetic essence. For me, Blake is
absolute.'
Leeds University Library

24
NEVILLE BODEN; born 1929
Procession through a split curve c.1965
Painted aluminium
183
Leeds City Art Galleries

25
NEVILLE BODEN; born 1929
White, grey, dark blue and black on white c.1965
Signed: Neville Boden 1/1
Lithograph
64.7 × 46.9
University of Leeds Art Collections

26
NEVILLE BODEN; born 1929
Band Relief c.1967
Painted aluminium
91.4 × 61 × 14
Boden was Gregory Fellow in Sculpture,
1965-8
University of Leeds Art Collections

27
DAVID BOMBERG; 1890-1957
Dancer 1913
Signed: David Bomberg
Watercolour and charcoal on paper
38.1 × 27.09
Read reviewed Bomberg in *Arts Gazette*, 13
Sep 1919
The Trustees of the Cecil Higgins Art
Gallery, Bedford

28
MARCEL BREUER; 1902-81
Dining table for Isokon Furniture Co,
London 1936
Plywood
70.6 × 137 × 69.5
The Board of Trustees of the Victoria and
Albert Museum, London

29
MARCEL BREUER; 1902-81
Long chair for Isokon Furniture Co,
London 1936
Moulded birch plywood, 'zebrano' veneer
79 × 61 × 99
Breuer lived in Isokon Flats, Lawn Road,
Hampstead, 1934-7
The Board of Trustees of the Victoria and
Albert Museum, London

30 (fig.113)
MARCEL BREUER; 1902-81 (attributed)
Tubular table* 1930
Metal and glass
73 × 66 × 52.2
Private collection

31
ALBERTO BURRI; born 1915
Untitled 1957*
Signed: Burri
Burnt and varnished paper, woven fabric
26 × 18.5 (on two sheets)
One of three works by the artist in
... *imprestami una battaglia*, a book of poetry
by Emilio Villa, published Rome 1955,
inscribed on page 1: A Herbert Read con
amicizia Alberto Burri Settembre 57 Roma
Private collection

32 (fig.141)
REG BUTLER; 1913-81
Head 1948-9*
Forged and welded iron on wood base
80 × 30 × 38
Ill: H. Read, *Contemporary British Art*, 1951,
pl.60
Private collection

33
REG BUTLER; 1913-81
Girl and Boy 1951
Iron
206 × 66.5 × 84
Exh: British Pavilion, Venice *Biennale*, 1952
(111)
Arts Council Collection, The South Bank
Centre, London

34 (fig.137)
REG BUTLER; 1913-81
*Working model for a Monument to The Unknown
Political Prisoner* 1955-6
Forged and welded iron, painted black,
bronze with plaster base
223.8 × 88 × 85.4
One of several studies related to the
international competition held in 1952-3;
the original, final maquette, shown in the
exhibition *The Unknown Political Prisoner*,
Tate Gallery, London, 14 March-30 April
1953 (14) and awarded Grand Prize, was
vandalised
Tate Gallery. Presented by Cortina and
Creon Butler 1979

35
REG BUTLER; 1913-81
Girl c.1957
Bronze
147.3 × 45.5 × 37
Butler was Gregory Fellow in Sculpture,
1950-3
Leeds City Art Galleries

36
ALEXANDER CALDER; 1898-1976
Untitled mobile c.1938-9
Painted metal, wire, wood and string
105 × 120
Private collection (on loan to Leeds City Art
Galleries)

37
TINO DI CAMAINO; c.1285-1337
Virgin and Child between 1323-37
Marble
47.6 × 37.2
H. Read, *The Art of Sculpture*, 1956, pl.75
illustrates a similar Camaino relief.
Trustees of the Victoria and Albert
Museum, London

38
LYNN CHADWICK; born 1914
*Maquette for a Monument to The Unknown
Political Prisoner* 1953
Welded iron
43
Exh: *The Unknown Political Prisoner*, Tate
Gallery, London, 14 March-30 April 1953
(15)
Collection of the artist

39 (fig.101)
LYNN CHADWICK; born 1914
The Stranger 1954
Bronze
73
Ill: H. Read, *Lynn Chadwick*, Bodensee-
Verlag, Amriswil, 1960, pl.8
Collection of the artist

40
SERGE CHERMAYEFF; born 1900
Radio cabinet Ekco Model AC 74, made by
E.K. Cole Ltd, Southend-on-Sea, Essex
1933
Bakelite case, chrome, four valves
45.5 × 38 × 26.5
Ill: H. Read, *Art and Industry The Principles of
Industrial Design*, 1934, p.121
The Board of Trustees of the Victoria and
Albert Museum, London

41
Chinese
Pair of candle-holders in the form of
monsters, probably Northern Wei Dynasty
Black earthenware with white slip
13.4 × 22 (each)
An example of sensuous distortion,
discussed in: H. Read, *The Meaning of Art*,
1931
Leeds City Art Galleries

42
Chinese, Hopei or Honan Province
Vase, probably Sung or Yüan Dynasty AD
960-1368
Grey stoneware with transparent glaze over
creamy white slip, painted with dark brown
slip
28
An example of irregular, intuitional form,
discussed in H. Read, *Art and Industry The
Principles of Industrial Design*, 1934, p.31
Leeds City Art Galleries

43 (fig.45)
JEAN COCTEAU; 1889-1963
Night of the Night 1926*
Inscribed: Le bain de lumière (maison de
santé) 1926 Jean Night of the Night amical
Souvenir au professeur Read: de Jean
Cocteau
Pen and ink on paper
31.5 × 24.2
Ill: H. Read, *Art Now*, 1933 frontispiece
Private collection

44
WILLIAM CONGDON; born 1912
Piazza San Marco No.2
Signed: WC
Oil on board
30 × 35
Given to Read by Peggy Guggenheim, 1963
Private collection

45
CONGO; born 1955
Fan Pattern
Gouache on paper
37 × 52
?Exh: Institute of Contemporary Arts,
London, 'Paintings by Chimpanzees', Sep-
Oct 1957
Private collection

46 (fig.96)
CONGO; born 1955
Split Fan Pattern
Gouache on paper
39 × 52
?Exh: Institute of Contemporary Arts,
London, 'Paintings by Chimpanzees', Sep-
Oct 1957
Private collection

47
DENNIS CREFFIELD; born 1931
Leeds from the University I 1964
Signed and dated: Dennis Creffield 64
Charcoal on paper
55.9 × 77.5
University of Leeds Art Collections

48
DENNIS CREFFIELD; born 1931
Leeds from the University II 1964
Signed and dated: Dennis Creffield 64
Charcoal on paper
55.9 × 77.5
University of Leeds Art Collections

49
DENNIS CREFFIELD; born 1931
Leeds from the University III 1964
Signed and dated: Dennis Creffield 64
Charcoal on paper
55.9 × 77.5
University of Leeds Art Collections

50
DENNIS CREFFIELD; born 1931
Halifax 1964
Signed and dated: Dennis Creffield 64
Charcoal on paper
55.9 × 77.5
The John Jones Collection

51 (fig.155)
DENNIS CREFFIELD; born 1931
Leeds 1965
Oil on canvas
91.4 × 101.6
Creffield was Gregory Fellow in Painting,
1964-7
Leeds City Art Galleries

52
STANLEY CURSITER; 1887-1976
Princes Street 1913
Signed and dated: Stanley Cursiter 1913
Oil on canvas
50.8 × 61
Cursiter was Director of the National
Gallery of Scotland during Read's
occupancy of the Watson Gordon
Professorship at Edinburgh University,
1931-3
James Holloway

53 Not in exhibition

54
HUBERT DALWOOD; 1924-76
Screen 1959
Alloy with black support
55 × 99.7 × 14.6
University of Leeds Senior Common Room
Club

55
HUBERT DALWOOD; 1924-76
Object: Open Square 1959
Aluminium
42 × 34.5 × 13
Leeds City Art Galleries

56
HUBERT DALWOOD; 1924-76
Double Casket c.1960
Aluminium
20.3 × 35.6 × 20
Dalwood was Gregory Fellow in Sculpture,
1955-9
The John Jones Collection

57
GEORGE DANCE THE YOUNGER; 1741-1825
Portrait of Samuel Taylor Coleridge 1804
Signed and dated: Geo. Dance March 21st
1804
Pencil on paper
19.7 × 16
The Wordsworth Trust, Centre for British
Romanticism, Grasmere

58
ALAN DAVIE; born 1920
Blood Creation 1952
Inscribed: 155215452
Oil on hardboard
182.9 × 182.9
The Ronnie Duncan Collection

59
ALAN DAVIE; born 1920
Image of the Fish God 1953
Signed: Alan Davie
Oil on paper
30.5 × 20
The Ronnie Duncan Collection

60 (fig.156)
ALAN DAVIE; born 1920
In the Face of the Witch 1955
Signed on verso: Alan Davie 55
Oil on board
99.7 × 116.8
Leeds City Art Galleries. Given by the
Contemporary Art Society 1962

61
ALAN DAVIE; born 1920
Untitled c.1957
Oil on brown paper
20.3 × 91.4
Davie was Gregory Fellow in Painting
1957-9
The Ronnie Duncan Collection

62 (fig.144)
JOHN WARREN DAVIS; born 1919
*Double Figure** c.1960
Bronze on wood base
28 × 11 × 8
Private collection

63 (fig.74)
PAUL DELVAUX; born 1897
L'Appel de la Nuit/The Call of Night 1938
Signed and dated: Delvaux.3-1938
Oil on canvas
110.8 × 28.9
Ill: H. Read, *A Letter to a Young Painter*, 1962,
p.96
Private collection, England. On loan to the
Scottish National Gallery of Modern Art,
Edinburgh

64 (fig.13)
VALENTINE DOBRÉE; 1895-1974
*To Grace Darling**
Collage on board
24.5 × 16
Private collection

65
Egypt, Akhmim
Figure of Tjeti 6th Dynasty/*c.*2400 BC
Inscribed on base with name and titles of
sitter
Wood (originally painted), crystalline
limestone, black obsidian, copper
75.5
H. Read, *The Art of Sculpture*, 1956, pl.58
illustrates a similar standing figure in wood
dating 1580-1090 BC
The British Museum, Department of
Egyptian Antiquities

66
Egypt, Saft El-Hinna
Fragment, Standing Figure of Nectanebo I
30th Dynasty/*c.*358 BC
Inscribed on back with names and titles of
sitter
Grey granite
64.4
H. Read, *The Art of Sculpture*, 1956, pl.154
illustrates a similar figure group attached to
the back of a stele
The British Museum, Department of
Egyptian Antiquities

67
England
Two donor figures: William and Matilda
Cele 2nd half 14th century
Inscribed: VILLMS CELE ET MATILDA
UXOR EI
Clear and coloured pot-metal glass painted
in black with yellow silver-stain
52.8 × 45
Ill: H. Read, *English Stained Glass*, 1926,
pl.26
The Board of Trustees of the Victoria and
Albert Museum, London

68
England
Drinking glass, first quarter 18th century
Lead glass
29.8
Items like this and catalogue no.181 feature
in Read's manuscript travel notes on
historic glass in Italy and France, compiled
while a curator in the Department of
Ceramics, Victoria and Albert Museum,
1922-31
Leeds City Art Galleries

69
England, Staffordshire
Figure of a Cat 1740-50s
Press-moulded salt-glazed stoneware, deep
brown and white 'agate' splashed with blue,
brown slip
13
Read illustrates an almost identical piece in
Staffordshire Pottery Figures, 1929, pl.10,
bottom
Leeds City Art Galleries

70
England, Staffordshire
Teapot and lid 1750s
Blue, brown and white 'agate' earthenware
15
A similar object is illustrated in B. Rackham
and H. Read, *English Pottery Its Development
from Early Times to the End of the Eighteenth
Century*, 1924, fig.163
Leeds City Art Galleries

71
England, Staffordshire
Teapot and lid 1760s
Creamware, press-moulded and cast,
stained blue, green and yellow glaze
14
An almost identical object is illustrated in
B. Rackham and H. Read, *English Pottery*,
1924, fig.160
Leeds City Art Galleries

72
England, Staffordshire
Teapot and lid 1760s
White salt-glazed stoneware, painted in
enamel colours
13
A Punch-Pot of the same material and
technique with similar decoration is
illustrated in B. Rackham and H. Read,
English Pottery, 1924, fig.10
Leeds City Art Galleries

73
HANS ERNI; born 1909
*Two Women 1958**
Signed and dated: hans dec 58
Oil on paper
52 × 65
Private collection

74 Not in exhibition

75 (fig.82)
MAX ERNST; 1891-1976
La Ville Petrifiée/The Petrified Town 1933
Signed: Max Ernst
Oil on paper stuck down on board
50.5 × 60.9
Read once owned a similar painting by
Ernst
Manchester City Art Galleries

76
France, School of Paris
Virgin and Child 14th century
Ivory
35.5
Ill: H. Read, *The Art of Sculpture*, 1956, pl.77
The Board of Trustees of the Victoria and
Albert Museum, London

77 (fig.162)
SAM FRANCIS; born 1923
Over Yellow 1957-8
Oil on canvas
290 × 200
Ill. H. Read, *The Origins of Form in Art*, 1965,
ill.57
Staatsgalerie Stuttgart

78
RUTH FRANCKEN; born 1924
Composition 1954-5*
Gouache on paper
36.5 × 51.5
Francken was the original recipient of *A
Letter to a Young Painter*, published in 1962
Private collection

79
TERRY FROST; born 1915
Yellow Verticals 1954
Oil on canvas
72.5 × 128.5
The Ronnie Duncan Collection

80 (fig.154)
TERRY FROST; born 1915
*High Yellow c.*1955
Oil on canvas
121.9 × 121.9
Leeds City Art Galleries

81
TERRY FROST; born 1915
Red, Black and White 1956
Signed and dated on verso
Oil on board
128 × 103
Painted after a visit to Stonegrave while the
artist was Gregory Fellow in Painting
(1954-6); he recollected 'a walk I had with
Herbert Read ... when I saw the sun setting
behind a wood in winter'
Private collection

82
TERRY FROST; born 1915
Untitled 1956
Signed and dated: Terry Frost 56
Lithograph
45 × 57
University of Leeds Art Collections

83
TERRY FROST; born 1915
Red, White and Black 1957
Oil on canvas
121.9 × 121.9
University of Leeds Senior Common Room
Club

84
TERRY FROST; born 1915
Umber, Black and Red December 1959-
February 1960
Inscribed on verso: Umber, Black and Red
Terry Frost Dec-Feb 60
Oil on canvas
76.2 × 63.5
Frost was Gregory Fellow in Painting,
1954-6
University of Leeds Art Collections

85 (fig.152)
MARTIN FROY; born 1926
Nude in a Window 1953
Oil on board
152.4 × 121.9
Wakefield Museums, Galleries and Castles

86
MARTIN FROY; born 1926
*Yorkshire Landscape c.*1955
Oil on board
121.9 × 91.4
Leeds City Art Galleries

87
MARTIN FROY; born 1926
Composition, Nudes and Landscape 1957
91.4 × 71.1
University of Leeds Art Collections

88
MARTIN FROY; born 1926
*A Seated Nude c.*1959
Pencil and gouache
31.6 × 24
Froy was Gregory Fellow in Painting,
1951-4
Leeds City Art Galleries

89
NAUM GABO; 1890-1977
Construction in Space : Soaring 1929-30
Brass, painted black and white, plexiglass,
wood
112
Leeds City Art Galleries. Allocated by the
Heritage Minister following the
recommendation by the Museums and
Galleries Commission which administers the
Acceptance in Lieu Scheme 1989

90
NAUM GABO; 1890-1977
*Model for a Monument to The Unknown Political
Prisoner* 1952
Plastic with stainless steel wire mesh on
plastic and slate base
38.1 × 8.9 × 9.5
Exh : The Unknown Political Prisoner, Tate
Gallery, London, 14 March-30 April 1953
(30)
Tate Gallery, London. Presented by the
artist 1977

91
NAUM GABO; 1890-1977
Op.4 1950*
Inscribed: Op.4 for Herbert Gabo 50
Wood engraving
15.7 × 13.7
Private collection

92 (fig.23)
MARK GERTLER; 1892-1939
Portrait of Sir Michael Sadler
Oil on canvas
61 × 54
University of Leeds Art Collections

93 (fig.117)
ERIC GILL; 1882-1940
Working model for Prospero and Ariel 1931
Caen stone
127 × 45.7 × 35.6
Tate Gallery, London. Purchased 1935

94
HAROLD GILMAN; 1878-1919
*Leeds Warehouses c.*1913
Inscribed on verso: The Factories (2)
H Gilman
Pencil on paper
22.8 × 28
University of Leeds Art Collections

95
CHARLES GINNER; 1878-1952
Factories and Barges, Leeds 1916
Oil on canvas
50.7 × 61
Exh : Leeds Arts Club, Oct 1916
Private collection

96 (fig.19)
CHARLES GINNER; 1878-1952
*Leeds University Buildings c.*1916
Signed: C. Ginner
Ink and crayon on paper
36.4 × 27 (image size)
University of Leeds Art Collections

97
THOMAS GIRTIN; 1775-1802
Bolton Abbey 1800
Signed and dated: Girtin 1800
Watercolour on paper
32.4 × 47.7
Leeds City Art Galleries

98
EMILIO GRECO; born 1913
Seated Figure 1949
Bronze
86.3
Leeds City Art Galleries

99 (fig.123)
Greece, Amorgos, Cyclades
Cycladic figure of schematic type (amulet)
late 3rd millenium BC
Marble
12.1
Ill: H. Read, *The Art of Sculpture*, 1956,
pl.31a
The British Museum, Department of Greek
and Roman Antiquities

100 (fig.124)
Greece
Figure of Hermes Wearing a Sun Hat
100 BC
Bronze
48.9
This figure is representative of the new
humanism introduced into Greek bronze
figures discussed in H. Read, *The Art of
Sculpture*, 1956
The British Museum, Department of Greek
and Roman Antiquities

101
BENJAMIN ROBERT HAYDON; 1786-1846
Life Mask of William Wordsworth 12 May
1815
Plaster cast
22.5 × 15 × 13
The Wordsworth Trust, Centre for British
Romanticism, Grasmere

102
STANLEY WILLIAM HAYTER; 1901-88
Couple 1952*
Signed and dated: S W Hayter 52
Etching
44.5 × 29.5
Read wrote the introduction to Hayter's
New Ways of Gravure, 1949
Private collection

103 (fig.75)
JEAN HÉLION; 1904-87
Composition 1935*
Signed and dated: Hélion 35
Watercolour on paper
27 × 21
Read wrote on Hélion in *Axis*, no.4, 1935
Private collection

104 (fig.50)
DAME BARBARA HEPWORTH; 1903-75
Kneeling Figure 1932
Signed and dated: b.r. B.H. 1932
Rosewood
69 × 28.8 × 32
Ill: H. Read, *Carvings by Barbara Hepworth*,
Arthur Tooth & Sons, London, 9 Nov-
3 Dec 1932; H. Read, *Barbara Hepworth
Carvings and Drawings*, 1952, pl.2
Wakefield Museums, Galleries and Castles

105 (fig.72)
DAME BARBARA HEPWORTH; 1903-75
Single Form 1937*
Holly wood
78.8
Ill: H. Read, *Barbara Hepworth Carvings and
Drawings*, 1952, pl.52
Leeds City Art Galleries, Bought with
grants from the National Heritage
Memorial Fund and the Henry Moore
Foundation, 1990

106
DAME BARBARA HEPWORTH; 1903-75
Forms in Red : Drawing for sculpture with colour
1941*
Signed and dated: Barbara Hepworth 1941
Pencil and gouache on paper
23 × 29.5
Private collection

107 (fig.5)
DAME BARBARA HEPWORTH; 1903-75
The Poet Reading to his Children 1948
Signed and dated: Barbara Hepworth 1948
A Poet reading
Pencil and oil on board
38 × 53.8
A portrait of Read, with Thomas, Sophie
and Piers
Leeds City Art Galleries

108 (fig.98)
DAME BARBARA HEPWORTH; 1903-75
Concourse 1948*
Signed and dated: Barbara Hepworth
1/1/48
Pencil and oil on board
25.2 × 35.5
Ill: H. Read, *Barbara Hepworth Carvings and
Drawings*, 1952, pl.107
Private collection

109
DAME BARBARA HEPWORTH; 1903-75
Pierced Form (Toledo) 1957
Mahogany and string
90
Gimpel Fils, London

110 (fig.160)
PATRICK HERON; born 1920
Still Life 1947*
Signed and dated: Heron II:47
Oil on canvas
62.5 × 75
Private collection

111
PATRICK HERON; born 1920
Sketchbook containing the first study for the
portrait of Herbert Read 1950
Pencil
26 × 35
Patrick Heron

112 (fig.159)
PATRICK HERON; born 1920
Portrait of Herbert Read 1950
Signed and dated: Patrick Heron 1950
Oil on canvas
76.2 × 63.5
National Portrait Gallery, London. Given
by Barbara Hepworth and Henry Moore
1968

113
PATRICK HERON; born 1920
*Portrait of Thomas Stearns Eliot: study from
memory* 1947-8
Signed and dated on verso
Oil on canvas
91.5 × 63.5
Patrick Heron

114
IVON HITCHENS; 1893-1979
*Henry Moore in His Parkhill Road Studio c.*1930
Oil on canvas
58.4 × 82.5
Leeds City Art Galleries. Purchased with
grants from HM Government and the
Henry Moore Foundation 1983

115 (fig.146)
JOHN HOSKIN; 1921-90
*Insect c.*1960*
Welded metal
9 × 32 × 6.5
Private collection

116 (fig.22)
FRANCIS ERNEST JACKSON; 1872-1945
*Portrait of Alfred Orage c.*1920
Signed: F. Ernest Jackson FEJ
Lithograph
28.1 × 21.7
Leeds City Art Galleries. Bought 1921

117
FELIX KELLY; born 1916
The Three Sisters 1943*
Signed: Felix Kelly
Oil on canvas
22 × 25.5
Read wrote the introduction to *Paintings by
Felix Kelly*, 1946, in which this work is
reproduced, pl.24
Private collection

118
PAUL KLEE; 1879-1940
Rauferei 1926*
Signed: Klee; inscribed: 1926 J. I. Rauferei
Pencil on paper
21.5 × 15
Read's first article on Klee appeared in
1931 and he continued to write about him
till the end of his life
Private collection

119 (fig.20)
MAX KLINGER; 1857-1920
Portrait bust of Friedrich Nietzsche 1904
Signed: MK
Bronze
52.6 × 24.5 × 33
Museum der bildenden Künste, Leipzig

120 (fig.148)
BRYAN KNEALE; born 1930
Portrait of Sir Herbert Read 1958
Signed and dated: Bryan Kneale 58
Oil on canvas
101.6 × 75
York City Art Gallery. Presented by the
Friends of York City Art Gallery

121
OSKAR KOKOSCHKA; 1886-1980
Prague Nostalgia 1938
Oil on canvas
56 × 76
Private collection

122
OSKAR KOKOSCHKA; 1886-1980
*Two Fishes**
Inscribed: OK für Herbert Read
Watercolour on paper
39 × 58
'Love is a soiled word. In Kokoschka it is
instinctive identity; identity with the colour
of the flower, the irridescences of fish scales
and shells, the fluctuation of light over hills,
or its splendour as it strikes the massed roofs
of some city.' From Foreword by Read to
E. Hoffmann, *Kokoschka: Life and Work*,
1947
Private collection

123 (fig.24)
JACOB KRAMER; 1892-1962
*Portrait of Herbert Read c.*1914*
Signed: Kramer
Pencil on paper
25.5 × 21
Private collection

124
JACOB KRAMER; 1892-1962
*The Rabbis c.*1919
Oil on canvas
76.5 × 50.8
Ferens Art Gallery, City of Kingston-upon-
Hull Museums and Art Galleries

125 (fig.25)
JACOB KRAMER; 1892-1962
Rite of Spring (Musical Theme) 1920
Signed: Kramer 1920
Oil on wood
63.5 × 76.2
Private collection

126
BERNARD LEACH; 1887-1979
Small vase 1931
Impressed with two St Ives seals
Stoneware
12 × 8.5
Southampton City Art Gallery

127
PERCY WYNDHAM LEWIS; 1884-1957
Great War Drawing No.2
Watercolour on paper
38.1 × 54.2
Southampton City Art Gallery

128 (fig.32)
PERCY WYNDHAM LEWIS; 1884-1957
Mr Wyndham Lewis as a Tyro 1920-21
Oil on canvas
76 × 45.4
'A great and scandalously ignored painter'
H. Read, *Nation & Athenaeum*, 1927
Ferens Art Gallery, City of Kingston-upon-
Hull Museums and Art Galleries

129 (fig.97)
JAMES LLOYD; 1905-74
Children at the Edge of a Wood 1957*
Signed and dated: J. Lloyd 57
Gouache on paper
30 × 27
Read wrote the Foreword for Lloyd's first
exhibition at the Arthur Jeffress Gallery in
1958, in which this work was shown,
cat.no.13
Private collection

130
RENÉ MAGRITTE; 1898-1967
Untitled 1936*
Signed and dated: magritte 1936
Pencil on paper
28.5 × 23
Discussed in H. Read, 'Magritte', *London
Gallery Bulletin*, no.1, April 1938, p.2
Private collection

131 (fig.127)
ARISTIDE MAILLOL; 1861-1944
*Bather**
Signed: AM
Bronze
30 × 11 × 10
Ex-collection: Peter Gregory
Private collection

132 (fig.80)
ANDRÉ MASSON; 1896-1987
La Messe à Pampelone/Mass at Pamplona 1937?
Inscribed: La messe a Pampelone. André
Masson
Black pen and ink on paper
50.8 × 64.8
Ill: G. Woodcock, (Ed.), *Now*, no.7, Feb-
March 1947, opposite p.49
Private collection

133 (fig.134)
BERNARD MEADOWS; born 1915
Black Crab 1953
Bronze
26.7
Similar to works shown in the British
Pavilion, Venice *Biennale*, 1952 (135-6)
Private collection

134
Mexico, Mexcala
Mask 10th century AD
Stone
19 × 15
Read illustrates similar stone masks in *Art
and Society*, 1937, pl.52 and *The Art of
Sculpture*, 1956, pl.141
The Henry Moore Foundation. On loan to
Leeds City Art Galleries

135
JACOB MILIAN
Composition 1967*
Signed and dated: Milian 67
Paint on paper
35 × 25.5
Private collection

136 (fig.81)
JOAN MIRÓ; 1893-1983
Composition 1934*
Inscribed: à Monsieur Herbert Read, très
affectueusement, Miró, 934
Gouache and ink on paper
62 × 45
Private collection

137 (fig.78)
LÁSZLÓ MOHOLY-NAGY; 1895-1946
Emery Paper Collage 1930
Collage with poster paint
20.3 × 28.3
Similar to a work by the artist once owned
by Read, *Trolitpicture* (1930)
Whitworth Art Gallery, University of
Manchester

138 (fig.79)
PIET MONDRIAN; 1872-1944
Composition with Red and Blue 1935
Oil on canvas
55 × 55
Mondrian lived at 60 Parkhill Road,
Hampstead 1938-40
Private collection

139 (fig.119)
HENRY MOORE; 1898-1986
Reclining Figure 1929
Brown hornton stone
84 × 57.2 × 38
Ill: H. Read, *Henry Moore Sculptor An
Appreciation*, 1934 and *The Art of Sculpture*,
1956, pl.205
Leeds City Art Galleries

140 (fig.49)
HENRY MOORE; 1898-1986
Half-figure 1932
Armenian marble
127 × 45.7
Ill: H. Read, *Henry Moore Sculptor An
Appreciation*, 1934
Tate Gallery, London. Bequeathed by
E. C. Gregory

141
HENRY MOORE; 1898-1986
Carving 1936
Travertine marble
47.5
Ill: D. Sylvester, *Henry Moore Sculpture and
Drawings 1921-1948*, with an Introduction
by H. Read, 1949 (164)
The Henry Moore Foundation

142
HENRY MOORE; 1898-1986
Reclining Figure 1938
Bronze
14.5 × 32.4
Ill: H. Read, 'Three English Sculptors', *XX
Siècle*, 11è année, no.1, 1939, p.23 (lead
version, now in the Museum of Modern Art,
New York)
Leeds City Art Galleries

143
HENRY MOORE; 1898-1986
At Coal-Face – Man Fixing Props 1942
Signed and dated: Moore 42
Pen, ink, chalk, crayon, wash and
watercolour on paper
34.8 × 56.2
Moore's series of coal-mining drawings
(1941-2) were made at Read's suggestion
Leeds City Art Galleries. Presented by HM
Government through the War Artists
Advisory Committee 1947

144 (fig.6)
HENRY MOORE; 1898-1986
'1945' 1946*
Signed and dated: Moore 46
Gouache and wash on paper
18 × 27.5
An illustration to Read's poem of the same
title
Private collection

145
HENRY MOORE; 1898-1986
Composition for H. Read's poem '1945'
c.1946 (printed 1966)
Signed: Moore
Etching and aquatint
34.9 × 27.6
The Henry Moore Foundation

146
HENRY MOORE; 1898-1986
Single Standing Figure 1950
Fibreglass
221
Ill: H. Read, *The Art of Sculpture*, 1956,
pl.209 (Double Standing Figure, bronze
version)
The Henry Moore Foundation

147 (fig.122)
HENRY MOORE; 1898-1986
Working model for Time/Life Screen 1952
Bronze
101
H. Read, *The Art of Sculpture*, 1956, pl.11,
illustrates the full-size, Portland stone screen
on the Time/Life Building, London, 1952-3
The Henry Moore Foundation

148
HENRY MOORE; 1898-1986
King and Queen 1952-3
Bronze
164
Ill: H. Read, *Henry Moore A Study of his life
and work*, 1965, pls 176-7
The Henry Moore Foundation

149 (fig.99)
HENRY MOORE; 1898-1986
Maquette for the UNESCO Reclining Figure 1957
Bronze
22
Leeds City Art Galleries. Bequeathed by
Lady Hendy 1993

150
THEO MOORMAN; born 1907
Cushion cover 1935
Woven wool
61.5 × 61.5
The Board of Trustees of the Victoria and
Albert Museum, London

151
JAMES MORLEY; active in Nottingham
*Jug c.*1700
Buff stoneware with a lustrous golden-
brown glaze
10.2
A similar piece is illustrated in B. Rackham
and H. Read, *English Pottery*, 1924, fig.134
Leeds City Art Galleries

152
EDWARD NASH; 1778-1821
*Portrait of William Wordsworth c.*1818
Inscribed on verso: Wordsworth drawn for
Southey
Pencil
23 × 17
The Wordsworth Trust, Centre for British
Romanticism, Grasmere

153 (fig.31)
PAUL NASH; 1889-1946
We Are Making a New World 1918
Oil on canvas
61.1 × 91.4
The Trustees of the Imperial War Museum,
London

154
PAUL NASH; 1889-1946
Ruined Country: Old Battlefield, Vimy c.1918
Watercolour on paper
27.9 × 38.7
The Trustees of the Imperial War Museum,
London

155 (fig.70)
PAUL NASH; 1889-1946
Northern Adventure 1929
Oil on canvas
91.7 × 71.6
Ill: H. Read, *Paul Nash*, 1937, pl.6; H. Read
Paul Nash, 1944, pl.28
Aberdeen Art Gallery

156
PAUL NASH; 1889-1946
Harbour and Room 1936
Oil on canvas
91.4 × 71.1
Ill: H. Read, *Surrealism*, 1936, pl.63. Exh:
International Surrealist Exhibition, New
Burlington Galleries, London, 11 June-4
July 1936 (240)
Tate Gallery, London. Purchase 1981

157 (fig.77)
PAUL NASH; 1889-1946
*Study for Encounter on the Downs | in the
Afternoon* 1936*
Inscribed: Souvenir for Herbert Read from
Paul Nash
Pencil, watercolour and wash on paper
19 × 28
Ill: H. Read, *Surrealism*, 1936, pl.62. The
finished version in oil on canvas shown at
the *International Surrealist Exhibition*, New
Burlington Galleries, London, 11 June-4
July 1936 (241)
Private collection

158
PAUL NASH; 1889-1946
Minotaur (Monster Pond) 1939*
Signed: Paul Nash
Watercolour on paper
28 × 38
Private collection

159
BEN NICHOLSON; 1894-1982
Still-life with Guitar 1933
Oil on canvas
76.2 × 63.3
Incorporating a portrait of Hepworth,
while she and the artist were Read's
immediate neighbours in The Mall,
Parkhill Road, Hampstead
Leeds City Art Galleries. Presented by the
Contemporary Art Society 1950

160 (fig.69)
BEN NICHOLSON; 1894-1982
Profile 1933*
Signed and dated: Ben Nicholson 1933
Linocut
43 × 35
The profile is that of Barbara Hepworth
(see cat. no.159)
Private collection

161
BEN NICHOLSON; 1894-1982
Foxy and Frankie (4) 1933*
Signed and dated: Nicholson 33
Linocut
15.5 × 15
Private collection

162 (fig.73)
BEN NICHOLSON; 1894-1982
Gouache 1936*
Signed and dated: Ben Nicholson 1936;
inscribed: for Herbert & Ludo Xmas 1938;
inscribed on verso: Version 3/12 hand
painted by B.N.
Gouache on paper
30 × 42
Private collection

163
BEN NICHOLSON; 1894-1982
Printed fabric
Signed: BN
59.7 × 84.5
See fig.3 for a similar fabric used as
curtaining in No.3 The Mall, Parkhill
Road, Hampstead, occupied by Read,
1933-7
Private collection

164
BEN NICHOLSON; 1894-1982
St Ives 1940 and 1961
Inscribed on verso: St Ives, Cornwall by
Ben Nicholson 1940 (part of foreground
worked on 1961/BN)
Oil on board
32.8 × 38.7
Private collection

165 (fig.93)
BEN NICHOLSON; 1894-1982
September '53 Aztec 1953
Oil on canvas
68.5 × 56
Ill: H. Read, *Ben Nicholson; Work Since 1947*,
vol.2, 1956 (5)
Formerly in the collection of Barbara
Hepworth
Private collection

166
BEN NICHOLSON; 1894-1982
Oct 26-54 (Rievaulx No.2) 1954
Pencil and oil wash on paper
32.5 × 51.5
Ill: H. Read, *Ben Nicholson; Work Since 1947*,
1956 (51). Executed while staying with the
Reads at Stonegrave, Yorkshire
Private collection

167 (fig.12)
BEN NICHOLSON; 1894-1982
Tenement 1960*
Signed and dated: BN 1960
Mixed media on paper
43 × 50.5
A work accompanying Read's poem of the
same title
Private collection

168 (fig.51)
EMIL NOLDE; 1867-1956
Die Familie/The Family 1931
Signed: Emil Nolde
Oil on canvas
111.5 × 74
Ill: H. Read, *Art Now*, 1933, pl.5
Stiftung Seebüll Ada und Emil Nolde,
Neukirchen

169 (fig.52)
EMIL NOLDE; 1867-1956
*Marschlandschaft mit Mühle | Marshland with
Mill* 1931
Signed: Nolde
Watercolour on paper
30.5 × 45.7
Ill: H. Read, *Art Now*, 1933, pl.24
Stiftung Seebüll Ada und Emil Nolde,
Neukirchen

170 (fig.53)
EMIL NOLDE; 1867-1956
*Paar (Blau und Violett) | Couple (Blue and
Violet)* 1931-5
Signed: Nolde
Watercolour on paper
45.6 × 30.5
Ill: H. Read, *Art Now*, 1933, pl.4
Stiftung Seebüll Ada und Emil Nolde,
Neukirchen

171 (fig.147)
SIR EDUARDO PAOLOZZI; born 1924
Forms on a Bow 1950
Brass
48.3 × 63.5 × 21.6
Exh: British Pavilion, Venice *Biennale*, 1952
(143)
Tate Gallery, London. Presented by the
Contemporary Art Society 1958

172
SIR EDUARDO PAOLOZZI; born 1924
*Maquette for a Monument to The Unknown
Political Prisoner* 1952
Plaster
43.2 × 61 × 6.4 (base size), 28 (height of
largest piece)
Exh: *The Unknown Political Prisoner*, Tate
Gallery, London, 14 March-30 April 1953
(21)
Private collection

173
Papua New Guinea, Sepik River
Mask*
Wood
57 × 22
Private collection

174 (fig.30)
STASS PARASKOS; born 1933
Lovers and Romances 1966
Oil on board
42 × 50
Private collection

175 (fig.94)
VICTOR PASMORE; born 1908
Abstract in White, Black and Green 1955
Transparent construction in painted wood
and plastic
45.5 × 51 × 14.5
Private collection

176
PABLO PICASSO; 1881-1973
*Poverty c.*1901
Pen and ink and wash on paper
37.4 × 26.7
Whitworth Art Gallery, University of
Manchester

177
JOHN PIPER; 1903-92
Forms on a White Ground 1935
Signed, dated and inscribed on verso: John
Piper 1935, oil Forms on a White Ground
Oil on canvas mounted on board
51 × 61
Piper was a member of Axis and Circle
Private collection

178
LUCIEN PISSARRO; 1863-1944
Wells Far Bridge 1907
Signed with monogram and dated 1907
Oil on canvas
45.7 × 54.5
The acquisition of this work by the Leeds
Art Collections Fund was arranged by
Frank Rutter in 1913
Leeds City Art Galleries

179
JOHN PLANTA; active c.1798-1802
Spinning-wheel
Printed label in drawer: Made by John
Planta, at Fulneck, near Leeds
Mahogany, oak, box, rosewood, ivory
94
An almost identical version of this piece in
the Victoria and Albert Museum is
illustrated in H. Read, *Art and Industry*, 1934,
p.17
Leeds City Art Galleries

180 (fig.92)
PORTOCARRERO; 1912-c.1985
Head 1967*
Signed and dated: Portocarrero 67
Watercolour on paper
53 × 42.5
Private collection

181
GEORGE RAVENSCROFT; 1618-81
*The Goring Tazza c.*1675
Lead glass
34.3 diameter
Leeds City Art Galleries. Bought with the
aid of grants from the MGC/V&A Purchase
Grant Fund, the NACF and NADFAS 1986

182
RUDOLF RAY; 20th century
Composition 1954*
Signed and dated: Rudolf Ray 54
Oil on canvas
31.5 × 24.2
Private collection

183 (fig.114)
ALFRED BURGESS READ
Table lamp (for Troughton & Young
Lighting Ltd) 1950*
Satin chrome, stove enamel
46 × 50 × 41
Ill: H. Read, *Art and Industry*, 1963, p.99
Private collection

184 (fig.18)
SIR HERBERT READ; 1893-1968
Ethical Volition 1916*
Signed and dated: H. Read 16
Watercolour and ink
11.5 × 9
Private collection

185 (fig.17)
SIR HERBERT READ; 1893-1968
Figure Composition No.1 1916*
Signed and dated: H.E.Read, 1916
Watercolour and ink
15.5 × 10
Private collection

186 (fig.26)
SIR HERBERT READ; 1893-1968
Impression de Croisilles 1917*
Signed and dated: H.E.Read, 1917
Watercolour and ink
12.8 × 17.7
Private collection

187
SIR HERBERT READ; 1893-1968
Desk c.1931*
Wood
72 × 152 × 102
Private collection

188
HANS RICHTER; 1888-1976
Composition 1961*
Signed and dated: H Richter 61
Watercolour on paper
28.5 × 18.5
Private collection

189 (fig.129)
AUGUSTE RODIN; 1840-1917
The Walking Man 1877-8
Bronze
84 × 57 × 28
Read discusses Rodin in *The Art of Sculpture*,
1956 and *The Concise History of Modern
Sculpture*, 1964
This particular cast was formerly in the
collection of Henry Moore
The Trustees of the Irina Moore
Grandchildren's Settlement

190
R.D. RUSSELL
Sideboard for Gordon Russell Ltd 1933
Brazilian Rosewood, mahogany, oak
85 × 165 × 52.7
The Board of Trustees of the Victoria and
Albert Museum, London

191
KURT SCHWITTERS; 1887-1948
Merzbild 1944*
Signed and dated: Kurt Schwitters 44
Collage on paper
21 × 16.5
Private collection

192
KURT SCHWITTERS; 1887-1948
Merzbild 'Dundrennan' 1947*
Signed and dated: Kurt Schwitters 1947
Mixed media on paper
23 × 20
Read was one of Schwitters's very few
supporters in England
Private collection

193
JOSEPH THADDÄUS STAMMEL; 1695-1765
*A Figure Symbolizing Fear c.*1750-65
Boxwood
36.8
Ill: H. Read, *The Art of Sculpture*, 1956,
pl.110
Trustees of the Victoria and Albert
Museum, London

194
JOHN CECIL STEPHENSON; 1889-1965
Bright Triangles 1938
Inscribed on verso: J. C. Stephenson
Tempera 1938
Oil and tempera on canvas mounted on
board
Stephenson features in *Circle: International
Survey of Constructive Art*, 1937. Read wrote
the introduction to the Memorial
Exhibition of Cecil Stephenson, Drian
Galleries, London, 22 Nov - 23 Dec 1966
Private collection

195 (fig.100)
GRAHAM SUTHERLAND; 1903-80
Thorn Trees 1945-6
Oil on canvas
127 × 101.5
Read owned a related work entitled *Study,
Crown of Thorns*, 1948
The British Council

196 (fig.83)
YVES TANGUY; 1900-55
*Untitled c.*1936
Gouache on paper
8.9 × 26.7
Tanguy features in H. Read, *Surrealism*,
1936, and Read once owned a similar work
by the artist
Private collection. Courtesy of The Mayor
Gallery, London

197
ANTONI TÀPIES; born 1932
Prova d'Artista 1960*
Inscribed: prova d'artista a Herbert Read
un recuerdo afectuoso
Etching
75 × 106
Private collection

198
DAVID THISTLEWOOD; born 1944
Kirkgate Market, Leeds 1959
Oil on board
40 × 50
Selected by Read for inclusion in the
National Children's Art Exhibition, London,
1959-60
The artist

199
HARRY THUBRON; 1915-85
Trees
Signed: H Thubron
Oil on board
63 × 77.5
Private collection

200
THOMAS TOFT; 17th century
North Staffordshire Dish 1674
Signed and dated: Thomas Toft 1674
Red earthenware covered with white slip
and trailed with light- and dark-red slip
under yellowish glaze
55.9 diameter
A similar, signed dish by this potter is
illustrated in B. Rackham and H. Read,
English Pottery, 1924, fig.37
Leeds City Art Galleries

201 (fig.1)
FELIKS TOPOLSKI; 1907-89
*Portrait of Sir Herbert Read c.*1961
Black chalk and coloured washes on paper
43.6 × 29.7
Her Majesty The Queen and HRH The
Duke of Edinburgh, Royal Library,
Windsor Castle

202
FRANCIS TOWNE; c.1739-1816
Lake Como 1781
Inscribed on verso: Lake of Como Light
from the left hand August 27th 1781 No.28
Francis Towne
Pen and brown ink, grey wash on paper
15.5 × 21
Towne was a particular favourite of Read's
among the English watercolourists. In 1934
he recommended *The Mer De Glace from
Montanvert*, 1781, to an English collector
Leeds City Art Galleries

203
BRUCE TURNER; c.1894-1963
Portrait of Pavlova 1912-14
Signed: BS Turner
Oil on canvas
51 × 61
Private collection

204
JOSEPH MALLORD WILLIAM TURNER;
1775-1851
*The Foot of the St Gothard c.*1842
Watercolour
48 × 60.7
Leeds City Art Galleries

205
FRITZ VAN DEN BERGHE; 1883-1939
Portrait of Permeke 1922-4
Oil on canvas
105 × 80
Works by this artist are illustrated in
H. Read, *Art Now*, 1933
Museum van Elsene/Musée d'Ixelles,
Brussels

206
EDWARD WADSWORTH; 1889-1949
Roofs 1919*
Woodcut
19.5 × 11.5
The first work of art acquired by Read (in
1919, from Frank Rutter's Adelphi Gallery,
London)
Private collection

207 (fig.27)
EDWARD WADSWORTH; 1889-1949
Slag Heaps 1920
Signed and dated: Wadsworth 1920
Ink and gouache on paper
78.1 × 61.6
Leeds City Art Galleries. Presented by Sir
Michael Sadler 1944

208
JOHN WALKER; born 1939
Study 1967
Signed and dated: J Walker 67
Chalk and coloured wash on paper
50.8 × 78.1
University of Leeds Art Collections

209
JOHN WALKER; born 1939
Study 1968
Oil cut-out on watercolour base on paper
151.1 × 101
University of Leeds Art Collections

210
JOHN WALKER; born 1939
Study for Conceal 1 1968
Signed and dated: John G Walker 68
Chalk and coloured wash on paper
57.4 × 86.4
Walker was Gregory Fellow in Painting,
1967-70
University of Leeds Art Collections

211
ALFRED WALLIS; 1855-1942
Boat Entering Harbour
Oil on board
7 × 16
A gift to Read from Ben Nicholson
Private collection

212
ALFRED WALLIS; 1855-1942
Horseman
Signed: A Wallis
Oil on board
14 × 17.5
Private collection

213
ALFRED WALLIS; 1855-1942
Landscape
Signed: Alfred Wallis
Oil on cardboard
20.5 × 35
Private collection

214 (fig.10)
RICHARD WESTALL; 1765-1836
Portrait of George Gordon, Lord Byron 1813
Signed and dated: 1813
Oil on canvas
91.4 × 71.1
Read wrote the British Council booklet on
Byron, 1951
National Portrait Gallery, London

215
ETHELBERT WHITE; 1891-1972
Illustration for H. Read, *Eclogues* 1919
Watercolour on paper
15.2 × 12.7
The Fine Art Society, London

216
JAMES AND CHARLES WHITEHEAD, Hanley,
or ENOCH WOOD, Burslem, Staffordshire
'Cream-bowl' and lid 1780-90s
Plain creamware with a finely-crazed
greenish glaze
23
Ill: B. Rackham and H. Read, *English
Pottery*, 1924, fig.191
Leeds City Art Galleries

217
FRANK AVRAY WILSON; born 1914
Composition 1962*
Signed and dated: avray wilson 62
Oil on board
60.5 × 50.5
Private collection

218
SCOTTIE WILSON; 1889-1972
Composition
Signed: Scottie
Pen and ink on paper
27.5 × 37
Private collection

219
RALPH WOOD THE YOUNGER, probably after
a model by John Voyez, Staffordshire
Figure of a Shepherd Carrying a Lamb 1775-80
Creamware
23
Ill: H. Read, *Staffordshire Pottery Figures*,
1929, pl.36 left (another cast, in the
Gwynne Collection)
Leeds City Art Galleries

220 (fig.46)
MARTA WORRINGER
*Kinder**
Signed: Marta Worringer
Gouache on paper
27.5 × 20.5
The artist was the wife of the philosopher of art, Wilhelm Worringer
Private collection

221
AUSTIN WRIGHT; born 1911
Bowling Torso 1961
Bronze
76.5
University of Leeds Senior Common Room Club

222
AUSTIN WRIGHT; born 1911
*Housing Scheme c.*1962
Aluminium
198.1
University of Leeds Art Collections

223 (fig.139)
AUSTIN WRIGHT; born 1911
*Moon c.*1962
Aluminium
363 × 85 × 65
Leeds City Art Galleries

224
AUSTIN WRIGHT; born 1911
Mother and Child
Lead on wood base
32 × 10 × 10
Wright was Gregory Fellow in Sculpture, 1961-4
Private collection

Lenders

Figures refer to catalogue numbers

Her Majesty The Queen and HRH The Duke of Edinburgh 201

Aberdeen Art Gallery 155
Kenneth Armitage 11
Bedford, the Board of Trustees, Cecil Higgins Art Gallery 27
Brussels, Museum van Elsene/Musée d'Ixelles 205
Lynn Chadwick 38, 39
The Ronnie Duncan Collection 8, 19, 58, 59, 61, 79
Grasmere, The Wordsworth Trust 57, 101, 152
Peggy Guggenheim Collection, Venice. The Solomon R. Guggenheim Foundation 74
Patrick Heron 111, 113
James Holloway 52
Kingston-upon-Hull Museums and Art Galleries, the Ferens Art Gallery 124, 128
The John Jones Collection 50, 56
Leeds City Art Galleries 24, 35, 41, 42, 51, 53, 55, 60, 68, 69, 70, 71, 72, 80, 86, 88, 89, 97, 98, 105, 107, 114, 116, 139, 142, 143, 149, 151, 159, 178, 179, 181, 200, 202, 204, 207, 216, 219, 223
University of Leeds, Art Collections 20, 21, 22, 25, 26, 47, 48, 49, 82, 84, 87, 92, 94, 96, 208, 209, 210, 222
—University Library 23
—National Arts Education Archive, Bretton Hall 5
—Senior Common Room Club 54, 83, 221
Leipzig, Museum der bildenden Künste 119
London, Arts Council Collection, The South Bank Centre 33
—The British Council 10, 195
—The British Museum 3, 4, 65, 66, 99, 100
—The Fine Art Society 215
—Gimpel Fils 9, 109
—The Board of Trustees, Imperial War Museum 153, 154
—The Museum of London 6
—The National Portrait Gallery 112, 214
—New Art Centre 9
—The Board of Trustees, the Tate Gallery 34, 90, 93, 140, 156, 171
—The Board of Trustees, the Victoria and Albert Museum 1, 28, 29, 37, 40, 67, 76, 150, 190, 193

Manchester, City Art Galleries 75
—University of Manchester, Whitworth Art Gallery 137, 176
The Montreal Museum of Fine Arts 7
The Henry Moore Foundation 105, 134, 141, 145, 146, 147, 148
The Trustees of the Irina Moore Grandchildren's Settlement 189
Neukirchen, Stiftung Seebüll Ada und Emil Nolde 168, 169, 170
Private collections 2, 12, 13, 14, 15, 16, 17, 30, 31, 32, 36, 43, 44, 45, 46, 62, 63, 64, 73, 78, 81, 91, 95, 102, 103, 106, 108, 110, 115, 117, 118, 121, 122, 123, 125, 129, 130, 131, 132, 133, 135, 136, 138, 144, 157, 158, 160, 161, 162, 163, 164, 165, 166, 167, 172, 173, 174, 175, 177, 180, 182, 183, 184, 185, 186, 187, 188, 191, 192, 194, 196, 197, 199, 203, 206, 211, 212, 213, 217, 218, 220, 224
Southampton City Art Gallery 126, 127
Staatsgalerie Stuttgart 18, 77
David Thistlewood 198
Wakefield Museums, Galleries and Castles 85, 104
York City Art Gallery 120

List of Illustrations

Illustrations are arranged alphabetically by artist (or by title where artist is unknown). Paintings by Herbert Read and documentary photographs appear under Read. References in parentheses are to illustration numbers.

Acknowledgements

Contributors

The exhibition organisers acknowledge the generosity of the many lenders, who are listed elsewhere in this publication. We are particularly grateful to Her Majesty The Queen and HRH The Duke of Edinburgh, the Read family, the British Museum, Tate Gallery and Victoria and Albert Museum for agreeing to important loans, and to the Museums and Galleries Commission for organising Government Indemnity cover for the exhibition which has helped to facilitate loans from Continental Europe and America. Leeds University Photographic Services have been immensely helpful and efficient, while the facilities of the Book, Conway and Witt Libraries at the Courtauld Institute of Art, University of London have proved as irreplaceable as ever. The following have also helped in many valuable ways: Bernard Adams, Katherine Aldred, Dr Robert Anderson, Michael Archer, Kenneth Armitage, Joanna Barnes, Leonard Bartle, Felicitas Baumeister, Mrs Leslie Benson, Dr Peter Beye, Dr M. L. Bierbrier, Neville Boden, Alan Borg, Elke von Brentano, Ann Bukantas, Mrs J. H. R. Carver, Eva Chadwick, Maurice Chapman, B. F. Cook, Dennis Creffield, the Rt Hon Lord Croft, Dr Penelope Curtis, Mary Moore Danowski, Jill Davies, Georgina Dobrée, Gregory J. Eades, Dr Patrick Elliott, Elizabeth Esteve-Coll, Terry Frost, Luke Gertler, René Gimpel, Elizabeth Goodall, Dr Wolf Goeltzer, Richard Gray, Halina Graham, Richard Green, Dr Herwig Guratzsch, Robert Hall, Harry Hare, Kate Hare, John Hayes, Max Hebditch, Margot Heller, Katharine Heron, Patrick Heron, A. Hidalgo, Nicole d'Huart, Sally Johnson, Isobel Johnstone, Alex Kader, Agi Katz, Louise Lalonde, Cathy Limb, Richard Littlewood, B. J. Mack, Dr J. D. Manson, Corinne Miller, David Mitchinson, Richard Morphet, Edward Morris, Theresa-Mary Morton, Andrew Murray, Antony Penrose, John R. Porter, Oleg Prokofiev, James Putnam, Mr and Mrs Cyril Reddihough, Paul Reiles, Dr Manfred Reuther, Andrea Rose, Reinhard Rudolph, Nicholas Serota, Christopher Sheppard, Dr and Mrs J. Sherwin, Peyton Skipwith, Alistair Smith, Ian McKenzie-Smith, Julie Summers, Michael Sweeney, John Taylor, Pierre Théberge, Antonino Vella, Nigel Walsh, Dr Philip Ward-Jackson, Angela Weight, Anthony Wells-Cole, Christopher Wilk, Rowena Willard, Paul Williamson, Heather Wilson, Matthew Winterbottom, Dr Robert Woof and Anna Wyner.

SIR ALAN BOWNESS is Director of the Henry Moore Foundation and former Director of the Tate Gallery, London

ROBERT BURSTOW is Senior Lecturer in Historical & Theoretical Studies at the University of Derby

DR ANDREW CAUSEY is Senior Lecturer in the History of Art at the University of Manchester

DR JUDITH COLLINS is Curator of the Modern Collection at the Tate Gallery, London

DR HILARY DIAPER is Curator of the University Art Collections, the University of Leeds

DR TERRY FRIEDMAN is former Principal Keeper, Leeds City Art Gallery and the Henry Moore Centre for the Study of Sculpture

MICHAEL PARASKOS is a Leeds WEA Tutor and Lecturer at the South-East Essex College of Arts and Technology

BENEDICT READ is Henry Moore Lecturer in Sculpture Studies at the University of Leeds

DR DAVID THISTLEWOOD is Reader in the School of Architecture, The University of Liverpool